civil-military
SMARTBOOK

3

thelightningpress.com

Disaster
Preparedness

Surviving Disasters On Your Own Terms

The Lightning Press
Ferlemann

The Lightning Press

2227 Arrowhead Blvd.
Lakeland, FL 33813
24-hour Voicemail/Fax/Order: 1-800-997-8827
E-mail: SMARTbooks@TheLightningPress.com
www.TheLightningPress.com

Civil-Military Smartbook 3: Disaster Preparedness
Surviving Disasters On Your Own Terms

Copyright © 2014 The Lightning Press
ISBN: 978-1-935886-48-8

Printed and bound in the United States of America.

Note to Reader

BE AWARE, PREPARED & RESILIENT

Disasters can happen at any time but with some careful thought and little preparation you can make choices before a disaster strikes that can directly improve your situation.

- Learn to understand the different kinds of disasters and their effects.
- Learn how to make your own plans and preparations that are right for you and your family.
- Build personal resiliency and give yourself options even when facing the worst situations.
- Know what kinds of help you can expect from government responses before, during and after the disaster.
- Discover what the government should provide after a disaster, how government plans to provide for people's needs and where the government will focus its efforts in response to a major disaster.

Civil-Military/Disaster Preparedness SMARTbooks

Disaster management (or emergency management) is the term used to designate the efforts of communities or businesses to plan for and coordinate all the personnel and materials required to either mitigate the effects of, or recover from, natural or man-made disasters, or acts of terrorism. Defense support of civil authorities (DSCA) is support provided by federal military forces, Dept of Defense assets, and National Guard forces in response to requests for assistance from civil authorities for domestic emergencies, law enforcement support, and other domestic activities, or from qualifying entities for special events.

The Lightning Press offers four specific Civil-Military/Disaster Preparedness SMARTbooks and a Homeland Defense & Defense Support to Civil Authorities (HD/DSCA) SMARTbook, plus more than a dozen related and supporting titles:

SMARTbooks - DIME is our DOMAIN!

SMARTbooks: Reference Essentials for the Instruments of National Power (D-I-M-E: Diplomatic, Informational, Military, Economic)! Recognized as a "whole of government" doctrinal reference standard by military, national security and government professionals around the world, SMARTbooks comprise a comprehensive professional library designed with all levels of Soldiers, Sailors, Airmen, Marines and Civilians in mind.

SMARTbooks can be used as quick reference guides during actual operations, as study guides at education and professional development courses, and as lesson plans and checklists in support of training. Visit **www.TheLightningPress.com**!

Introduction: Disaster Preparedness

A Real Worst-Case Scenario

In June of 2002, FEMA director Joe Allbaugh states that the potential effects of a hurricane on a major city cause him "great concern." New Orleans is one of the cities on his list. On Friday, August 26, 2005, his worst fears are realized: Hurricane Katrina is building power in the Gulf of Mexico and headed right for the coast of Louisiana and Mississippi. Late in the afternoon of August 27, orders to evacuate New Orleans are confused with separate authorities' calling for voluntary and mandatory evacuations. It was generally agreed that people should leave the low-lying areas. Many citizens take advantage of the short window for departure and heed the evacuation order. Many others do not or cannot. Traffic is slow on clogged highways for the next 24 hours. Many highways become one-way to accommodate the exodus. Early on the 28th, Katrina becomes a Category 5 Hurricane; evacuation orders become mandatory. But for many still in the city, it is too late to leave. The city opens 10 "shelters of last resort," including the Superdome. Other strong points in the city become unofficial shelters. Some 100,000 people are still in the city. The National Weather Service predicts the levees may be "overtopped" by the storm surge.

Katrina makes landfall at 6:10AM on Aug 29. Over the next 24 hours, many of the city's levees fail, flooding 80% of New Orleans in up to 20 feet of water; hundreds perish. As the worst of the storm passes, the city is left in pandemonium. The rule of law disintegrates as looting and violence sweep through the streets. 25,000 people are trapped in the Superdome, and 52,000 more arrive at Red Cross shelters and relief stations. Over the next several days, police are called away from search and rescue efforts to deal with the continuing lawlessness. Other rescue efforts are suspended due to sporadic gunfire endangering rescue helicopters and boats. Explosions and fires are seen across the city. By September 1, there are 45,000 refugees in the city shelters. Despite rescue efforts, hundreds more die in the aftermath, lacking security, sanitation, food and water, medical attention, and evacuation. The federal government responds with thousands of armed National Guardsmen followed by active-duty personnel to provide security and support the national rescue effort. The New Orleans city government is unable to restore services or support the few services that remain. Feeling frustrated, helpless, and abandoned, hundreds of New Orleans police officers walk off the job. The failure is epic: some officers commit suicide. By September 3, some 40,000 National Guard troops have deployed to the Gulf Coast states to assist in the relief and restore order. On September 4, the Superdome is officially evacuated, and soon only stragglers remain. By September 6, the streets are mostly secure. The city begins the long road to recovery. Reports vary, but around 1,500 to 2,000 city residents are dead or missing. It is the highest death toll in any U.S. city in over one hundred years (Brookings inst.).

Why was New Orleans affected so severely? Hurricane Katrina had a significant impact not just on the City of New Orleans, but also on the entire bottom third of the state of Louisiana, half of the state of Mississippi, significant portions of Alabama, and parts of the Florida panhandle. Cities like Gulfport, Mississippi, were devastated, but did not suffer the same aftermath as New Orleans. What made this one city the worst-case scenario?

This event was not a surprise. The government had advanced warning and had taken action to prepare response efforts and preposition supplies. 10,000 National Guard troops were standing by along the Gulf Coast ready to respond. Despite the best intentions and efforts, as a nation, we were unable to respond to the magnitude of this event. It will happen again.

The question is, "Do you want to be part of the next Katrina?"

By picking up this book, you have shown an interest in your survival. It may seem to be a simplistic idea, but in reality disaster survival is determined well before the disaster strikes. You have engaged your most important survival tool, your brain. The ideas offered here are not focused on survivor skills, although some of that kind of information is included in the discussions. It is more about what happens before the disaster and how you can make choices now that will affect you later. It is also about choices you will want to think about now so you will be able to make informed decisions during and after a disaster.

Sometimes things go badly and all our hopes and plans fail us. Our illusions are shattered, our expectations are beyond anyone's capacity to fulfill, and our demands go unanswered. When this time comes, what will you do?

> "Want of foresight, unwillingness to act when action would be simple and effective, lack of clear thinking, confusions of counsel, until the emergency comes, until self-preservation strikes its jarring gong — these are the features that constitute the endless repetition of history."
> — Winston Churchill

What Mr. Churchill was talking about is procrastination, the unwillingness of people to think about unpleasant things in the future and prepare for them. These words are a warning from a man who led his people out of the fear and pain of World War II. More importantly, he was a man who made people do the things they needed to do to survive and learned important lessons from the experience. First was the idea that a little preparation goes a long way and there comes a point when you cannot make up for lost time. Second was the idea that, although the people he saved were very appreciative that he had saved them, they disliked him at times for what he made them do in order to survive. These two themes are directly applicable to you, the reader, in the event of a disaster. You will need to make some choices for yourself based on these two important themes.

This is not a pleasant, comfortable, or easy discussion to have. It is about scary, uncomfortable, difficult, frustrating, and dangerous situations and how you can survive them, both physically and emotionally. It will ask you to think about and decide upon issues now, when you have the time to think and prepare, rather than waiting until your options are few (or none). This is not about science or statistics, although those things will be used to support some points. The intent is that the ideas presented should act as a catalyst for a conversation you should have with yourself and your family. The information provided is both general and accurate, which is all it needs to be to help you make your choices.

Personal Resiliency

Anytime you are reading about survival, you are reading about resiliency. Resiliency is the ability to recover quickly from setbacks. Preparation for emotional or physical challenges is part of the process, but there is no magic formula for resiliency that will make a disaster less destructive, disruptive, or devastating. True resiliency is more than just having a plan: it is a mindset, a decision made before the crisis that you have chosen to survive.

Continued on next page

In a true disaster you will experience loss, be stressed, and be physically and mentally challenged. Different people respond in different ways, and because survival is about choices, you can decide now how you will build your own personal resilience. It is said that courage is not the absence of fear, but what you do with it. The question for you to answer is how do you choose to develop your confidence, courage, and resiliency? How do you choose to survive?

When we make our choices, we can start by giving ourselves options for survival through preparation and learning, we build confidence and awareness by understanding what is happening around us, and we can decide now to actively participate in our own survival. These are the most basic of actions and the easiest to do. Prepare in those ways that are simple and effective while you have the time and resources to do them. Take the time to learn about the potential hazards and threats in your area and plan accordingly. Make decisions on those things that you can decide upon now, and know what decisions you may need to make later.

Still, none of this matters until we make the greatest choice of all: when we decide that we will survive and that we will do it without desperation, fear, or cruelty, but as decent human beings. By being truthful with yourself and endeavoring to meet your real needs during a disaster, you can gain a level of independence that will allow you to recover more effectively from setbacks when they happen (and they will happen).

Attitude: It could be argued that when people are trapped in a disaster they are helpless victims, completely unable to respond to the situation or to save themselves. I submit to you that *this is not the case* and that the public can educate themselves and prepare for disasters in a variety of ways. In short, you have choices, and more important, *if you choose not to make them for yourself, someone else will make them for you.*

Beginning the Discussion

This book is designed to provide for the reader who may not have studied this before.

In Section I, *Understanding Disasters and the Role of Government*, we will cover the effects and scope of different types of disasters. Once we can describe a disaster in terms of effects, then we can look at how local, state, and federal agencies react to the different types of disasters. We will do this in two ways: first by looking at the language used by emergency managers and government officials, and second by reviewing how local, state, and federal governments respond to disasters.

We will discuss the rules governing jurisdictions and Declarations of Emergency because control and money are vital to government and become big factors in disaster response. We will also look at the specifics of how agencies work within the established National Response Framework because understanding how emergency management works is important in determining what kinds of services you can expect to see during a disaster response. This is true at the national level also, and we will examine the government's plans currently in place to preserve the nation and to provide for the population in times of catastrophic national disaster.

Section II, *Mental Resiliency and Making Your Choices*, outlines options you have for developing a level of preparation that fits your lifestyle, resources, and level of comfort. This involves an in-depth discussion on how to make plans that will actually work for you and ways to determine appropriate preparation, determine realistic expectations, and deal with unknown factors, both those things we can control and those we can't. A big part of this will include insights and discussion on different types of frustrations you may encounter and positive ways of preparing to keep a cool head.

It may seem like the long way around to get to the question of, "What do I want to do to protect myself and my family?" but there is method in the madness. To make the kinds of informed decisions you will want to make, it is important to have a framework of how government responds to disasters. Once you have a good understanding of what kinds of threats you may encounter and how the government will respond to assist you, you will be ready to make your own plans.

Section III, Descriptions of Disasters and Things You Need to Know About Disasters, provides you with information you will want and need when making your plans and preparations.

Be prepared and stay aware.
Know what to do and when to do it.
Smart is resilient,
Resilient survives!

Choices and Challenges

As you progress through this discussion, you will have the opportunity to consider three questions.

Question 1: *What threats are you willing to live with?*

Question 2: *To what level are you willing to be dependent on others for assistance after a disaster?*

Question 3: *What level of preparation and planning will you need to make to be as ready as you believe you should be?*

When you make and act upon these three choices, you will have significantly increased your probability of survival in the event of a disaster.

Information Sites

There is a treasure trove of survival and preparedness information that will be useful to the reader available on government websites provided just for that purpose. The information comes from the expertise of the highly educated, experienced, and capable subject-matter experts who have dedicated themselves to effective disaster communication. In most cases information is taken directly from government websites. The government does not copyright this data and asks only that persons referring to the information give due credit for where the information was acquired. This author has taken full advantage of their kindness. The purpose is not to regurgitate the information found on the World Wide Web, but rather to consolidate it and put it into perspective. You can find all of this information on the government websites listed at the end of this introduction and at the beginning of each disaster description. You are highly encouraged to do so.

If you have access to the Internet, the website locations provided with each disaster description can provide excellent information and important updates. If you do not have access to the Internet, this book provides an accurate, concise, and relevant summation of pertinent information. The intent is to provide the reader with a quick reference, to get you started if you have time to research the disaster in question or to provide the bare essentials of the available required information when you do not.

National Oceanic and Atmospheric Administration (NOAA) — http://www.noaa.gov/
National Weather Service (NWS) — http://www.weather.gov/
Federal emergency management Administration (FEMA) — http://www.ready.gov/
Center for Disease Control and Prevention (CDC) — http://www.cdc.gov/

Acknowledgements & Recognitions

re•sil•ience (noun)
1. *the power or ability to return to the original form, position, etc., after being bent, compressed, or stretched; elasticity.*
2. *the ability to recover readily from illness, depression, adversity, or the like; buoyancy.*

This was a collaborative effort and special thanks go to those who labored in its completion. As always, to my wife Pamela who has been my proof reader, graphics designer, conscience and best supporter for all these years; to my mother Mimi Hall with her years of experience as an editor and, in this case, her service as a disaster novice content reader. To the team of subject matter experts who worked diligently on this endeavor; Mr. Jim Green for emergency management, Captain Tim Cochran for police and fire response, and to Lieutenant Larry Collins for weapons considerations. Mr. Adam Bois was the manuscript proof reader and is responsible for the consistency of style which makes the book so much easier to read.

This effort would not have been possible without the diligent and dedicated people who work in and with the government agencies responsible for our health and safety; the Federal Emergency Management Administration (FEMA), the National Oceanographic and Atmosphere Administration (NOAA) and National Weather Service (NWS), the Centers for Disease Control (CDC), the National Geological Survey (NGS), the Red Cross and all the other governmental and non-governmental organizations who make it their business to keep the public informed of potential threats and ways to survive them.

We must recognize those brave souls, who, when all seems lost, will come to our aid; firefighters, police and emergency medical technicians of our cities, counties, tribes and states, the doctors, nurses and care providers, the Soldiers and Airmen of the National Guard and active duty, the linemen, plumbers and builders who enter the tangled wreckage of our communities to contain the wrath of broken infrastructure, the ever present American Volunteer and our neighbors who will pitch in to help even when they themselves have lost everything.

We should all remember those who plan and prepare for our safety. Even thought we rarely ever see them or even know they exist, there are legions of planners and emergency managers whose sole purpose is to prepare for the worst and plan how to save lives, mitigate threats and hazards, and protect what infrastructure we have left so we can do what we always do when our world is torn down; begin to rebuild.

Finally to you, who has made the choice to participate in your own preservation.

Table of Contents

Chap 3: Federal Disaster Response 3-1

Section III:
Things You Need to Know About Disasters

Section I:
Understanding Disasters and the Role of the Government

Understanding Disasters

Most disasters are the results of things we live with every day as acceptable risks: the West Coast has earthquakes, the Central Plains has tornadoes, and the East Coast has hurricanes. The very nature of the changing earth conflicts with man's desire to build permanent things. We know it is not only possible, but *probable* that a disaster will affect us because we have come to understand those natural changes. We also realize that disasters are low-probability and high-effect, and so we have come to accept the hazards and threats of these events and have adapted responses to help.

(FEMA photo/ Anita Westervelt)

It is the predictable nature of disasters that allows us to prepare for them in meaningful ways. With this knowledge we can make choices prior to an event and make decisions on some very important things. We can choose where we will live and how we will respond to the disaster probabilities we have chosen to live with. To help you understand what happens in a disaster, the first part of this chapter will discuss what disasters are and the real effects they may have on you. The second part of the chapter will discuss the importance and meaning of the words used in disaster communication.

What are Disasters and How Do They Affect Us?

In the business of emergency management, there are many things that can be communicated to the public prior to a disaster. Although authorities sometimes do not know exactly when a disaster will take place or exactly *how* bad the damage may be, there is other information that can help identify the possibility, probability, and extent of a natural or man-made event. Names like "Tornado Alley," "hurricane season," and "100-year flood plain" represent a level of understanding that can be conveyed to the public to their advantage.

The word "disaster" is defined in the Merriam-Webster dictionary as a sudden calamitous event bringing great damage, loss, or destruction, or more broadly, a sudden or great misfortune or destruction[1]. The application of the word is not limited in scope and is commonly used to describe both the catastrophic deaths of thousands in natural events, like an earthquake-triggered tsunami, or mundane man-made events, like an unsuccessful dinner party. This causes a difficulty: because it is used in so many ways, the word "disaster" does not convey the real impact of an event when we try to use it to describe something that is incredibly dangerous and disruptive.

So what do we do with this situation of loose definition? The answer is to think about what makes an event into a disaster and then think about how those events will affect us and our loved ones. When you think about it, there is a lot of information about disasters that can be discovered prior to the event that is helpful in making choices, plans, and preparations *before* the event. What information about the storm is useful to people before the storm happens?

The "BIG 8": Disaster Qualifiers

When people talk about disasters, they talk about causes and effects. The terms we use to describe a disaster and the methods we use to measure its effects become the definition of the disaster. For example, F5 tornado, Category 3 hurricane, and 8.0 earthquake. But these are generalized descriptions that do not give us enough information to protect ourselves.

There are eight questions to consider when thinking about any disaster: where can it happen, what will happen when, how big will it be, how long will it last, how much reaction time will I have, what will be left, who can help me, and what comes next? Although you may not be able to answer all eight questions for any given situation, it is very rare that you will not be able to answer, or make a good guess on, five or more of them. By gathering information on as many of these questions as you can answer, you make an informed plan and decision on just about any situation, man-made or natural.

See facing page for further discussion and an overview.

#1. Areas of Known Occurrence, Possibility (Where can it happen?)

Areas of Known Occurrence are determined by historical records and known science, which identify the possibility of a disaster based on situation, location, season, or a combination of the three. There is little mystery here, and this information allows us to make choices well in advance of an event. Locations near volcanoes and on fault lines are directly susceptible to the effects of eruptions and earthquakes. Coastlines are susceptible to tsunamis and seasonally susceptible to storm surges and hurricanes. Inland areas can be susceptible to seasonal dangers of tornadoes and fires. If you live in the central U.S., each spring you will need to be aware of tornadoes. The area from Texas through Oklahoma, Kansas, Nebraska, and into Iowa is called Tornado Alley for a good reason. Tornadoes are also possible in all other parts of the U.S., but are not as frequent. If you live in California along the San Andreas Fault, you know you will eventually be affected by earthquakes because you live in an Earthquake Zone. If you live in the mountains or the high plains, you know that there is a high probability of seasonal blizzards and ice storms. You can use this knowledge to determine the possibility of your being affected by a particular type of disaster.

#2. Scales and Measurements, Predictability (What will happen when?)

Disasters are measured in different ways, not just in the difference of the aspects of the event as in a flood being different than a fire, but also in *what* is actually measured and *when* it is measured. For this reason some disaster measurements are useful prior to the event and others are not. Measurements taken for slow-devel-

The "BIG 8": Disaster Qualifiers

When people talk about disasters, they talk about causes and effects. The terms we use to describe a disaster and the methods we use to measure its effects become the definition of the disaster. For example, F5 tornado, Category 3 hurricane, and 8.0 earthquake. But these are generalized descriptions that do not give us enough information to protect ourselves.

There are eight questions to consider when thinking about any disaster: where can it happen, what will happen when, how big will it be, how long will it last, how much reaction time will I have, what will be left, who can help me, and what comes next? Although you may not be able to answer all eight questions for any given situation, it is very rare that you will not be able to answer, or make a good guess on, five or more of them. By gathering information on as many of these questions as you can answer, you make an informed plan and decision on just about any situation, man-made or natural.

We can take these eight questions and express them in quantifiable, or measurable, terms: Areas of Known Occurrence, Events and Measurements, Area of Effect, Duration of Effect, Quick or Slow Onset, Destruction of Infrastructure, Disruptions of Services, and Aftermath. Although history will record each of these aspects in full after a disaster, by looking at each question, we can discern the potential for some of the answers before the event.

1. Where can it happen — Areas of Known Occurrence

2. What will happen when — Scales and Measurements

3. How big will it be — Area of Effect

4. How long will it last — Duration of Effect

5. How much reaction time will I have — Quick or Slow Onset

6. What will be left — Destruction of Infrastructure

7. Who can help me — Disruptions of Services

8. What comes next — Aftermath

The point here is to build your ability to look at a situation and analyze the information you have, to think about what is happening and be able to make an informed decision based on your specific situation and the general knowledge of how the events usually progress.

oping events or events where the threat is determined by the measurement of pre-event conditions, as in the case of wildfire and volcano warnings, can provide useful information prior to the event in respect to the magnitude of a potential disaster. In the case of events where it takes time for the event itself to build up the energy required to become a disaster, such as hurricanes, warnings are based on measurements and movements of the existing storm, once again very useful information prior to the event. At the other end of the spectrum are tornadoes and earthquakes, which are measured after the event and based on the amount of damage done or energy released.

This has a lot to do with the predictability and onset time of an event. The longer it takes for an event to develop into a disaster situation, the more time there is to assess the situation and predict the event's effects. Keep this in mind as it is a major clue to the amount of time you will have to respond to the event.

These criteria work just as well for man-made disasters as for natural ones, although in the case of man-made disasters, they tend to be quick-onset and long-duration based on two factors: first is our occasional overconfidence in the control we have over nature and technology, and second is man's tendency to default to the kinetic tools of political diplomacy, i.e. conduct war and commit terrorism. Any war, just or villainous, causes disaster conditions. Information on the methods of measurement for specific disaster types can be found with the disaster summaries.

#3. Area of Effect (How big will it be?)

Area of effect has two major considerations: first is how far people have to travel to escape the area of effect, and second, how much relief, in the form of rescuers, equipment, and material resources, must move into the area of effect in order to effectively help the population after a disaster.

This aspect can be highly variable or very specific based on the type of event. It is best used in conjunction with other criteria such as destruction, disruption, and duration. As an example, when considering if emergency services will be available after a disaster, there will be differences between different events. Consider these three scenarios: a 30-second earthquake that is felt in several states, but does relatively little damage; a tornado that is a quarter-mile wide, is on the ground for 30 minutes, and travels along a 15-mile path in a highly populated urban area before rising back into the clouds; and a hurricane core that is 30 miles wide, lasts for three days, and travels slowly inland for 100 miles, dropping four days of rain, causing massive flooding well beyond the coastal storm surge. The short-term effects of the tornado may cause the greatest number of deaths, the hurricane the greatest amount of property damage and disruption of services, and the earthquake the greatest area of effect. From this we learn that area of effect is not directly tied to intensity or level of devastation, but can relate to how far people or services will have to travel to get into or out of the area of effect.

#4. Duration of Effect (How long will it last?)

Duration of effect refers to not only how long the causal event lasts, but also how long the effects last. This is not as simple as it may seem: a hurricane that brings a week of rain may only have a core landfall of 12 hours before dissipating into a storm front that lasts for another three days. This would have three distinct phases of effect: first being the wind and storm surge damage from the hurricane core, lasting several hours; second would be potential flooding from the rains, which may take weeks to recede; and third is how long it would take for all the infrastructure damaged in the storm to be fixed or replaced so that people could get back to normal living. An important point here is that duration of effects can be sequential, with multiple events causing effects over an extended duration.

#5. Quick or Slow Onset (How much reaction time will I have?)

This aspect is not prediction. Onset is the amount of time you have with the direct knowledge of an upcoming event. This can be a week's warning from watching a simmering volcano or a tropical storm developing into a hurricane, or it can also be an instantaneous earthquake. Warning time has improved with scientific equipment, such as seismographs to record earth movement and Doppler radar to look into storms to see hook echo indications of cloud rotation and tornadoes. This in combination with more-advanced warning communication systems, such as tornado and tsunami sirens, distribution of weather alert radios, and mass communication applications for personal devices, has improved our ability to communicate threats with as much advanced warning as possible. That said, some events lend themselves to identification better than others. Two examples of extremes are hurricanes, which are seasonal and take many days to develop, on one end of the spectrum, and on the other, destructive earthquakes and tsunamis, which can be separated by hundreds of years but can happen at any time with very little, if any, warning. It is important to remember that duration of effects (how long it lasts) is not always related to a quick or slow onset (how fast it arrives).

#6. Destruction of Infrastructure (What will be left?)

Infrastructure (also called systems) are those permanent structures built by man: houses, buildings, roads, cell phone towers, electrical lines, water treatment plants and city water systems, both clean water delivery and waste & storm water removal, and all the other things built for our public and private use. When these things are destroyed by disasters, it is not just an interruption, but a destruction of the capacity of these systems to provide their intended services. These capacities are important. They provide shelter, food, water, sanitation, transportation, and facilitate services like police protection, fire rescue, and emergency medical response. Once they are destroyed, it can take months or even years to rebuild them.

#7. Disruptions of Services (Who can help me?)

Services are defined as the activities needed for communities to function. Not just limited to government services, this also includes business and economic activities. It has two aspects: first is the availability of the personnel that perform the services, and second is the infrastructure and equipment required to perform the service.

Services are often identified by priority. For this discussion, let's call them essential services and stability services. Examples of essential services are police security, fire, and emergency medical response. Essential services are directly linked to public safety, security, and emergency response. Stability services include business, healthcare, water and electrical service, waste water and trash removal for sanitation, courts and legal activities, and mail delivery. Stability services provide the things we need to keep our communities peaceful, clean, healthy, and economically active.

Providing these essential and stability services involves two major aspects: first is the ability to support the service providers in terms of pay, equipment, vehicles, fuel, and other sundry arrangements that allow the service providers to perform their respective duties, and second is the ability to physically get to the areas where they need to provide services. The loss of either one of these two aspects will cause the service to be limited (how much can be done) or delayed (how quickly can it be done).

#8. Aftermath (What comes next?)

Aftermath involves the follow-on effects of a disaster and refers to what happens after there is destruction of infrastructure and a disruption of services. Aftermath manifests itself only partially in the actual loss of the infrastructure and disruption of services. Think about aftermath as things *other than the disaster itself* that keep you from getting the things you need to survive. It is more closely tied to the government's response to the disaster and the people's reaction to that response. The aftermath of a disaster can be just as bad as or worse than the disaster itself. An effective way to describe aftermath is to look at the term "governance." Governance is different from government. Legitimate and effective governments provide three basic functions of governance: providing security, delivering public goods and services, and providing political participation and accountability.

Why should you care about governance? This will be important to you because you will want to know if you are in a safe and secure place or in a dangerous place, if the government has the ability to provide for your needs or not, and whether you have access to the legal system to protect your life, property, rights, and freedoms. The absence of security, services, and civil protections will be important indicators of different kinds of threats you may encounter.

The first aspect of governance is providing security: public security in the form of police, fire, and emergency medical services to protect people, homes, and businesses. This aspect roughly equates to essential services. The potential for civil unrest, looting, and violence becomes a very real threat after a disaster. Security entails more than just the presence of police and National Guard personnel. It also requires the acceptance by the population that the government is in legitimate and capable control of the situation and able to respond to maintain order without suspending individual rights or unreasonably restricting civil liberty. The loss of security in the aftermath of a disaster manifests as limited or no capacity to provide police response for the public, which can result in looting, violence, and other forms of lawlessness.

The second aspect of governance is to deliver the stability services that allow for a functioning society: commerce, health, education, electricity, water, and sanitation. Critical in post-disaster areas are the aspects of health, water, and sanitation. Education can be temporarily suspended, separation from electricity can be endured for a short period of time, but health services, water, and sanitation are paramount. The loss of these services has a direct impact on health and life and will eventually cause security issues, because when a government fails to provide health services, water, and sanitation, they may be seen as a failed or ineffective government. The loss of services in the aftermath of a disaster manifest as disrupted medical services, untreated injuries, exposure to disease, and potential shortages of water and food. You can see how, if these important services were allowed to fail for too long, it could cause dissatisfaction within the affected population.

The third aspect of governance is providing access to political participation and accountability. Before a disaster, this has to do with the right to vote, free speech, and effective courts. But after a disaster, this translates directly to access to justice (due process in a court of law) and is an important part of the idea of legitimacy addressed in providing security. The combination of security and *access to justice* is collectively called rule of law. The loss of rule of law in the aftermath of a disaster manifests as loss of access to due process of law (proper law enforcement) and no access to courts to address civil grievances. This directly impacts on public trust and the public's perception of the legitimacy of government.

In many cases a disaster will include multiple destructive elements, as in the case of both Hurricane Katrina and Super Storm Sandy, where there were hurricanes, storm surges, flooding, the destruction of infrastructure, the disruption of services, lack of food and water, loss of sanitation, and exposure to disease. Despite these similarities, each hurricane had aspects unique to its situation. In the aftermath of Katrina, the dangers included the loss of rule of law, civil unrest, looting, and dangerously hot temperatures. The aftermath of Super Storm Sandy was marked by shortages of medicine, fuel for heating homes, and dangerously cold temperatures. In the aftermath of a disaster, you may be exposed to a variety of threats, such as injury and lack of medical care, exposure to disease, separation from emergency rescue and police pro-

The Bottom Line (The "BIG 8")

The idea behind the Big 8 is to provide a framework to define a disaster in real effects. Think of disaster effects as things that separate you from the protection, systems, and services provided by governance. Use this information to make your plans, for both before and after an event, to help you accomplish your most important task: to get yourself and your loved ones to a safe and secure location where there is security, rule of law, and stability services. Most of the bad things about disasters (the loss, the pain, the fear, and the uncertainty) involve separation from these aspects of governance.

Another important point to remember is that the definition or measurements of a disaster are less important than the effects. The names and descriptions are all attempts to describe how much potential power is in an event, but the names are not a direct indicator of the amount of damage that an event can cause. A Category 1 hurricane and a microburst tornado can still cause massive destruction and should not be taken lightly. Knowing how to use the Big 8 to keep yourself informed of your situation will help you make better choices.

What can you do? Be prepared and stay aware.

What does it mean to be prepared and aware? It sounds simple enough: have some supplies, and listen to the radio for news. Having the right supplies is not difficult or expensive. We will address this later in the book. Listening to the radio becomes the difficult task. Understanding the words that are being used during an emergency in respect to what they mean for you is the key to your survival.

This chapter will introduce you to some important language used in emergency management, not just in definitions, but in what they will mean to you during a disaster. When you have completed reading this chapter, you will have improved your ability to understand the nature and scope of different kinds of disaster situations and be better able to choose what will be best for you and your family's preservation.

We will start the definitions with the phrase "Prepared and Aware." In respect to preparedness it may help to use the military term *readiness*. Readiness means at any time the service member is prepared with an understanding of the mission, educated on the tasks required to complete the mission, and equipped with all the required tools and resources they may need to complete the mission. They are also mentally prepared to work as part of a team or operate independently depending on the situation.

In order for you to be *prepared*, you should understand the types of threats and hazards you may encounter, have the supplies you will need readily available for use, and be ready to take the actions you need to keep yourself and your loved ones safe. A key aspect of this idea is that better understanding allows you recognize your situation sooner, act sooner, and use fewer supplies. The earlier you act, the less expensive in time and resources your actions will be. When you act on your own time schedule, rather than just reacting to things as they happen, you will be less likely to be restricted by the situation.

To be aware is the ability to perceive and understand what is going on around you, the capacity to see, hear, and understand those things that will affect you. It implies not only that you know what is happening around you, but also that you are ready and willing to make informed decisions and take action on your own behalf.

The discussions and definitions that follow will help you in being prepared and aware.

tection, separation from the rule of law, and being left without resources to protect or sustain yourself. Disasters are bad, aftermath can be worse, and the potential threats can be different for each situation, even when the disaster elements are very similar.

One would think that aftermath is unavoidable, but this is not the case. The disaster is only the catalyst for aftermath, but not the cause of it. After a disaster, the people will have an expectation of what the government will do to help them. When the state has the capacity to gather and provide resources and the political will to use the resources to meet the expectations of the people, then the situation becomes highly resilient (but not completely immune) to the effects of aftermath. If government fails in gathering the capacity to respond or lacks the will to act to meet the expectations of the people, then the aftermath is a separate disaster in itself.

The Language of Disaster

The word disaster originally referred to an astrologically unfavorable aspect to a planet or star that foretold of a great misfortune. This original use holds an important key to the meaning of the word disaster as it is used today. It refers to something that we know can and may happen that will affect us in a negative fashion. If a disaster is an event that is both *possible* and to some extent *probable*, it is *predictable*. Anything we can predict, we can prepare for. The words we will cover are called "So What" words. They are provided to offer food for thought and to inspire you to consider both what they mean and what they mean to you and your survival.

See facing page for further discussion.

Disaster

There are some common themes in the myriad definitions for disaster. Laurie Pearce[3] and Terry Cannon[4], experts in the field of emergency communication, both note that much of the definition has to do with both the impact and the scale of the event. This idea of initial damage, duration, and area covered is important not just in defining a disaster, but in recognizing an event as a disaster. Keep these things in mind:

- Disasters are non-routine, low-probability, and high-consequence events that are *perceived* as being exceptional and requiring external assistance for recovery by *both those affected and those outside of the area*. This can be a legalistic view, as in the case of Designated Flood Zones and Flood Hazard Areas. In this example the government absolves itself of the responsibility of any response beyond emergency rescue by not recognizing floods in these areas as disasters. These maps can change over time, as do other federal definitions and area classifications. Be aware of changes and stay up to date.

- Disasters lead to increased mortality, illness, and injury, destroy or disrupt people's livelihoods, *and* exceed the capacity of the affected area to respond to it in such a way as to save lives, preserve property, and maintain the social, ecological, economic, and political stability. By these criteria not all destructive or disruptive events are disasters, even if your house is completely destroyed. This will become important when you are deciding how to prepare for different types of disasters and how much help you can expect to receive, if any.

- Disasters can also refer to somebody or something that fails. In the "So What" category, this is important. The failure of those outside an event to recognize and respond to mortality, illness or injury, and disrupted livelihood can be a completely separate disaster in itself. The best example of this is the delays in assistance to the city of New Orleans in response to Hurricane Katrina. Even though, in that case, it was political gamesmanship that caused the delay, it made no difference to the 100,000 people trapped and dying in the city in the summer of 2005. Despite the best intentions of rescuers and federal response agencies in many cases, the response arrived too late, did not meet the needs of survivors, or exposed survivors to secondary threats.

"SO WHAT" Words

The word disaster originally referred to an astrologically unfavorable aspect to a planet or star that foretold of a great misfortune. This original use holds an important key to the meaning of the word disaster as it is used today. It refers to something that we know can and may happen that will affect us in a negative fashion. If a disaster is an event that is both *possible* and to some extent *probable*, it is *predictable*. Anything we can predict, we can prepare for. The words we will cover are called "So What" words. They are provided to offer food for thought and to inspire you to consider both what they mean and what they mean to you and your survival.

The language of disaster is somewhat confusing. There are several different definitions and mixed meanings not only for the word disaster, but also for related words like hazard, risk, and threat. The issue of a lack of consensus on the concise definition of key terms is a major point of discussion in emergency management. As of the writing of this book, there is no definitive set of definitions for the common terms used in emergency management. The use of these common terms in government disaster plans is mostly concerned with jurisdictions, planning responsibilities, criteria for government emergency assistance, and other things that define what local, state, and federal government is responsible for doing before, during, and after a disaster. "Which definitions and concepts will be used depend less on their inherent or scientific merits but more on political considerations."[2] This is very important when thinking about political will and aftermath.

The real problems arise when the same words are used to communicate different meanings depending upon the context in which they are used. This means some words used to communicate disaster information will have more than one meaning depending upon when they are spoken, before or after a disaster takes place. This makes it particularly important to understand what the words meant *at the time* they were spoken.

For this reason it is important to look at the words used to describe disasters and determine what it is they are trying to convey, the "So What" factor. There are a few words that will be particularly vital for you to understand and that may have a significant effect on your ability to survive. These "So What" words are disaster, survivor, capacity, capability, hazard, threat, risk, watch, warning, mandatory, rescue, relief, assistance, and relocation. This list is a starting place for your understanding, and as you study your own situation, you may want to add more words and definitions to this list.

Each one of these words has a meaning that is linked to two important aspects: first, how you choose to prepare and respond when you hear the words used, and second, how the government uses the word to describe what they are capable of doing and willing to do in response to a disaster.

- Disaster
- Survivor
- Capability
- Capacity
- Hazard
- Threat
- Risk
- Watch
- Warning
- Mandatory
- Rescue
- Relief
- Assistance
- Relocation

Survivor

A survivor is someone who lives through a disaster and recovers their life. It could be someone who makes informed choices before a disaster and knows what to do during an event to avoid threats or someone who is just lucky. This may just be semantics, but it is important. The media likes to refer to all those affected by a disaster as victims to enhance the drama of the situation. This is not necessarily true. Victims die or fail to recover from the effects of a disaster, and survivors live through the effects of a disaster and recover in some way that allows them peace of mind. Your choices prior to a disaster and your attitude when affected by a disaster will be one of the major factors to your survival. To avoid becoming a victim, think like a survivor.

Capability

Capability refers to what can be done: the authority, power, or practical ability necessary to do something. The importance of this word is that it only addresses ability (can) and not capacity (how much). People can fall into the mistake of assuming capability (can) will translate directly into action (will). If you hear the word capability, the next word to listen for is capacity.

Capacity

Capacity refers to limits of capability, the maximum amount of output or productivity.

The "So What" factor of capacity is to understand that existing services may not be available to you in an emergency. This word will translate into how much time you will need to survive on your own until the capability can reach you. Also understand that capacity will often go to the greatest number of people first. This "triage effect" comes from the responders' desire to get the greatest number of people as quickly as possible. You may be asked to wait for rescue while watching rescue vehicles pass you by to get to a location with a greater number of people or people in a more desperate or dangerous situation than you are in. Remembering the definition of disaster, in many cases the capacity will not be enough to meet needs. Adjust your expectations to meet the reality of the situation you see and the emergency communications you hear.

Hazard

A hazard is something that has the potential to physically affect a person negatively. This can be anything from a deadly gas to a pointy object. The "So What" factor for hazards is the need to identify the hazard and then separate or distance yourself as much as possible. We live around hazards every day — caustic chemicals, uneven sidewalks, office workers with colds or the flu — and we survive quite well. The government helps by identifying hazards and suggesting ways to mitigate or contain the hazard. The Occupational Safety and Health Administration (OSHA) requires all chemicals and effects to be documented in areas where chemicals are used. They identify and regulate best practices to ensure a safe workplace.

Although it may seem cumbersome in day-to-day life, OSHA hazard information is, in reality, very helpful, most especially in the form of signs and placards. Although common sense tells us to watch our step when walking through post-disaster rubble, the ability to read and understand the warning signs on vehicles and buildings can come in very handy. OSHA placards identify explosives, gases, flammables, poison and inhalation hazards, acidic and corrosive materials, and radioactive substances by word, picture, and color code. This is important after a disaster because contained things tend to leak out of, or escape, their containers. Knowing how to read these hazard signs is just one hazard identification skill, but it is a very useful one.

For more information on posted hazard information, go to the OSHA web site or visit http://www.compliancesigns.com. Hazards that escape confinement and go from potential to possible have become threats.

Threat

A threat is something that has the *possibility* to physically affect a person negatively. Where hazards are contained, threats are on the loose; a threat is an exposure to a hazard. Exposure to a threat, or multiple threats, in a disaster situation is serious business, and threats should not be ignored. The "So What" for threats is the nature of the threat because it will affect how you respond as well as how the government responds.

Threats can be situational or environmental. Examples of situational threats are looting, lawlessness, and violence, as in the case of civil unrest. Examples of environmental threats are heat, cold, contaminated food, and diseased water. During the aftermath of the earthquakes and tsunami in Japan in 2011, the situational threat of violence was low in all areas, but the environmental threat of radioactive exposure was high in some areas. Your part in response to a threat is to avoid it and move away from it when you can. This may seem simplistic, but staying away from trouble has a lot to do with not getting into it.

Governments warn of hazards, but they respond to threats. When they do respond, it is often with a broad brush. This is important to remember because, to the government, threat response is not the same as rescue. When civilian law enforcement and federalized military forces move into an area to reestablish rule of law during civil disturbance, they will be more aggressive than when responding to a flood or tornado. Similarly the government will be much more demanding of public cooperation during a mandatory evacuation for a radiological event than they would be for the enforcement of a mandatory hurricane evacuation order because they would have a greater desire to get everyone out of the area to avoid the threat themselves.

Risk

Risk is a vague word indicating an undefined possibility or chance of a negative outcome. It is most often used when logic and experience tell us something could go wrong, but we are not entirely sure when or how. *Risk becomes a very important word when we are thinking about danger and how we will react to that danger.* When used in plans, the word risk helps in the description of exposure to hazards that may become threats (i.e. low risk vs. high risk). It addresses neither a person's actions nor the government's. The words risk and threat are often used as having the same meaning, and this can cause confusion during disaster communication. When you hear the word risk used before an event, it refers to possibilities. When you hear the word risk used during or after a disaster is identified, then look and listen for information on identified hazards or threats.

Watch

A watch is an official recognition that conditions are right for a dangerous situation to develop and indicates a need for specific awareness. The intent of issuing a watch is for the public to change its behavior to reduce possible exposure to dangerous conditions and to confirm preparations for the identified threat. A good example of this is storm watches. Government meteorologists know enough about atmospheric conditions to be able to predict when storms are likely to occur. The "So What" of a watch is that it provides awareness and valuable preparation time. Awareness includes changes in your regular activities that may put you or your family at risk of exposure to harm. As an example, don't go out on the lake or play golf during a severe thunderstorm warning due to the increased likelihood of lightning strikes.

During watches, you should also take the time to ensure your preparations are complete and your supplies and are in place: in the case of tornadoes, access to shelter, and in the case of snow and ice storms, blankets and food. When an agency takes the time to issue a watch for any condition, from snow storms to tsunamis, you can choose to use that time to prepare, confirm your preparation, and adjust your activities to protect yourself.

Warning

A warning is a confirmation that a dangerous situation exists. The purpose of a warning is to get you to *take action to protect yourself*. Many times a warning will follow a watch and represents the development of an undefined risk into a specific threat. In many cases warnings come on short notice and you will not have time to prepare after the warning is issued. When a warning is issued, you should be able to go immediately to your preparations and supplies. The number-one rule for responding to a warning is *don't panic*. The number-two rule for responding to a warning is not to ignore it. Doing the right thing — calmly, smoothly, quickly, and without a fuss — is the key to success and survival. Once you have moved to a safe place, be calm enough to listen for more information. This information can come from the media or listening to the sounds of the storm. DO NOT go to look. That will just expose you to the danger you have been warned about. You have a choice in your response to a warning: you can look for excitement, or you can look for safety.

A Note on Watches and Warnings: There is a growing concern in emergency management that the public has become complacent to warnings. To help communicate the dangers of warnings more accurately, words like "mass devastation," "un-survivable," and "catastrophic" will be used to explain to people how severe the storm's impact is expected to be.

Mandatory

Mandatory is a very important word, and when you hear it you should act upon it. By definition mandatory involves an instruction *required* to be complied with, usually because of an official recognition that things may go badly. It is the official requirement part that is of concern to you, and failure to comply or take action can have serious consequences. From the government's perspective the word is used when emergency managers determine a situation will have one or both of the following effects: first, that the anticipated effects pose a very real threat to human life; second, the disaster situation will limit or surpass the government's capacity to respond.

This means that within the area affected by a disaster, the government may not be able to provide security or services. This can include the inability to rescue people or get food and water into the affected area. The mandatory order will be an attempt to distance the public from a dangerous or undesirable effect. It could be an evacuation order to get you away from a destructive disaster or a "stay in your homes" order to limit your exposure to disease or civil unrest.

The "So What" of mandatory is that you should have a much lower expectation of rescue or incoming services in the area covered by the mandatory order. *If you choose to ignore mandatory instructions, you should consider yourself on your own and not expect assistance to arrive in time to save you*, not because the government will not try to help, but because the demand for rescue and assistance will be so great from all the other people who chose to ignore the mandatory order that your chances of getting help may be greatly reduced.

Rescue

A rescue is the act of saving somebody or something from an *immediately dangerous or harmful situation*. The "So What" of rescue is that in almost every case a rescue will leave you alive but unhappy. Remember that a successful rescue will only remove you from the immediate threat, and in most cases, rescues that are considered successful are uncomfortable, frustrating, exhausting, and scary, but ultimately successful. Think of rescue in three categories:

- **Self rescue** offers you the most choices, uses the least amount of resources, and is the most preferable. When confronted with a threat, having the ability and resources to respond to the threat, for example to have a medical kit and provide first aid until you can move away from the threat on your own, is a huge advantage.

- **Assisted rescue** is where you need some help, but are not totally dependent on the assistance of others for your survival. This can include food, water, medical attention, and transportation. Understand that the intent of assistance is to help as many people as possible. This may conflict with your desire to get everything you feel you need. The instructions you receive from an assistance organization will be designed to meet your *immediate needs* and to provide relief to the greatest number of people possible. Sometimes meeting your immediate needs is very helpful, but if you ask for help from others, you will need to be ready to wait for your turn.

- **Dependent rescue** is the least preferable and sometimes your only option. Rescuers will do everything they can do, which may not be much more than removing you from the immediate threat and providing minimal first aid, minimal food and water, uncomfortable and overcrowded shelter, and absolutely no privacy, but you will survive. If you receive help from rescuers, one of the biggest things you can do for yourself is to follow the instructions of emergency personnel. If you want their help, you must cooperate with them and not make demands for more than you absolutely require.

Relief

Relief is what comes after rescue and is usually still within the timeframe of post-disaster recovery. Relief provides minimal security, basic first aid, food and water, uncomfortable and overcrowded shelter, and (most likely) absolutely no privacy — only the basic resources and services you need to survive provided in a location other than your home. The "So What" of relief is that you should not expect comfort from a relief effort. You may self-rescue, but still need relief assistance. It is preferable to separate yourself from relief as soon as you can reasonably do so. This is a balance between staying long enough to get enough resources to move on and staying too long and becoming dependent on relief in order to survive.

Assistance

Disaster assistance is much like relief, but without the immediate threat. It is most often associated with rebuilding after the disaster and provided to people who have returned to their homes or to some other form of permanent or semi-permanent housing. This can include food, water, medical attention, shelter, transportation, or even money. The "So What" of assistance is that it may not give you everything you need in order to keep what you have left. It may take months or years for a community to return to pre-disaster conditions of infrastructure and economic opportunity. When the effects of a disaster limit government services and economic opportunity for an extended period of time, the assistance may only be enough to help you survive when what you truly need is to rebuild and thrive. Assistance can be very helpful, but if you're not careful you can become dependent on assistance. Assistance will keep you going, but it will not help you back up. You will need to do that on your own. Use assistance for what it is, and then get away from it as soon as you can. This is sometimes easier said than done.

Relocation

Relocation is to move to a new place on a long-term basis. This is different from an evacuation, where you expect to be able to return to your home after the threat has passed. Disaster relocation involves not coming back to your home for months, or even ever again. This may be because your home is destroyed or because long-lasting effects of a disaster and aftermath keep the area from economic recovery. Much of your property may be left behind. You may be faced with leaving everything but a few of your most-valued personal belongings and your important documents. If you live in an area where catastrophic disaster is a possibility, you will want to think about where you would relocate and have your ideas well thought out before you are faced with the necessity.

(FEMA photo/Marty Bahamonde)

Conclusion

The descriptions of the effects of disasters and definitions of disaster language provided in this chapter do not paint a pretty picture. This is not intended to cause you to give up hope, but just the opposite. We cannot stop natural disasters, and the accidents that lead to man-made disasters are the unintended failures of man's attempts to control his environment. What we can control is how we prepare and educate ourselves for the known eventualities of our changing planet.

You have been provided with some basic tools for how to understand disaster situations and how to see, hear, and understand the things you will want to know about. Some choices will be required, and you *will* choose. Even deciding not to choose is a choice.

How Response Works (Response Capability)

Before we get into individual planning and preparation, we need to take a look at the local, state, and federal response capabilities that will be activated during a disaster. The roles, responsibilities, capabilities and resources of first responders and incident-response agencies should be defined so that appropriate and realistic expectations can be made for their performance. Starting from the local level and moving to organizations from higher echelons of government, an accurate picture can be portrayed of the capabilities of the different levels of responders. This does not include the wide variety of assistance that states and communities will receive to rebuild communities after the immediate threats of the event are mitigated.

(U.S. Army photo by Spc. Joseph Davis/Released)

The Goal of Response

As you read through these explanations of the capabilities of the different jurisdictions of government, understand that each responding element will have specific tasks they want to accomplish and an order in which they will want to get them done. The plan of every response effort will *always* follow this simple set of priorities: Security, Rescue, Relief, and Recovery.

Security

Before anyone can be rescued, the responding agency will make sure that the rescuers will not be unreasonably exposed to hazards and threats that may cause them to be injured or killed in their attempts to save people's lives. This includes protecting both the public and responders from environmental hazards and threats in addition to protection from violence and civil unrest. When an area is too dangerous to enter, rescue is delayed.

What is too dangerous? Generally speaking there are two qualifiers. First, although there is risk in any rescue scenario, the responder has to have a greater chance of successful rescue than of death or injury to themselves. This also includes preservation of the equipment and the capacity to continue their mission. The men and women who take these jobs are brave and capable and will face considerable personal risk to save a person in danger. Secondly, the area must be free of violent attackers. The threat of violence will stop a rescue effort because responders will not expose themselves or their equipment to a significant threat of violence; this is not the kind of risk they are willing to take. Rescuers will not be allowed to do their jobs until law enforcement has made the area safe for them to enter. In the case of a major disaster, it may take hours or days to establish security.

Rescue

The first priority after security is established is to rescue people in immediate danger from death or injury. Putting out fires, removing people from flood waters and collapsed buildings, providing first aid, transportation to medical facilities, and dealing with other immediate threats, post-disaster hardships are the rescuers' major concerns. An important distinction is that "rescue" only saves people from an immediate threat; once your life is no longer in danger, rescue stops. Some people may have an expectation that their rescuers will do other things they may need, like transport them to a relief center or provide them with food. Helping people not in immediate danger is called relief and is not the goal of rescue.

Relief and Recovery

Relief and recovery can take place at the same time, but encompass slightly different aspects. Relief provides for the basics of survival, primarily in the form of shelter, water, and food, but also in the form of medical care for injuries that are not life-threatening, transportation to safer or better resourced locations, and assistance in reuniting families separated by the disaster. In many cases these services will be provided by religious or community organizations. Not all relief locations will be the same, and different providers will be capable of filling different needs. In recovery, responders will work on the collection and proper handling of the dead, clearing of streets, and restoration of utilities like power, water, and sanitation. If you survive a disaster without major injury or need for rescue, you may have to be patient and wait until the rescue phase is over for recovery to start so you can get to relief. Keep these ideas in mind as you read through the capabilities' descriptions below.

Tiered Response (Local, State, Federal)

Tiered response means that disasters are managed and responded to at the lowest level and only when it is determined that more help is required are higher levels of assistance requested for the response. This is important because the local government is responsible for disaster response and will use its own capabilities before asking for help from the state. Most disasters can be responded to with local resources. Some disasters require state assistance. Few disasters are so large that they require federal resources for a complete and timely response effort. Understand that federal disaster response is different from federal disaster relief. In relief the federal government allocates money to the state to help with recovery after the disaster is over. In response the federal government sends people and resources to assist with saving lives and stabilizing the situation. Examples of federal response are Hurricane Katrina, Super Storm Sandy, and the BP oil spill.

In any disaster response there is a specific set of rules for what level of government (or their related assistance agencies) has the responsibility to respond first, who is allowed to assist, and what must be done to ask for more help. As you read through all the things each level of government does, understand that all levels of government are motivated by the same goal: public safety, relief, and economic recovery. The questions start when the issue of method is addressed. Governments are motivated by two major considerations when it comes to methods of mitigation. These two aspects are not always synchronized. The first is, "Is there money?" *And* the second is, "Who gets to spend it?".

The first motivator is the availability of money to pay for the response. How much of the collected taxes and funds provided by local resources, state funds, and federal treasure will be required to conduct the response? This is manifest in the capability and capacity of police, fire, and other emergency response that is ready for the local government to use in a disaster response. Do not think badly of your local civic leaders and state representatives. By keeping a close eye on costs, they ensure the community, county, or state will have enough funds remaining in the public coffers to get the local economy up and going after a disaster. This is an expensive necessity that must be considered.

The second motivation is authority. The level of government that holds jurisdiction has the authority to direct the rescue, relief, and recovery effort. It also has the power to spend the money that pays for those efforts. In the end, the real question is of how federal agencies and federalized military forces are used in response to a disaster. Can the federally empowered personnel tell the locally elected sheriff or mayor what to do? In a few chapters, when you are reading about how cities and counties request state assistance and how states request federal assistance, understand that these questions are fixed in the minds of each level of government.

Local government will do all it can first, and only when it determines that it needs help will it ask for it. The same is true of states and territories. A governor will not ask for federal assistance without some soul-searching because the cost to the state is not only in dollars but in responsibility for everything that happens or fails to happen, and the political cost to the state (not just the person in the office) can be great. That said, the county emergency manager or the governor will not hesitate to ask for assistance from higher levels if lives are in danger.

As you are making your plans, you may be able to influence where you get your help. One aspect of using the government resources is choosing whether you go to the FEMA relief camp for federal help, the municipal center for city government assistance, or the local church for community assistance. The Red Cross and other national relief agencies operate at all three levels. If you have a preference as to what level of government provides your assistance, you should keep this in mind and plan accordingly. Just remember that you may not have a lot of choices in the middle of the disaster, and ensure that preferences for one type of relief do not become exclusions of another.

Local Response

In the event of a disaster, the initial assistance on the scene will most likely be the local first responders. Local police, EMT, and fire departments were the first on the scene at the World Trade Center, the Pentagon, and in the fields of Pennsylvania on September 11, 2001.[6] This was also true of the Alfred P. Murrah federal building in Oklahoma in 1995. These agencies and departments are designed to respond to the immediate needs of the public.

The local municipality provides police and fire response. The police provide protection for people and their property under the laws of the local jurisdiction. Fire departments responded to threats and hazards to the public and their property. Employees from both types of organizations can perform basic first aid. Fire departments carry specialized equipment for responding to a variety of situations including, but not limited to, fires, hazardous material spills, and extraction and rescue. This rescue equipment often includes specific tools for responding to automobile accidents and for confined-space or limited-oxygen environments. These departments vary in their capabilities based upon their levels of funding and training. Funding is highly dependent on the tax base of the area they serve. Smaller communities tend to have less funding and less response capacity. Larger communities and major metropolitan areas can have departments employing thousands of police and firefighters who utilize the most advanced equipment. The size of the department will not always correspond to the ability of the responders or the sophistication of the equipment they use.

These departments are designed to provide for the general public and, to a limited extent, private industry. Although they operate twenty-four hours a day, they are limited in the duration of their response. In the case of a major disaster involving massive property damage or large numbers of casualties, communities can mass their response assets to mitigate damage, but this response will draw from the total response capability and, in all but the largest communities, maximum continuous response may not be sustainable for more than 8 to 12 hours without outside assistance.

In addition to the requirements identified by their respective local governments, local response agencies are also subject to federal mandates on their response capabilities. An example of this is the Nunn-Lugar-Domenici Defense Against Weapons of Mass Destruction Act of 1996.[6] This federal mandate sets requirements for cities, counties, and states for levels of training and response capability in order to respond to a weapon of mass destruction (WMD) attack in the United States. Mandates like these, although prudent and necessary, draw resources from already-strained response budgets.

Private industry is also involved in first-response capability. Privately owned hospitals and independent ambulance services provide medical response for the stabilization and transportation of injured persons to hospitals within the community. These transportation assets include mostly fleets of wheeled ground ambulances but can also include helicopter air-transport assets as well. Because these hospitals are in most cases financially self-sustaining or for-profit organizations, they do not maintain significant open space for mass casualties or the medical staff to treat large numbers of victims. These hospitals and ambulance companies can mass their resources for a limited time, but are constrained by the same issues of finite resources and manpower that limit prolonged operations of community responders. Most healthcare organizations have reciprocal agreements, allowing them to transport persons beyond their service capacity to other hospitals. Accredited personnel from hospitals outside the community can also augment medical staff in situations of high demand. This has been the case in many disaster situations.

Commercial industry is required to provide infrastructure to support the protection of their property and the safety of the surrounding community. This infrastructure comes in the form of ensuring proper water capacity for fighting fires and specialized equipment for any specific needs the industry may have. In some cases, the private facility is required to provide trained security, firefighting, or Emergency Medical Technician (EMT) personnel to meet the needs of their particular industry. This is especially true of industrial or chemical manufacturing facilities.

As local requirements and federal mandates become greater (taking up more resources), regional cooperative agreements are becoming more prevalent. Coordination of this kind, both public and private, is often made at the county level. Communities pool their assets in order to build greater capability within their county or region. This level of cooperation varies from region to region, but in the best cases communities divide the responsibilities up and each provides a separate service to the whole. In rural areas it is not uncommon to find the responding departments consolidated at the county level and not specifically associated with an individual community at all.

In order to coordinate between these separate agencies, the local responders use an integrated coordination system called the Incident Command System (ICS). This system is used nationally by civilian responders at the local, state, and national levels in order to allow for effective leadership and mitigation of any situation based upon the requirements of the situation and the level of agency responding. If local assets are not sufficient to meet the emergency response requirements, a community can request state (or regional) assets through the state Office of Emergency Services (or the equivalent state agency).

State Response

The state has a variety of agencies that can respond to almost any need. The state's uniformed law enforcement agency is the highway patrol (sometimes known as state police). An example of a highway-patrol mission statement is provided by the Kansas Highway Patrol: "[We] are committed to providing protection of life and property through enforcement of traffic and other laws of the state of Kansas."[7] Although recognized primarily as a transportation control organization, the highway patrol plays a much larger role than just enforcement of traffic laws. Their close ties to local law enforcement — the state's Department of Transportation, the investigative branches of the state enforcement agencies, the state's National Guard, and the state's Office of Emergency Services — make them a vital resource for the state. The highway patrol has several significant aspects that make it a real response multiplier. It has jurisdiction throughout the state and can exercise concurrent (both authorized to act) jurisdiction with local law enforcement anywhere within the state. It has personnel distributed throughout the state 24 hours a day, 7 days a week, and can consolidate those forces rapidly. It does suffer from the same limitation as local law enforcement, having a restricted duration of continuous, massed operations, but can apply force to a situation for up to several days before requiring assistance. The duration of sustained operations is dependent on the size and funding of the individual department. Most state police have a dedicated, independent communications system that is operational along all major state highways across the length and breadth of the state. It can use these assets of speed, massing of personnel, and communication to meet the requirements of communities in need. In Kansas these assets are managed through their Emergency Operations Section, General Headquarters, which is responsible for planning, policy, and training for critical incidents in which the highway patrol is involved. Each state has a similar organization for command and control of state law-enforcement elements. The highway patrol and state police are well trained in the Incident Command System and can fall in on that program as a contributing member agency with no difficulty at all.

The highway patrol, state police, or Department of Public Safety, depending upon what state you are in, works closely with the State Bureau of Investigation (SBI). The SBIs are much the same in purpose and structure as the Federal Bureau of Investigation, but serve their respective governors rather than the president. Their mission is to provide professional investigative and laboratory services to criminal justice agencies, and the collection and dissemination of criminal justice information to public and private agencies for the purpose of promoting public safety and the prevention of crime within their respective states.[8] This agency becomes prominent when a disaster is found to have been caused by criminal activity and discourages criminal activity after a disaster. These agencies will not provide significant manpower, but will provide subject-matter experts in a wide variety of investigative disciplines.

The agency most likely to provide the largest amount of assets to a community during a significant event is the state's National Guard. The National Guard is the state's military assets. They often consist of both Air Force and Army units. They answer directly to the governor and can be mobilized at the state level. They are federally equipped, trained, and recognized as U.S. military forces. They can be called to service by the president in times of national emergency for domestic or overseas service, but are in reality the traditional militia of the state. Because they work directly for the governor, the National Guard is integrated into the state's Office of Emergency Services (or each state's equivalent). The highest-ranking member of the state's National Guard is called the adjutant general. In some cases the adjutant general, or a civilian emergency manager who works closely with the National Guard, serves as the state's director of emergency management and advises the governor on how to best use the state's civilian and military assets in response to a disaster.

The National Guard of each state has different types and numbers of Army and Air Force units. This state-specific list of resources is referred to as the state's force structure. Where force structure is available, the National Guard can provide communities with supporting vehicles, equipment and manpower, generators to power vital public services, bulk clean-water hauling and storage, personnel for medical assistance, engineer assets to clear roads and remove debris, armed or unarmed soldiers for security patrols to protect lives and property, facilities to temporarily shelter those made homeless by disaster events, and helicopters to move personnel and materials as required within the state. These units operate from facilities called armories, which are located throughout the state. Each armory has a radio system linked to the state's National Guard headquarters and office of emergency services. This can provide statewide communications when civilian systems may have failed. The National Guard can provide significant manpower, equipment, logistical support, and operational control for extended durations as the situation dictates with no degradation of capabilities. The specific capabilities of the units vary dependent on the force structure within the state, but the ability to respond and assist is universal.

Because they are organized in the same manner as federal forces, they use the same style of chain of command. This can be problematic as this military command and control systems do not automatically translate to the Incident Command System. To help the military effectively coordinate with civilian agencies, the National Guard uses a method called the Unified Command. This close coordination allows two not-completely dissimilar systems to work together with each agency protecting their operational and jurisdictional interests while collectively working towards the common goal of life saving and disaster mitigation. Unified Command works well because National Guard and the civilian agencies they work with spend a good bit of time communicating with each other, learning how the other organization works and practicing the skills required for effective cooperation.

Some military units in the National Guard are designed specifically to work with the civilian agencies and are well versed in the Incident Command System. These units are called Civil Support Teams. These are federally funded units that are distributed regionally throughout the nation. They are controlled by the state for assistance in response to events involving weapons of mass destruction or unidentified hazardous materials. Specifically, they respond to chemical, biological, radiological, nuclear, and high-yield explosive (CBRNE) threats or any incident suspected to be such. These Civil Support Teams provide very specialized skills that would be beyond the normal resources of a state to provide in a rapid response capacity. They also have specialized equipment and can decontaminate limited amounts of their own personnel, vehicles, and equipment that have been contaminated in a CBNRE environment. The military aspect of this team allows them to operate in a physically hostile environment.

The state's substantial resources, to include the National Guard called to state emergency duty status, are coordinated through pre-event state response and contingency plans and are normally managed by the state's office of emergency services. Should the situation arise that the state's assets are not sufficient to meet disaster-response requirements, the governor can request assistance through several federal action centers and agencies.

Federal Response

Federal response is linked to the powers of states and legal jurisdictions to such an extent that Chapter 3 is dedicated to the workings of federal assistance to states. But for now the intent is just to explain who from the federal government will be coming to help.

Response
Capability

In responding to a disaster caused by a terrorist or criminal action,[9] federal departments and agencies rapidly deploy the needed federal capabilities to the scene, including specialized elements for dealing with specific types of disasters resulting from the threat or actual use of weapons of mass destruction (WMDs). These teams have set criteria for what they will respond to and the timeline for response. In many cases these teams will be on scene within 8 to 12 hours of notification. To coordinate the federal response, the Federal Bureau of Investigation (FBI) and FEMA have been assigned lead agency responsibility for crisis and consequence management, respectively, in response to a domestic terrorist attack or disaster incident.

The FBI is the lead agency for crisis management in response to criminal acts or domestic terrorism, which includes measures to identify, acquire, and plan for the use of resources needed to anticipate, prevent, or resolve a criminal threat or act of terrorism. Because many of the types of criminal or terrorist activity that cause mass destruction or disruption are covered in the exclusive or supreme (one-agency) jurisdiction of federal law, the United States assigns primary authority to federal agencies to prevent and respond to these events. State and local governments provide assistance as capability allows within the Incident Command System. Despite federal lead in a situation, the local and state concurrent jurisdictions are respected and utilized to their fullest extent.

Crisis management includes active measures for prevention, immediate disaster response, and post-disaster response to an event. Activities include command and control of resources on-scene as the lead agency for a disaster in coordination with other federal agencies and state and local authorities. The FBI also provides guidance on responses to situations requiring the use of classified plans or information. Two examples of this are the FBI Nuclear Incident Contingency Plan and the FBI Chemical/Biological Disaster Contingency Plan.

FEMA is the lead agency for the federal efforts in consequence management, which entails both preparedness for and dealing with the effects of a natural disaster or the consequences of a terrorist incident after the criminal or threat has been dealt with. Although the affected state and local governments have primary jurisdiction for emergencies, a disaster involving weapons of mass destruction or hazardous material could create a situation beyond the scope of local response capability. If this were to happen, FEMA would work with local authority to coordinate the response to deal with the effects of the disaster, to protect public health and safety, to assist in the restoration of essential government services, and to provide emergency assistance. FEMA would implement the Incident Response Plan in cooperation with state and local emergency response agencies.

The difference between a law-enforcement response, like the FBI, and an emergency-management response, like FEMA, is that in a natural disaster, consequence management — the final authority to make decisions on-scene regarding the response to a disaster (rescue and treatment of casualties, protective actions for the affected community) — rests with the local disaster commander. This type of resource augmentation and assistance is fundamentally different from the FBI leadership response in a criminal or terrorist situation,[10] where the federal command structure would be the lead agency for crisis management.

A note about FEMA: Two major events have shaped the way FEMA works over the last ten years: the 1993 Mississippi floods and the 2005 Hurricane Katrina. FEMA took a lot of criticism over shortcomings in the handling of both of those disasters, but they did learn important lessons and, more importantly, acted upon them to ensure improvement. In 2012 when Hurricane Isaac made roughly the same landfall as Katrina, FEMA was ready and moved with purpose and positive effect in rescue and recovery operations. The same was true during Super Storm Sandy and the storms that followed. Do not confuse mission difficulty with inability to respond, and do not discount FEMA or their ability to provide timely and substantial assistance to large numbers of displaced persons in times of need. When worse comes to worse, FEMA will most likely be the agency most capable of getting rescue and relief to those who need it; FEMA knows it, and they take that responsibility very seriously.

Some agencies within the Department of Defense (DoD) and the government laboratories from the Center for Disease Control (CDC) can also be called upon to respond with specialized equipment and capabilities. These facilities can identify chemical weapons and infectious diseases and transport patients with illnesses caused by either biological warfare agents or highly infectious diseases requiring significant levels of containment or isolation to institutions equipped to deal with this level of threat.

Federal Military Forces in Response Efforts

There are four separate types of military structures in the United States. This is different from the branches of the military, which are the Army, Navy, Marines, and Air Force. These structures are separated by *description* in Section 8 of the Constitution and by federal law in the United States Code (USC). They are the raised armies and navy and the militia. Each type of military structure serves a different purpose within the federal and state goal of defense.

The raised armies are what we today call the regular, or active-duty, forces: Army, Navy, Air Force, and Marines. These are the standing forces used for federal defense and are regulated under Title 10 of the U.S. Code. They are under the command of the president and funded by Congress.

The militia is separated into three parts. Although originally the militia were all able-bodied male citizens who could be called to service for limited durations, over time the militia has separated into three distinct forces. The differences between these formations have to do with who pays for and controls the forces. They are the United States Reserves, the National Guard, and the state's militia.

The United States Reserves are forces whose sole purpose is to augment the active-duty. They are regulated by Title 10 of the U.S. Code and are under the command of the president. They are subject to all the rules and limitations of use that control active-duty (Title 32 USC) forces.

The National Guard is the military formation within the states and territories. They are equivalent in structure and equipment to the active-duty, but are regulated under Title 32 of the U.S. Code. They are under the command of the governors of their respective states and territories. They are trained and equipped by the federal government so that in times of war they can be lent to the president by the governors and integrated into the active-duty force. They can be recalled from the president's control by the lending state's governor at any time.

The states' militias are the able-bodied citizens of the respective states and territories. They are more like the original militia as described in the Constitution. These forces are under the command of the governor and are trained, equipped, and paid for by the individual states and territories. In many cases states' militias are funded by the members themselves, as has been the tradition from the earliest years of our nation. These forces are authorized by the Constitution, but regulated by state law rather than the U.S. Code. These forces are never released to federal service and remain under the command of the governor. Their levels of training, equipment, and readiness are not uniform. In states where they are effectively integrated into state response plans, they are often called upon by governors to assist in state response efforts and sometimes loaned to other governors in a similar manner to how National Guard forces are lent to the president. This was the case between Louisiana and Massachusetts during Hurricane Katrina, when the militia of Massachusetts, known as the Massachusetts State Defense Force, provided trained and certified medical personnel to fill in at National Guard mobile military hospitals.

Posse Comitatus and Martial Law

Posse Comitatus

Originally a part of ancient law, Posse Comitatus, or power of the county, was used to call able-bodied men to the defense of the community. On the American western frontier, a sheriff could call up a posse of local men to assist him in law enforcement. Although not used often in modern times, many county sheriffs across the U.S. still have the authority to "command and take with him the power of the county or a part thereof, to aid him in the execution of the duties of his office." This specifically means private citizens with personal weapons under the command of the sheriff and conducting law enforcement under his authority.

When we talk about Posse Comitatus today, we usually are making reference to the Posse Comitatus Act of 1879 and related amendments. Basically this law says that a local sheriff can't go to a military installation, base, or camp and ask for active-duty personnel, weapons, ammunition, or equipment to augment his department or office. Those requests have to go through the governor to the president. The National Guard is not subject to the Posse Comitatus Act when called up by the governor. When the president calls on federal troops, they are not subject to Posse Comitatus either. In both cases the soldiers provide passive support, which means they are not given the full authority of police discretionary powers.

They are limited in their authority to search or arrest and are often used to augment civilian law enforcement. They are authorized to detain and defend. The military ability to detain civilians is formidable, and detention does not provide all of the same legal rights and protections as arrest. The authority to defend is equally powerful. Soldiers can deny civilians access to designated areas regardless of the status of the area as public or private and have a specific set of rules for the use of force they use to determine how much force can be used to enforce the restriction of movement or defense of resources, equipment, or themselves.

The rules for the use of force are used in the support of domestic law enforcement because Rules of Engagement are for combat and not to be used when dealing with the American public. It is important to recognize and appreciate that the military takes care to make that distinction. Soldiers nonetheless have the authority to use force when appropriate within the use of force continuum. This graduated scale of response to threat actions on the part of hostile or aggravated citizenry ranges from self-defense to use of deadly force.

Martial Law

Martial law is not automatically a bad thing. When an aftermath situation degrades to the point of complete loss of rule of law and there is a threat of violence against the population (even if from within the population itself), then the balance between the competing aspects of liberty and security must favor security. That said, marital law is a very dangerous tool that should be used in only the most dire of circumstances and then only for a short amount of time. A short description of martial law will explain why.

Martial law is when the president or the governor suspends local government and constitutional civil liberty for the necessity of security. This places the whole process of rule of law, including law enforcement, arrest authority, and confinement in the hands of the military. This is a uniformly disliked and highly discouraged last-resort solution. It suspends jurisdiction of local elected authority and places a huge burden on the federal forces that are made responsible for all rule-of-law functions. Given the level of preparation and professional capability of local and state governments, the enactment of martial law is extremely unlikely in any situation other than widespread rampant lawlessness or violent civil unrest. Even then there would need to be some indication of organized insurrection before civil liberty and constitutional protections would be superseded by this extreme measure.

NOTE: There are some groups of civilians that form paramilitary groups and claim allegiance to the Constitution rather than service to the people and laws of the states where they muster. By not recognizing the authority of the governors, who are lawfully elected by the people of the represented states, these paramilitary organizations are not militia in the sense of the definition provided in the Constitution. Any formation of military or paramilitary power that does not recognize the legitimate elected government is a competitor and rival to legitimate government of the people, by the people, and for the people.

In times of disaster the three federally standardized force structures of the National Guard, reserve, and regular forces can provide military support to civilian authority in two ways: active-duty and reserve units under Title 10 of the U.S. Code and National Guard units on state active duty under Title 32 of the U.S. Code. For all intents and purposes, the only difference between the two is the governor can call out the National Guard of their respective state and, if the situation calls for it, the president can call out regular and reserve forces in response to a state's request for assistance. Control over and funding of military elements is a big issue during response efforts.

Overall, the consensus is that the local preparedness for response to a WMD terrorist disaster is nominal, meaning effective but very limited. To the extent that hazardous material preparedness applies to the CBRNE arena, some basic protective and containment skills are planned, resourced, and practiced. However, attention must be applied to resource management, planning, and training for the unique nature of CBRNE terrorist disasters. Until a much higher national standard is reached through training and funding of local agencies, there will be a requirement for assistance from federal laboratories in the identification and mitigation of CBRNE or catastrophic hazardous-material events. If federal military forces are the only level of government that can operate effectively in a CBRNE area of effect, that area is, by default, under the control of the military, even if not officially under martial law.

Event preparation and response planning for natural disasters and accidents is based on educated assumptions on the needs of the area and the level of resources available for preparation. The current level of planning is prudent and allows for an adequate response to a vast majority of situations and events that may be encountered by first responders. What is generally agreed upon is that a terrorist attack will quickly overwhelm any first-responder element and most likely the state response as well. Only through open communication and effective cooperation can local, state, and federal agencies come together to coordinate adequate responses to catastrophic events.

Incident Command System, National Incident Management System, & Unified Command

Topics that are important tend to have lots of rules and regulations to govern them. Examples of this are human resources hiring practices and tax law; both are important to government, and both are incredibly boring to read when you are not specifically interested in the subject matter. The same is true of Incident Command. What follows is a rather dry and just as important explanation of the Incident Command System and Unified Command. Although you are not in a disaster now, when one comes along you will have a specific interest in how ICS works. It is a short section and has information worth knowing.

The command and control system used by civilian agencies to respond to almost any kind of disaster situation is called the Incident Command System (ICS). According to the 2003 National Response Team Incident Command System/Unified Command (ICS/UC) Technical Assistance Document, civilian agencies must use a command-and-coordination method designed specifically to interact with other agencies.[11]

How the Incident Command System Works

ICS is now a standardized on-scene incident-management concept designed specifically to allow responders to fit into an integrated organizational structure. It can expand to meet the complexity and demands of any single incident or multiple incidents without being hindered by jurisdictional boundaries.[12] The ICS enables integrated communication and planning by establishing a manageable span of control, and it divides an emergency response into five manageable functions essential for emergency response operations: Command, Operations, Planning, Logistics, and Finance & Administration.

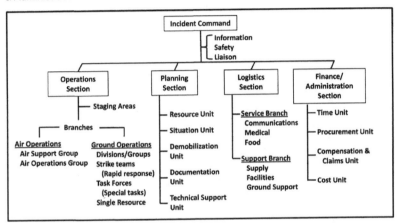

The modular organization of the ICS allows responders to scale their efforts and apply the parts of the ICS structure that best meet the demands of the incident. There are no hard and fast rules for when or how to expand the ICS organization. Many incidents will never require the activation of planning, logistics, or finance/administration sections, while others will require some or all of them to be established. A major advantage of the ICS organization is the ability to fill only those parts of the organization that are required for the response. The ICS organization adheres to a "form follows function" philosophy. The organization should reflect only what is required to meet planned response objectives.

The Lightning Press offers two specific specific Civil-Military SMARTbooks and a Homeland Defense & Defense Support to Civil Authorities (HD/DSCA) SMARTbook covering ICS and NIMS:

Civil-Military Smartbook 1:
National Incident Management System (NIMS)
NIMS is a systematic, proactive approach to guide departments and agencies at all levels to work together seamlessly and manage incidents involving all threats and hazards.

Civil-Military Smartbook 2:
Incident Command System (ICS)
ICS is a standardized on-scene incident management system to allow responders to adopt an integrated organizational structure equal to the complexity and demands of any crisis.

A product of the 1970s, the ICS is the agency standard for response operations in the civilian sector. Its inception was the result of a season of devastating wildfires in Southern California. To fight the blaze, local fire companies came from all of the surrounding counties with assistance from state and even federal agencies. The result was a disaster. Despite the efforts of experienced fire captains and dedicated firefighters, the effort just could not get organized. The uncoordinated efforts suffered from a variety of difficulties. The problems centered on certain areas: command and control, communication, coordination of support, and unity of effort. In military terms, this translates to command and control (C2), signal, logistical resupply, and massing of combat power — the same issue military leaders face when working in task-organized formations. In response to these shortcomings, the agencies involved formed an organization called Fire Resources of Southern California Organized for Potential Emergencies (FIRESCOPE) to identify the resources and systems required to effectively coordinate all the resources of the different agencies. FIRESCOPE developed the first version of ICS. Although it was originally designed for response to wildfires, FIRESCOPE has evolved into an all-risk management system.

Although a single incident commander normally handles the command function, an ICS organization may be expanded into a Unified Command (UC) if there is more than one incident commander responding to an event. The UC is a structure that brings together the incident commanders of all major organizations involved in the incident in order to coordinate an effective response while at the same time carrying out their own jurisdictional responsibilities. Each element conducts operations in support of a common response goal. Similarly, each member of the UC works to develop a common set of incident objectives and strategies, share their information, maximize the use of available resources, and enhance the efficiency of the individual response organizations.

The Unified Command does not function as a committee. When time is of the essence, the principal leadership is there to command the response to an incident. UC should develop synergy based on the significant capabilities that are brought by the various representatives. The UC incident commander may not know what he has in the way of agencies or resources until they show up at the scene. There should be personal acknowledgement of each representative's unique capabilities, a shared understanding of the situation, and agreement on the common objectives. As in any stressful situation, there will be differences, but the necessity of mitigation will often guide the individual ICS commanders to a consensus. In one aspect, UC is like the military: they both require competent and firm leadership. While UC structure is an excellent vehicle — and the only nationally recognized vehicle — for coordination, cooperation, and communication, the duly authorized representatives must make the system work successfully. A strong commander, a single incident commander for a UC, is essential to an effective response. The incident commander is normally the senior responder of the organization with the preponderance of responsibility for the event (e.g. fire chief, police chief, or emergency medical).

This uniformity of response method at the local, state, and federal levels serves a very important purpose: it ensures that the agencies who will be working together all have the same expectation of who will be in control of the response to a disaster situation and a common understanding of the desired goals and outcomes. It also has the advantage of significantly improving the ability of responders to provide effective response and get the most benefit out of the available response capability.

Federal Disaster Response

The next three chapters will address what the government is going to do in a disaster and the rules that govern who is in control of restoring governance in the aftermath of a disaster. This is important because it speaks to the intent of the government and importance of our trusting that government has our best interests in mind and will be successful in assisting not just in our survival, but in our recovery from a disaster.

When we examine the plans for the national response to disasters, we will find the government is taking special steps to ensure that hope (security and economic opportunity), voice (representative form of government and open communication), and justice (rule of law) survive. This chapter looks at the specific plans and addresses, in a general manner, the goals and methods used in a recovery effort as articulated in the separate government plans. We will then see how the different plans fit together to guide and coordinate the efforts of people working from the highest levels of government leadership down to the efforts of state and local leadership, agencies, and service providers.

Note: Much of the information provided here is taken verbatim from plans and government documents or extracted from those documents and placed in context with information from other plans. Specific quotes and data neither have endnotes nor are individually referenced, but every source is identified in the body of the discussion. You are encouraged to go online or to their local government and get copies of these plans and read them themselves. There is significant confusion and misinterpretation of these plans that can be easily avoided just by reading the plans yourself instead of letting someone else tell you what they say. The reader can take the word of the author and the author's intent is to accurately inform. But, should you have questions and want to learn more on your own, this chapter can serve as a study guide should you wish to pursue your own in-depth review of the government's Continuity of Operation Plan (COOP) and Continuity of government (COG) plans. This is an important part of knowing for yourself, thinking for yourself, and making your own plans that will work for you.

Before we get into the individual plans, it would be prudent to examine what exactly government response plans *need* to accomplish. When we say need, we mean what the plans should accomplish to secure, rescue, relieve, and assist the people. We can then compare this to what the government planners *want* to accomplish and see how they match up. It is very important that we as citizens understand that what we need government to provide is what our government wants to accomplish. If these two aspects do not match up, then the government will not have the legitimacy of our consent as the governed. But when they do match up, we can understand that even though times are difficult, the government is in fact working in our best interests.

What we want and need the government to provide for us is governance. In our discussion from Chapter 1, we framed our definition of aftermath by the disruption of governance: the government's ability to provide security (police, fire service, and emergency rescue), public services (health, education, electrical, water, and sanitation), and political participation and accountability (the right to vote and access to courts and the justice system, the rule of law). When these things are disrupted, there is a general lack of opportunity to conduct economic activities and people will not have the stability required to make a living, exercise their individual or social liberties, or pursue good quality of life. As general as that sounds, life, liberty, and the pursuit of happiness are the desired goals. As we review the government plans, see if they meet your expectations. Choose for yourself whether or not you believe the plans to be trustworthy because it is important for you to have confidence in your government.

The U.S. government's plans are expressly written for the preservation of the U.S. form of government and the well-being of the U.S. population. The plans are linked, cooperative, and all focused on the same common goals. We know this for two reasons: first, that is the way the plans are written, and second, these are the very same methods our government uses in stability operations in the aftermath of armed conflict in other nations. Regardless of the fact that war is a political tool, it is still a form of disaster. The disruptions of governance found in armed conflict are very similar to those found during a large-scale natural disaster. By knowing what the government's goals are when reestablishing stability and governance in international post-conflict areas, we can anticipate the government's goals when reestablishing stability in a domestic post-disaster situation. It is very important to differentiate goals from methods when looking at international stability operations in relation to domestic disaster relief. We can see within the plans that the methods are very different. It may not be a comforting idea to some people, but the similarity of goals is an appropriate and realistic expectation.

Federal Plan Types and Tasks

Federal plans are designed to do different things at different times. When you find a plan that looks incomplete, think about what that plan was designed to do. No plan does everything, so when one plan appears lacking, the chances are good there is another plan to cover the issue you are concerned about. Federal plans fall into one of these three major categories: Continuity of Operation (COOP), Continuity of government (COG), and Enduring Constitutional Government (ECG). Each has special components to meet specific requirements. We will not go into great detail here to describe the mechanics of these plans, but knowing what each kind of plan is designed to accomplish is very helpful in understanding how the different plans work together.

Continuity of Operation Plan, or COOP

COOPs are *individual organizational efforts* within organizations, agencies, or departments within a branch of government and provide guidance, both specific and general, as to how the individual organizations, agencies, or departments are to ensure they can continue to perform their respective duties.

Continuity of Government, or COG

COG plans are *coordinated organizational efforts within branches of government* to ensure the eight National Essential Functions (which will be described in detail soon) are continuously protected, supported, and provided.

Enduring Constitutional Government, or ECG

ECG plans are *cooperative efforts between the three branches of government* — legislative, executive, and judicial — coordinated by the president, where each branch does its part in a mutually supporting and friendly manner to ensure the eight National Essential Functions are continuously protected, supported, and provided for the express purpose of preserving the constitutional framework under which the nation is governed.

Requirements of Governance

The goals of governance, as described in stability operations, are described in order of precedence, each stage advancing on the benefits gained from the preceding aspect. These are not separate or stand-alone phases as much as they are descriptions of emphasis during the evolution of effective governance. Some of the aspects will begin in one phase and evolve into the next. Two good examples of this are fire-response services and effective government. Fire response begins as an aspect of security, but expands into an aspect of services. Effective government starts by providing essential services, but evolves in its legitimacy through the application of systems that provide stability. Other aspects grow simultaneously. Economic opportunity is not dependent on legitimate government, but the two are mutually supporting under the benefit of rule of law.

Security

Security has two major aspects: the population is continuously secure, meaning they are safe from fire, crime, and violence, and there is full freedom of lawful movement, meaning there are no special requirements needed for travel or curfews limiting the regular exercise of civil liberties.

Essential Services

Essential services are built or restored. These include water and electrical services to homes and businesses; transportation networks including roads, rails, and airports; fire response; sanitation services including sewage treatment and trash collection; medical services from hospitals, clinics, and emergency medical personnel; and education opportunities from schools and universities.

Legitimate Government with Rule of Law

Legitimate government is made up of effective government institutions, including the establishment and enforcement of local laws and ordnances in addition to the ability to vote in open and legitimate elections. Rule of law entails a full and functional justice system of law enforcement and crime investigation (police), impartial and accessible courts (habeas corpus & trial by jury), and a humane prison system (jails).

Economic Opportunity

Economic opportunity includes having a functioning economy with freedom to conduct lawful commerce; the presence of commercial infrastructure (marketplaces and roads); the ability to move money into and out of the area (banks); the ability to manufacture goods and provide services; and the ability to grow, transport, and market agricultural products.

These things combined together make up the tenets of governance. As you read about the government plans here, or read the actual plans on your own, see if you recognize the tenets of governance in the plans. When you do see them, you will know it is a good plan.

Federal Response

Roles and Responsibilities

Checks and balances are a big part of how government works in the United States, and it is important to maintain this balance, especially in times of emergency. No one part of government is allowed to have sole authority over "Caesar's Trifecta" of manpower, material, and authority to command. We see this represented in the three separate branches of government. We can see these same ideas in the roles and responsibilities of disaster response, where it is less about defense of freedom and more about being able to concentrate on providing the different aspects of required services well. You will find that the providers within the plans fall within one of three major groups: service providers, material providers, and authority providers.

Service Providers and Technical Leadership

These groups will have the capability and skills to take action. They do not have the authority to take action without permission and do not provide their own long-term resources. Examples of service providers are the police, fire department, and military.

Material Providers and Control Elements

These groups have the resources in the form of money to pay for manpower and materials to do the things that need to be accomplished, but will not have the authority to take action and may not have the skills to use the materials they can provide. The best example of this is FEMA. They have resources and the ability to control large operations, but rely on local and state government to bring service providers and technical leadership.

Authority Providers

These groups have the power to start and stop the actions of service providers. This idea of needing authority to take action is a very important form of control and comes in the form of jurisdiction, which we will discuss in detail in a later chapter. Elected officials are authority providers.

With no one group having all three powers, each group is dependent upon the others to get the job done. Working together, the balance of power is maintained between local, state, and federal government. At the state, local-government, and private-sector level, it is important that resources be separate from government control. This is the strength behind how a representative republic and capitalism work together. Figure 2 provides a visual representation of the providers and their respective roles.

Group	Player	Provide
Federal Government	Executive Branch	Leadership & Resources for action (short term)
	Legislative Branch	Authority to spend or use resources (long term)
	Judicial Branch	Constitutional Rulings on Roles & Authority
State, Local, Territorial, and Tribal Government	Elected Officials	Leadership & Authority within Jurisdictions
	Emergency Services	First Response
	Public Services	Reestablishment of lost services
Private Sector	Owners	Leadership, Money, & Materials
	Operators	Skills and Labor

Figure 2.

Federal Plans

Each separate federal plan is one piece of a series of plans that interconnect to form what is collectively called the National Response. Reading a lone plan without the context of its relationship with other plans leaves the reader with an incomplete picture of the National Response as a whole. If you are reading a federal plan and see a void or aspect that is not addressed, it only means that you need to go find the plan that meets that part of the need in the National Response. Sometimes finding these plans is easier said than done, but here are a few of the federal plans that will have a significant impact on how things will work during a National Response. A short description of the general concepts and priorities and methods of each plan will be provided with notes on how they interconnect with other federal plans. For the purposes of our discussion, the goals of governance will be identified when they match a major aspect of the plan.

Presidential Defense Directive 67 (PDD 67): Enduring Constitutional Government and Continuity of Government Operations, 21 October 1998

This is a secret defense plan. The existence of the plan is not a secret, but the aspects of the plan are secret. It is the directive for all branches of government (including some programs and agencies that are not mentioned openly) and provides detailed standards for how the U.S. will respond to a major catastrophic event. The text of PDD-67 has not been released, and there is no White House fact sheet summarizing its provisions. It makes a certain amount of common sense not to openly display our defense and security plans. This is done to ensure the National Response plans for the U.S. are not countered by an opponent reverse engineering our plan in order to find (or create) vulnerabilities. What we do know about PDD 67 comes from the non-secret Continuity of Operation and Continuity of government plans that were written at the direction of PDD 67 for the subsequent branches of government. This is open-source (meaning unclassified and open to media release) information and can be quite revealing.

The president will coordinate the cooperative efforts of national response, not control or direct. This means the separate branches of government will stay separate, and the sovereignty of the states is preserved. This specification that the president will not have "special executive powers of authority" is important. We will see the theme of the preservation of authority within state- and local-level jurisdictions repeated throughout the plans. This is the best indication of the government's intention to help without taking over. The executive branch, being the largest branch of government, has well-defined plans that offer a good view of the goals and methods of the plans.

Federal Continuity Directive 1 (FCD 1): Federal Executive Branch National Continuity Program and requirements (Feb 2008)

This is the overall plan on how the executive branch of the federal government will respond to a major disaster. This is the order for what is to be done. It is a Continuity of Operation, or COOP, plan which means its purpose is to ensure that the essential functions of government do not completely break down by directing the organizations, agencies, and departments of the executive branch to identify their respective mission functions. Mission functions are important because they identify services that the government must provide to the people.

- **Primary Mission Essential Functions (PMEF)** are those tasks each organization must ensure continue in a seamless and immediate manner. Plans for PMEFs are made independently by each organization and simultaneously with other plans.

- **Mission Essential Functions (MEF)** are those tasks each organization must ensure they can continue to provide or resume rapidly after a disruption. Plans for MEFs are made independently by each organization and simultaneously with other plans.

It provides annexes to give specific direction on a variety of Who, What, When, Where, and Why issues. It issues standards, timelines, redundancies and testing requirements to ensure the separate parts of the executive branch can perform their duties in case of a disaster. What it does not say is how to do these things, leaving the details to the individual organizations.

There was some confusion when FDC 1 was released in 2008: the legislative and judicial branches were nowhere in the plan! They were not directed, included, or even addressed. Some people took exception to this and mistakenly believed that the president had made a plan for National Response without the benefits of the legislative or judicial branches. This, of course, is not true. Because FDC 1 is the Continuity of Operations Plan (COOP) for the executive branch, the plan only addresses the executive branch. The president has no authority to direct the legislative or judicial branches in any way. FDC 1 was designed to coordinate with the plans of the other branches of government as outlined in the Continuity of Government and Enduring Constitutional Government plans. This is a good example of the issue of a seemingly incomplete plan being misread by people who do not understand the purpose of each of the COOP, COG, and ECG plan types.

A review of FCD 1, Annex D: Essential Functions provides the details that appeared to be missing from the plan. It spells out exactly what the goals of the plan are along with the authorities and responsibilities of the different branches of government. As described earlier in this chapter, the participants in the plans are all three branches of the federal government, who hold the resources and moneys needed for National Response; the state, local, territorial, and tribal governments, who hold most of the authority; and private-sector critical-infrastructure owners and operators, who control the capability for production and manufacturing.

The national goals for federal response are outlined specifically in the eight National Essential Functions. See facing page for a listing and discussion.

Every plan that follows has at its core the requirement to meet these eight core goals. The plans, by direction, must be redundant and incorporated into the everyday functions of each government agency to ensure the seamless and immediate continuation of their respective Primary Mission Essential Functions.

Executive Order 12656, Assignment of Emergency Preparedness Responsibility

This document provides specifics on the areas of responsibility for the Departments of Agriculture, Commerce, Defense, Education, Energy, Health and Human Services, Housing and Urban Development, Interior, Justice, Labor, State, Transportation, Treasury, Environmental Protection Agency, Federal Emergency Management Agency (FEMA), National Aeronautics and Space Administration (NASA), National Archives and Records Administration, Nuclear Regulatory Commission, Office of Personnel Management, Selective Service System, Tennessee Valley Authority, United States Information Agency, United States Postal Service (USPS), the Veterans Administration, and the Office of Management and Budget. This is the order for who is to perform what tasks. For all intents and purposes, EO 12656 outlines the Primary Mission Essential Functions (PMEF) and Mission Essential Functions (MEF) for each executive branch function. There is not a lot left to the imagination in this order, and it represents a clear understanding from the White House of what it expects from each executive branch function.

National Essential Functions (NEFs)

The national goals for federal response are outlined specifically in the eight National Essential Functions. If you had any questions about what your government has in mind for you after the "big one," here it is. The National Essential Functions are provided here verbatim from the FDC 1 *with the author's addition* of a note for each NEF as to its place in governance at the end of each NEF.

NEF 1. Ensuring the continued functioning of our form of government under the Constitution, including the functioning of the three separate branches of government. This NEF includes Federal executive branch functions that respect the roles and maintain the check and balance relationship among all three branches of the Federal Government. (Legitimate government & rule of law)

NEF 2. Providing leadership visible to the Nation and the world, and maintaining the trust and confidence of the American people. This NEF includes Federal executive department and agency functions to demonstrate that the Federal Government is viable, functioning, and effectively addressing any emergency. (Legitimate government/ security)

NEF 3. Defending the Constitution of the United States against all enemies, foreign and domestic, and preventing or interdicting attacks against the United States or its people, property, or interests. This NEF includes Federal executive department and agency functions to protect and defend the worldwide interests of the United States against foreign or domestic enemies, honor security agreements and treaties with allies, implement military operations ordered by the President, maintain military readiness, and maintain preparedness to achieve national objectives. (Security)

NEF 4. Maintaining and fostering effective relationships with foreign nations. This NEF includes Federal executive department and agency functions to maintain American foreign policy. (Security)

NEF 5. Protecting against threats to the homeland and bringing to justice perpetrators of crimes or attacks against the United States or its people, property or interests. This NEF includes Federal executive department and agency functions to protect against, prevent, or interdict attacks on the people or interests of the Nation and to identify, neutralize, and prosecute those who have committed or intend to commit violations of the law. (Security)

NEF 6. Providing rapid and effective responses to and recovery from the domestic consequences of an attack or other incident. This NEF includes Federal executive department and agency functions to implement response and recovery plans, including, but not limited to, the implementation of the National Response Plan. These are outlined in the 15 Emergency Support Functions (ESF) as described in the National Response Framework (January 2008) and tie directly back to the tenets of governance. (Essential Services)

NEF 7. Protecting and stabilizing the Nation's economy and ensuring public confidence in its financial systems. This NEF includes Federal executive department and agency functions to respond to and recover from the economic consequences of an attack or other major impact on national or international economic functions or activities. (Economic Opportunity)

NEF 8. Providing for critical Federal Government services that address the national health, safety, and welfare needs of the United States. This NEF includes Federal executive department and agency functions that ensure that the critical Federal-level health, safety, and welfare services of the Nation are provided during an emergency. (Essential Services)

Homeland Security Presidential Directive 5 (HSPD 5): Management of Domestic Incidents

This document outlines and directs the requirements of the National Response Plan (NRP) and National Incident Management System (NIMS). It specifically addresses the manner in which the federal government will assist state, local, territorial, and tribal governments when those governing bodies request federal assistance.

Homeland Security Presidential Directive 7 (NSPD 7): Infrastructure Identification, Prioritization, and Protection (2003)

This document instructs the Departments of Agriculture, Health and Human Services, Environmental Protection Agency, Energy, Treasury, Interior, and Defense on exactly what critical infrastructure they are to protect within the United States.

Homeland Security Presidential Directive 8 (HSDP 8): National Preparedness (2011)

This document directs the executive branch departments and agencies on how to coordinate preparedness within their own departments, with other departments and agencies, and with the private sector, both corporate and community. It ties in directly to HSPD 5 as the National Incident Management System requires coordination between federal, state, and local governments.

Federal Stafford Act Disaster Assistance: Presidential Declarations, Eligible Activities, and Funding (also called the Stafford Act) (1974, amended thru 2011)

The Stafford Act comes into effect when things go so badly that a state or local government is unable to exercise the powers within its jurisdiction. It authorizes the president to issue major disaster or emergency declarations in response to catastrophes in the United States that overwhelm state and local governments. It does not allow the federal government to become the local government but only to act in the best interests of the security and well-being of U.S. citizens. This assistance comes in the form of the National Response Framework. It is important to recognize the difference between "able to come and help" and "authorized to seize control." The function may be the same, but the intent is very different.

National Response Framework (NRF): (2008)

All of the plans for National Response, in the form of federal disaster assistance, culminate in the federal coordination of support to state, local, territorial, and tribal governments. These tasks are performed through the conduct of specific functions that tie into the Incident Command System (ICS). The Incident Command System, which we will discuss in detail later, is the national standard for local-level response. It is the way we as a nation respond to any type of emergency. This idea of using the same methods to respond to any emergency is called an All-Hazards Response and is very effective. *All emergency-response plans have the same three priorities:*

- Save lives (Rescue people from danger and provide medical assistance)
- Stabilize the situation (Remove or control threats and hazards)
- Protect infrastructure, property and environment (Preserve what is left)

The National Response Framework outlines the specific ways the federal government will interact with state and local government through 15 Emergency Support Functions (ESF). These 15 ESFs are the methods the federal government uses to meet needs of state and local jurisdictions in their efforts to maintain the eight National Essential Functions identified in Federal Continuity Directive 1. ESFs may be selectively activated for both Stafford Act (federal help without asking) and non–Stafford Act (governor asks for help) incidents under circumstances as defined in HSPD-5 (the rules for how to help). They serve the needs of disaster response in preparation, rescue, aftermath mitigation, and recovery to provide the essential aspects of governance: security, essential services, and access to political process (rule of law).

All levels of emergency response will use these same 15 functions and will plan and prepare based on these functions. This is very helpful when a disaster response grows to require more resources and assistance from a higher jurisdiction because all the plans are written with the same support functions in mind. This makes it very easy for new responders to support and integrate into the existing efforts to rescue, relieve, and recover.

A description of the 15 ESF Functions are provided on the following pages.

As you read through these ESF descriptions, think about how they relate to the tenets of governance. You may notice that services are heavily represented over the other tenets. This is because services are what are most immediately required, in tandem with security (when it is required) and followed closely by political access & rule of law. These description points are taken exactly as they are written in the federal plan, with the addition of the author's additional note on which tenet of governance they primarily support and a discussion on each function.

Jurisdictions and Requests for Assistance

There are two last issues to address before we move away from local, state, and federal response, and they have to do with control. The first is jurisdictions. Jurisdictions are legally recognized areas of government authority. Names like "township," "city," "county," "state," "territory," and "federal" are just a few ways we recognize jurisdictions. There are different kinds of jurisdictions, and sometimes they can overlap. The important point to take away is that the local jurisdiction has the most authority. This is different from having the most power. The county can tell the state to stay away, and the state can tell the federal government to stay away. The system works this way because the different levels of government recognize that in the end it will be the local jurisdiction that has to deal with whatever happens. All emergencies, and for that matter all questions of local government and representation of the people, start locally and end locally. This is not to say that there is not debate on where jurisdictions start and end, but the premise that local authority has the final say is very important to a representative republic and emergency response.

The second aspect, which somewhat follows the idea of jurisdiction, is that in an emergency, the smaller jurisdiction must request assistance before a larger jurisdiction can come in to help. Counties must request help from states, and states must request help from the federal government. This keeps larger jurisdictions from overrunning smaller ones. This puts a lot of power in the hands of local officials and governors (which is a major strength of a representative republic). There are exceptions for when a situation is so bad that local jurisdiction is unable to request assistance. The ongoing debate on what these exceptions should be is the best indicator that the authority of local government and the sovereignty of states are seen as important and worth preserving.

Emergency Support Functions (ESFs)

The National Response Framework outlines the specific ways the federal government will interact with state and local government through 15 Emergency Support Functions (ESF). These 15 ESFs are the methods the federal government uses to meet needs of state and local jurisdictions in their efforts to maintain the eight National Essential Functions identified in Federal Continuity Directive 1. ESFs may be selectively activated for both Stafford Act (federal help without asking) and non–Stafford Act (governor asks for help) incidents under circumstances as defined in HSPD-5 (the rules for how to help). They serve the needs of disaster response in preparation, rescue, aftermath mitigation, and recovery to provide the essential aspects of governance: security, essential services, and access to political process (rule of law).

(Photo by Command Sgt. Maj. Dennis Green, Virginia National Guard/Released)

The 15 Emergency Support Functions are:

ESF #1 — Transportation (Essential Services)
ESF Coordinator: Department of Transportation

Aviation/airspace management and control

Transportation safety

Restoration and recovery of transportation infrastructure

Movement restrictions

Damage and impact assessment

Discussion: Transportation is part of a full spectrum of response being active in preparation, rescue, aftermath mitigation, and recovery. It can be generally rolled up into three main concepts: movement management, transportation safety, and movement restriction.

Movement management is a big part of logistics and covers everything from air traffic control to making sure parking lots don't get overcrowded with trucks bringing in supplies. It also includes clearing and repair of transportation infrastructure. In this capacity

ESF 1 works closely with ESF 3, Public Works and Engineering, and ESF 7, Logistics Management and Resource Support. When the government looks at movement, they will look at all options.

Transportation safety ensures that only safe infrastructure is used and transportation operations are conducted safely. This includes things like rules for driver rest, the number of trucks allowed on the road (vehicle density), and where different kinds of vehicles are allowed to go (weight limitations on roads and bridges).

Movement restriction is a significant issue when people are trying to return to their homes after a disaster. The areas in question must be determined safe and secure to ensure the public will not be in undue danger when returning to their homes. Restriction is primarily to protect life and preserve rescue and response resources. They will not open an area to the public when there is a significant chance they will have to rescue those same people to get them back out.

How people are moved: As resources move into a disaster area, transportation will be moving people out of the disaster area. This will include moving on your own to a collection point where you will be gathered with other survivors and transported by truck, bus, or whatever other means are available to a relocation center. At the relocation center you will wait for mass transportation to a relief center where you can stay until you are able to move again on your own. The names for collection point, relocation center, and relief center may be different, but the functions of transporting and sustaining the population will be the same.

The plans for disaster relief almost always include helping lots of people out of the affected area. This means collecting people up and moving them by the safest mass transportation method possible to a secure location where power, water, food, and shelter are available and sustainable. You need to think about this and be ready for it if you plan to use this method of movement. You will have restrictions on what you can carry. This may be as little as what you can fit on your lap. Once you are in the transportation process, you will need to follow instructions, which may include long periods of waiting in uncomfortable conditions until you are told to move. Your final destination will be determined by others and you will be informed of where you will be going, but this may change as the situation develops. The trade-off for this scary and uncomfortable experience is that you will be moved to security, shelter, and sustainment.

Continued on next page

ESF #2 — Communications (Essential Services)
ESF Coordinator: DHS (National Communications System)

Coordination with telecommunications and information technology industries

Restoration and repair of telecommunications infrastructure

Protection, restoration, and sustainment of national cyber and information technology resources

Oversight of communications within the federal incident management and response structures

Discussion: Communication is another full-spectrum response element (preparation, rescue, aftermath mitigation, and recovery) and a major contributor in disaster-response success. Because communications infrastructure is often destroyed in a disaster, there is a whole functional area dedicated to bringing in and standing up a completely separate communications infrastructure until the original systems can be repaired or replaced. There may be limitations on personal communication until public communication systems (cell towers and internet access) are back online. These limitations are not "denial of communication" or "denial of voice," but rather limitations on system availability and prioritized use given to emergency responders.

Continued on next page

Federal Response

Emergency Support Functions (Cont.)

ESF #3 — Public Works and Engineering (Essential Services)

ESF Coordinator: Department of Defense (U.S. Army Corps of Engineers)

Infrastructure protection and emergency repair

Infrastructure restoration

Engineering services and construction management

Emergency contracting support for life-saving and life-sustaining services

Discussion: This function deals with infrastructure and is prominent in post-disaster mitigation and recovery. They shut down what is broken to contain threats and remove hazards, like downed wires and leaking gas lines. They secure what is working so it does not break. Repair crews then begin to restore essential services, like power and water. This function also addresses levies, roads, bridges, harbors, and rails. These are the "go-to" guys for every other support function.

ESF #4 — Firefighting (Essential Services)

ESF Coordinator: Department of Agriculture (U.S. Forest Service)

Coordination of federal firefighting activities

Support to wild land, rural, and urban firefighting operations

Discussion: As a vital part of rescue and post-disaster mitigation, firefighting provides both safety and security. During recovery, firefighting returns to its more traditional prevention and safety role. This is not just for wildfires because almost every kind of disaster (including floods) generates fires and fire hazards.

ESF #5 — Emergency Management (Essential Services)

ESF Coordinator: DHS (FEMA)

Coordination of incident management and response efforts

Issuance of mission assignments

Resource and human capital

Incident action planning

Financial management

Discussion: Emergency management encompasses agencies (and more importantly the smart people in them) who coordinate for all aspects of disaster response and are active in planning, preparation, rescue, recovery, and all other aspects of disaster response. They are the subject-matter experts who coordinate the details from planning to actual response. It is important to understand that they are not in control, but work directly for the elected officials who have jurisdiction in the affected area to coordinate the effort. Emergency managers are the operational go-to people when the time comes to rescue, stabilize, and restore a community affected by a disaster.

ESF #6 — Mass Care, Emergency Assistance, Housing, and Human Services (Essential Services)

ESF Coordinator: DHS (FEMA)

Mass care

Emergency assistance

Disaster housing

Human services

Continued from previous page

Discussion: This function provides sustainment and care for the affected population and recovery personnel during rescue and post-disaster mitigation. This primarily consists of medical treatment, food, water, and shelter, but will also provide access to resources for family reunification, religious services, psychological assistance for traumatic experiences, and other aspects of human services. As with emergency management, the goal during recovery is to return the population to independent living. Economic recovery is dependent upon working people spending money in the local economy. A population who has become dependent upon relief facilities is not conducive to recovery.

How people are sustained: In an extreme disaster in which people require significant resources just to survive, the solution calls for self-sustaining relief facilities (buildings) or camps (tents). A relief facility has to provide for several things. It must be close to the disaster zone but not within the effects of the destruction. It must have access to roads to bring resources in and let people get out. It must be securable and able to control the population within it in order to effectively account for and distribute services. There must also be limitations and positive controls on how many people enter and leave the facility to ensure the resources available match the population.

If this option sounds like a better alternative than unprotected exposure to aftermath, then go inside and accept assistance. If on the other hand, you think this seems like a prison and don't like the restrictions that will, by necessity, be placed upon you in exchange for relief, then do not go inside. But you will still need to find some form of security and sustainment for yourself and your family. Just remember that putting controls on relief is not the same as denying liberty. Consider the benefits of accepting the rules that come along with the relief until you can move to a situation more to your liking.

ESF #7 — Logistics Management and Resource Support (Essential Services)

ESF Coordinator: General Services Administration and DHS (FEMA)

Comprehensive, national incident logistics planning, management, and sustainment capability

Resource support (facility space, office equipment and supplies, contracting services, etc.)

Discussion: This function is most active during preparation and recovery. Prior planning and preparation ensures the availability of the resources that will be required during rescue and other post-disaster recovery. It serves to shape the response to a disaster by managing national resources at the strategic level to coordinate for the availability of all logistical and administrative needs.

ESF #8 — Public Health and Medical Services (Essential Services)

ESF Coordinator: Department of Health and Human Services

Public health

Medical

Mental health services

Mass-fatality management

Discussion: This function provides two distinct and vital services. First, during preparation and rescue, it works closely with ESF 6 to plan for and provide medical services for survivors (the living). They run the hospitals that are located within the relief facilities. Second, during post-disaster mitigation, it provides separate services for victims (the dead). Collection and internment of the dead is always kept separate from services for the living. Because medical personnel certify death and medical facilities are the usual collection point or transition point from life to death, ESF 6 serves in this dual capacity.

Continued on next page

Emergency Support Functions (Cont.)

Continued from previous page

ESF #9 — Search and Rescue (Essential Services)

ESF Coordinator: DHS (FEMA)

Life-saving assistance

Search–and–rescue operations

Discussion: Search and rescue is the first element to arrive during rescue because in any disaster response the first priority effort is to save lives. They are followed closely by security elements when the need is identified. Search and rescue can be hindered by security issues because rescuers are not allowed to go into areas where they would be vulnerable to random or targeted violence. This is not just limited to civil unrest. During the Hurricane Katrina response, emergency personnel came under sporadic gunfire from unknown assailants. Rescue operations were suspended until security was reestablished. Search and rescue will come for you if there is a greater chance of them saving you than of losing their own lives or losing their ability to continue to rescue.

ESF #10 — Oil and Hazardous Materials Response (Security)

ESF Coordinator: Environmental Protection Agency

Oil and hazardous materials (chemical, biological, radiological, etc.) response

Environmental short- and long-term cleanup

Discussion: This post-disaster mitigation response deals with all the hazards that have, or potentially may, escape mechanical confinement. Containment vessels like tanks, pressure lines, and service conduits will fail during a disaster. Much of what Hazardous Material Response personnel will do is detect hazards and determine levels of exposure. Many of these hazards are odorless, colorless, or otherwise difficult to detect, making them extremely dangerous to survivors and responding personnel.

ESF #11 — Agriculture and Natural Resources (Security)

ESF Coordinator: Department of Agriculture

Nutrition assistance

Animal and plant disease and pest response

Food safety and security

Natural and cultural resources and historic properties protection

Safety and well-being of household pets

Discussion: This rescue and post-disaster mitigation response element coordinates animal rescue, treatment, and confinement, coordinates pet/owner reunification, and works to limit the spread of animal-borne diseases. They are also instrumental in ensuring food safety and work to preserve natural and cultural resources and historic properties.

ESF #12 — Energy (Essential Services)

ESF Coordinator: Department of Energy

Energy infrastructure assessment, repair, and restoration

Energy industry utilities coordination

Energy forecast

Discussion: One of the first priorities in recovery is to reestablish power generation and distribution. Even before a disaster is over, as in the final days of a hurricane,

Continued from previous page

power crews will be side by side with security personnel and engineers to ensure power is being restored as soon as possible. This is a vital component of recovery.

ESF #13 — Public Safety and Security (Political Access & Rule of Law)

ESF Coordinator: Department of Justice

Facility and resource security

Security planning and technical-resource assistance

Public safety and security support

Support to access, traffic, and crowd control

Discussion: This full-spectrum element is active in preparation, rescue, post-disaster mitigation, and recovery. The establishment of security and the rapid return to local jurisdictional rule of law is a firmly held expectation of the U.S. population. Access to justice is just as important as access to medical services and is considered an essential part of recovery.

ESF #14 — Long-Term Community Recovery (Essential Services)

ESF Coordinator: DHS (FEMA)

Social and economic community-impact assessment

Long-term community recovery assistance to states, tribes, local governments, and the private sector

Analysis and review of mitigation-program implementation

Discussion: As the name implies, long-term community recovery takes place during recovery. The ability for a community to reestablish a thriving private-sector economic environment is absolutely necessary for community recovery. To understand the impacts of this element, look up Greensburg, Kansas. After a tornado decimated the town, it rebuilt itself into a thriving community using the latest clean-energy technologies. This returned investment, jobs, and prosperity to a town that had been completely destroyed.

ESF #15 — External Affairs (Political Access & Rule of Law)

ESF Coordinator: DHS

Emergency public information and protective action guidance

Media and community relations

Congressional and international affairs

Tribal and insular affairs

Discussion: This ESF works to ensure communication between the responders, the public, and the legitimate elected officials by serving as a liaison between state, local, territorial, and tribal-elected public officials. Accordingly, DHS will employ pre-identified organizational processes to foster information-sharing and to deliver constituent services to ensure the people's elected representatives have access to the populations they serve.

Federal Response

Recovery Support Functions: Federal Assistance in Recovery (Before and After)

Reference: http://www.fema.gov/recovery-support-functions

Community recovery actually begins before the disaster strikes. This is one of the aspects of resiliency that the federal government spends so much time trying to promote. The ability of a community to recover from a disaster is established prior to the disaster. Like any effort, it is the strength of the plan, the preparation and training prior to the event, and finally, the ability of the population, business community and local government to effectively receive resources and put them to good use in a timely manner that determines how quickly a community can recover from a disaster. Notice how the focus is on communication between agencies at different levels of government. The lead agencies for federal recovery assistance are not necessarily all responders as you will see in the descriptions below.

FEMA Says: The Recovery Support Functions (RSFs) comprise the National Disaster Recovery Framework's (NDRF's) coordinating structure for key functional areas of assistance. Their purpose is to support local governments by facilitating problem solving, improving access to resources and by fostering coordination among State and Federal agencies, nongovernmental partners and stakeholders.

The Recovery Support Functions, created within the National Disaster Recovery Framework, bring together the core recovery capabilities of Federal departments and agencies and other supporting organizations — including those not active in emergency response — to focus on community recovery needs. The Recovery Support Functions are organized into six manageable components and through the Recovery Support Functions, relevant stakeholders and experts are brought together during steady-state planning and when activated post-disaster to identify and resolve recovery challenges. Recovery Support Functions and stakeholders organize and request assistance and/or contribute resources and solutions. Together, these Recovery Support Functions help facilitate local stakeholder participation and promote intergovernmental and public-private partnerships.

The objective of the Recovery Support Functions is to facilitate the identification, coordination and delivery of Federal assistance needed to supplement recovery resources and efforts by local, State, Tribal and Territorial governments, as well as private and nonprofit sectors. An additional objective is to encourage and complement investments and contributions by the business community, individuals and voluntary, faith-based and community organizations. These Recovery Support Functions activities assist communities with accelerating the process of recovery, redevelopment and revitalization.

Impact of Recovery Support Functions

The strength in these RSFs is in the ability to provide local governments and communities with concepts, actions and resources to build resiliency into the community prior to a disaster or event. It may, at first glance, seem that these "recovery functions" are unfocused but remember that none of these federal functions are arriving to take control of the process but are instead providing valuable resources to the community. They are outside infrastructure with ideas, tools and technical skills to assist communities in using their existing resources to the best advantage. Where the Emergency Support Functions deal with restoring infrastructure and reestablishing services, the Recovery Support Functions provide methods at the local level to promote the most effective use of the restored infrastructure and reestablished services.

There are two reasons for this expenditure on the part of the federal government. First it helps communities get back on their feet as quickly as possible. This may

Government Response to a Disaster

Success is found in individual responders and the population having a common understanding and everyone working towards a common set of goals. The concept of execution following a purposeful direction of centralized (federal) planning and decentralized (local) execution. Note how the planning spectrum begins and ends with the intent of preserving the life and liberty of the individual.

1. Preserve the Constitution and Government Operations (Personal Liberty)

- Enduring Constitutional Government Plans
- Continuity of Government Plans
- Continuity of Operation Plans

2. Plan to Provide Governance (Security, Essential Services & Rule of Law)

- Presidential Directives & Executive orders
- National Essential Functions (8)
- Primary Mission Essential Functions (PMEF)
- Mission Essential Functions (MEF)

3. Provide Federal Level Response Capability

- National Response Framework
- National Incident Management System (NIMS) – Linked to Incident Command System (ICS)
- National Disaster Response Framework
- Emergency Support Functions (15)

4. Prepare States and Communities

- Incident Command System (ICS) - Linked to National Incident Management System (NIMS)
- Recovery Support Functions (6)

5. Link Community and Non-Governmental (NGO) Agencies into the Response System

- NGOs - Red Cross, Salvation Army, Etc
- Community Organizations - Veterans of Foreign Wars, American Legion, Churches
- Community Preparedness Groups – Civil Air Patrol, Short Wave Radio, Etc
- On Line resources for education – Schools, Boy Scout & Girl Scouts of America

6. Individual and Family Awareness and Preparedness (Personal Liberty)

- FEMA Recommendations (books and on-line content)
- Local Emergency Management events
- Personal initiative and Family disaster planning & preparedness

take a much as five years in the case of major disasters like Hurricanes Katrina and Rita or Super-storm Sandy. This leads to the second reason; a community that can get back up on its own requires fewer resources from the federal government for a shorter duration. It is less expensive for the federal government to spend the money up front to help keep communities strong, resilient and as independent as possible.

Recovery Support Functions

The National Disaster Recovery Framework's (NDRF's) coordinating structure for these Recovery Support Functions (RSFs) are:

 Community Planning & Capacity Building

 Economic

 Health and Social Services

 Housing

 Infrastructure Systems

 Natural and Cultural Resources

Notice that these Recovery Support Functions are not numbered, they are not part of the Incident Command System and do not fall under any portion of the National Incident Management System. But the primary agencies executing these support functions all have a role in both ICE and NIMS. The skills and methods provided by the RSF are for building and restoring communities before and after a disaster. This demonstrates the federal government's commitment to states and communities. This is an excellent example of the scope of the National Response Framework & National Disaster Recovery Framework and the positive role the federal government can play in providing effective governance.

A. Community Planning and Capacity Building (Recovery Support Function)

Coordinating Agency
Department of Homeland Security/Federal Emergency Management Agency

Primary Agencies
Department of Homeland Security/Federal Emergency Management Agency and Health and Human Services

Recovery Support Functions (RSFs)

(FEMA photo/Andrea Booher)

Each function is outlined by identifying key aspects of its form and function. Prior to describing the function it is prudent to review what the identifiers really mean.

Coordinating Agency
Planners - Primary agency overseeing the execution of the support function.

Primary Agencies
Doers - Primary agency(s) executing the support function

Supporting Organizations
Stakeholder within the Government – Other Government agencies that will be affected by, or provide assistance in, these support functions.

Mission
This statement represents the agencies overall goal.

Function
This statement reflects the methods the supporting agencies will use to meet the goals identified in the Mission statement.

Pre-disaster function
Actions and resources made available to communities prior to a disaster to help them become more prepared for a disaster.

Post-disaster function
The actions for the actual recovery assistance part of disaster recovery.

Outcomes
This statement identifies the desired results of the recovery efforts.

Supporting Organizations

Corporation for National and Community Service, Department of Homeland Security, Department of Commerce, Department of Interior, Department of Justice, Department of Transportation, Environmental Protection Agency, General Services Administration, Housing and Urban Development, Small Business Administration, Department of Treasury and Department of Agriculture.

Mission

Supporting and building recovery capacities and community planning resources of local, State and Tribal governments needed to effectively plan for, manage and implement disaster recovery activities in large, unique or catastrophic incidents.

Function

The core recovery capability for community planning is the ability to effectively plan and implement disaster recovery activities, engaging the whole community to achieve their objectives and increase resilience. The Community Planning and Capacity Building RSF unifies and coordinates expertise and assistance programs from across the Federal Government to aid in restoring and improving the ability of Tribes, States and local governments to organize, plan, manage and implement recovery. The RSF assists States in developing a pre- and post-disaster system of support for their communities. This RSF also has an emphasis on integration of hazard mitigation throughout the continuum of pre- and post-disaster recovery planning and implementation. The RSF also serves as a forum for helping to integrate the nongovernmental and private sector resources into public sector recovery planning processes.

Pre-Disaster

- Coordinates the provision of preparedness planning and technical assistance support to aid Tribes, States and local governments to develop effective pre-disaster recovery plans that guide the full range of recovery efforts, both short- and long-term, and ensure all affected populations are included.
- Coordinates the resolution of outstanding Federal agency program and policy issues identified in after-action and other evaluations that present ongoing barriers or challenges for effective support for State, Tribal and local community planning and capacity necessary to facilitate an effective recovery process.
- Develops multidisciplinary recovery tools and best practices.
- Promotes resiliency measures and enhances coordination of programs that build local leadership capacity, community member involvement, partnerships and education on disaster preparedness for recovery.
- Identifies and leverages programs that assist communities to prepare, collect and analyze relevant existing and future data necessary to plan and manage complex disaster recovery
- Integrates mitigation, recovery and other pre-disaster plans and activities into existing local, State and Tribal community-wide planning and development activitites, such as comprehensive plans, land use plans, economic development plans, affordable housing plans, zoning ordinances and other development regulations through technical assistance.
- Coordinates educational and cross-training opportunities for key participants in community recovery planning and capacity support including, but not limited to: emergency managers; city managers; planning, economic development and other local officials; and nonprofit and private sector partners for recovery.
- Develops pre-disaster partnerships with others such as Federal agency extension programs, universities, national professional associations, and nongovernmental organizations, to facilitate recovery capacity-building activities and expansion of resources available to communities after a disaster for planning and decision making.

Post-Disaster

- Maintains robust and accessible communications throughout the recovery process between the Federal Government and all other partners to ensure ongoing dialogue and information sharing.
- Identifies the range and significance of the disaster's effects on Tribes, regions and local governments in the impacted area.
- Coordinates the provision of resources to units of government for recovery planning technical assistance and to support recovery capacity and surge needs in a variety of Tribal/county/city functional areas (e.g., city Management, financial management, hazard mitigation and risk assessment, damage assessment, building inspection and permitting); coordinates resources to address other skill sets that communities often lack capacity after large-scale and catastrophic disasters.
- Develops community-focused technical assistance teams for uniquely or heavily impacted Tribes or communities, integrating the use of Federal agency resources organized under other Recovery Support Functions.
- When activated by the Federal Disaster Recovery Coordinator, the primary and supporting departments and agencies deploy in support of the Community Planning and Capacity Building mission.
- Identifies and tracks resolution of gaps and conflicts in multiple Federal planning requirements and assistance programs, as well as programs that support and build community capacity and surge needs for recovery management.
- Coordinates the application and treatment of hazard mitigation and sustainability principles in Federally supported recovery planning efforts.
- Coordinates Community Planning and Capacity Building supported community-centric technical assistance teams with the establishment of local unmet needs committees or groups for assisting individuals and families.
- Aids local, State and Tribal governments to identify and integrate the consideration of all affected stakeholders, including vulnerable populations and persons with disabilities, and individuals with limited English proficiency into the public sector recovery plans and decision making process.
- Provides technical assistance and planning support to aid all levels of government to integrate sustainability principles, such as adaptive re-use of historic properties, mitigation considerations, smart growth principles and sound land use into recovery decision making and planning during the post-disaster period.
- Captures after-action recommendations and lessons learned.

Outcomes

- Through a coordinated effort that draws from resources of Federal departments, agencies and services, the Community Planning and Capacity Building RSF provides expertise to ensure:
- Enhanced interagency coordination of resources, requirements and support for building community capacity and community recovery planning.
- Increased community self-reliance and adaptability.
- Hazard mitigation and risk reduction opportunities have been integrated into all major decisions and reinvestments during the recovery process.
- An improved planning process that ensures a more effective and efficient use of Federal, State, nongovernmental and private sector funds.
- Communities are able to shorten the timeline and improve specific recovery outcomes through more effective decision making and management.
- Integration of socioeconomic, demographic, risk assessment, vulnerable populations and other important information into recovery planning and decision making.
- Increased community-wide support and understanding of sustainability and resiliency principles applicable to the opportunities presented during disaster recovery.

B. Economic (Recovery Support Function)

Coordinating Agency

United States Department of Commerce

Primary Agencies

Department of Homeland Security/Federal Emergency Management Agency, Department of Commerce, Department of Labor, Small Business Administration, Department of Treasury and Department of Agriculture

Supporting Organizations

Corporation for National and Community Service, Department of Interior, Environmental Protection Agency and Health and Human Services

Mission

The mission of the Economic Recovery Support Function is to integrate the expertise of the Federal Government to help local, State and Tribal governments and the private sector sustain and/or rebuild businesses and employment, and develop economic opportunities that result in sustainable and economically resilient communities after large-scale and catastrophic incidents.

Function

The core recovery capability for economic recovery is the ability to return economic and business activities (including agricultural) to a state of health and develop new economic opportunities that result in a sustainable and economically viable community. Economic recovery is a critical and integral part of recovery. Disasters not only damage property, but also entire markets for goods and services. The speed and effectiveness of returning a community to self-sufficiency and vitality depend upon quickly adapting to changed market conditions, reopening businesses and/or establishing new businesses. Businesses employ workers, provide for community needs and services and generate revenue once again, allowing the community, both its members and government, to provide for itself.

Considerable Federal funds are contributed to local, State and Tribal economic recovery as well as to other areas of recovery that necessarily strengthen the economy. The attraction of outside investment and the role of the private sector cannot be understated as foundational in a community's economic recovery. Thus, the role of the Economic RSF is to facilitate and enable that role by leveraging Federal resources, information and leadership. Informed management must accompany this capital investment to ensure its most effective use and compliance with all applicable Federal laws and regulations. This involves the coordination of Federal recovery programs and their integration with private sector efforts including those of nongovernmental and private volunteer organizations, nonprofits, investment capital firms and the banking industry.

The Economic Recovery Support Function facilitates the progression from direct Federal financial assistance to community self-sustainment. Importantly, the Recovery Support Function works closely with local community leadership who direct long-term economic recovery efforts. This requires the sustained engagement of possibly months or years by RSF leadership with the leadership of disaster-impacted jurisdictions. A complex undertaking, this RSF engages many entities utilizing government assistance as seed money. These actions encourage reinvestment and facilitate private-sector lending and borrowing necessary for the functioning of vital markets and economies. Effective economic recovery following a disaster is positively influenced by pre-disaster community planning including mitigation actions that increase community resilience.

When coupled with informed decisions by local officials, it provides the confidence building necessary for economic recovery.

Pre-Disaster

- Identifies statutory, regulatory and policy issues that contribute to gaps, inconsistencies and unmet needs in economic recovery.
- Seeks innovative solutions to address preparedness, mitigation and resilience issues before a disaster strikes including comprehensive land use policy.
- Appreciates the value of community and economic development planning in disaster recovery; encourages and facilitates this planning through appropriate State government agencies.
- Develops initiatives and incentives to facilitate the integration of Federal efforts and resources with private capital and the business sector.
- Creates, encourages and participates in local, State, Tribal and Federal disaster recovery exercises to enhance skills and develop needed techniques.
- Leverages mitigation programs to create strong communities resilient to disaster.
- Works with local, State and Tribal officials to implement disaster resistant building codes and incentivize business and individual pre-disaster mitigation and preparedness activities.
- Seeks to promulgate resiliency policies and practices in agency programs and stakeholder operations, wherever appropriate.
- Sustains pre-disaster engagement activities possibly for months or years with the leadership of jurisdictions that may be impacted by a disaster.
- Encourages the establishment of disaster information networks for businesses.

Post-Disaster

- When activated by the Federal Disaster Recovery Coordinator, the primary and supporting departments and agencies deploy in support of the Economic Recovery Support Function mission.
- Works to apply and integrate plans developed pre-disaster to most effectively leverage Federal resources and available programs to meet local community recovery needs while aggressively integrating with the private sector to facilitate early and productive engagement.
- Develops an interagency action plan for each disaster to ensure the coordinated action of all Federal agencies, stakeholders and supporting entities in the support of local, State and Tribal governments.
- Incorporates mitigation measures into redevelopment following a disaster to build the community back stronger to minimize future risk.
- Building upon the relationships developed during pre-disaster planning, works closely with local community leadership during disaster recovery to provide technical assistance and data related to economic development.
- Maintains robust and accessible communications throughout the recovery process between the Federal Government and all other partners to ensure ongoing dialogue and information sharing.
- Engages the workforce development system, including State vocational rehabilitation programs, as a means of helping individuals who acquire a disability as part of the disaster return to work with the appropriate supports, accommodation and retraining (if necessary).

Outcomes

Through the coordination of local, State, Tribal and Federal government programs and the private sector, the Economic Recovery Support Function and local leadership leverages, following a disaster, community development plans and stakeholder relationships to create a new post-disaster economic condition meeting community needs. The following actions encourage reinvestment and facilitate private sector lending and borrowing necessary for the functioning of vital markets and economies. Sustained pre- and post-disaster mitigation actions create a community less at risk, strengthen future economic stability and create possible insurance benefits. Specific outcomes may include:

- Workforce development initiatives are in place; jobs are created and retained.
- Entrepreneurial and business development initiatives are in place.
- Community-wide economic development plans are developed with broad input and consider regional economic recovery and resiliency.
- Strategies for quickly adapting to changed market conditions, reopening businesses and/or establishing new businesses are in place.
- Business initiatives to employ workers and generate revenue are in place.
- Management plans ensure that the most effective use of Federal funds is in place.
- Federal funds are withheld when discrimination on the basis of race, color, national origin, religion, sex, age, or disability are present.
- Private and public sector actors have information they need to make informed decisions about recovery.

C. Health and Social Services (Recovery Support Function)

Coordinating Agency

Department of Health and Human Sevices

Primary Agencies

Corporation for National and Community Service, Department of Homeland Security (Federal Emergency Management Agency/National Preparedness and Protection Directive and Civil Rights and Civil Liberties), Deparment of Interior, Department of Justice, Department of Labor, Education Department and Veterans Affairs

Supporting Organizations

Department of Transportation, Small Business Administration, Department of Treasury, Department of Agriculture, Veterans Affairs, American Red Cross, National Organizations Active in Disasters

Mission

The Health and Social Services Recovery Support Function mission is for the Federal Government to assist locally-led recovery efforts in the restoration of the public health, health care and social services networks to promote the resilience, health and well-being of affected individuals and communities.

Function

The core recovery capability for health and social services is the ability to restore and improve health and social services networks to promote the resilience, health, independence and well-being of the whole community. The Health and Social Services RSF outlines the Federal framework to support locally-led recovery efforts to address public health, health care facilities and coalitions, and essential social services needs. For the purposes of this RSF, the use of the term health will refer to and include public health, behavioral health and medical services. This Annex establishes (1) a Federal focal point for coordinating Federal recovery efforts specifically for health and social services needs; and, (2) a Federal operational framework outlining how Federal agencies plan to support local health and social services recovery efforts. This framework is flexible and can adjust during a disaster to complement local efforts, as needed.

Pre-Disaster

- Incorporates planning for the transition from response to recovery into preparedness and operational plans, in close collaboration with ESFs #3, #6, #8 and #11.
- Incorporates planning for the transition from post-incident recovery operations back to a steady-state into preparedness and operational plans.
- Develops strategies to address recovery issues for health, behavioral health and social services – particularly the needs of response and recovery workers, children, seniors, people living with disabilities, people with functional needs, people from diverse cultural origins, people with limited English proficiency and underserved populations.
- Promotes the principles of sustainability, resilience and mitigation into preparedness and operational plans.

Post-Disaster

- Maintains situational awareness to identify and mitigate potential recovery obstacles during the response phase.
- Leverages response, emergency protection measures and hazard mitigation resources during the response phase to expedite recovery.
- Provides technical assistance in the form of impact analyses and supports recovery planning of public health, health care and human services infrastructure.
- Conducts Federal Health and Social Services Recovery Support Function assessments with primary agencies.
- Identifies and coordinates Federal Health and Social Services specific missions with primary agencies
- When activated by the Federal Disaster Recovery Coordinator, the primary and supporting departments and agencies deploy in support of the Health and Social Services Recovery Support Function mission, as appropriate.
- Establishes communication and information-sharing forum(s) for Health and Social Services RSF stakeholders with the State and/or community.
- Coordinates and leverages applicable Federal resources for health and social services.
- Develops and implements a plan to transition from Federal Health and Social Services recovery operations back to a steady-state.
- Identifies and coordinates with other local, State, Tribal and Federal partners to assess food, animal, water and air conditions to ensure safety.
- Evaluates the effectiveness of Federal Health and Social Services recovery efforts.
- Provides technical assistance in the form of impact analyses and recovery planning support of public health, health care, and human services infrastructure.
- Identifies and coordinates with other local, State, Tribal and Federal partners the assessment of food, animal, water and air conditions to ensure their safety.

Outcomes

- Restore the capacity and resilience of essential health and social services to meet ongoing and emerging post-disaster community needs.
- Encourage behavioral health systems to meet the behavioral health needs of affected individuals, response and recovery workers, and the community.
- Promote self-sufficiency and continuity of the health and well-being of affected individuals; particularly the needs of children, seniors, people living with disabilities whose members may have additional functional needs, people from diverse origins, people with limited English proficiency, and underserved populations.
- Assist in the continuity of essential health and social services, including schools.
- Reconnect displaced populations with essential health and social services.
- Protect the health of the population and response and recovery workers from the longer-term effects of a post-disaster environment.
- Promote clear communications and public health messaging to provide accurate, appropriate and accessible information; ensure information is developed and disseminated in multiple mediums, multi-lingual formats, alternative formats, is age-appropriate and user-friendly and is accessible to underserved populations.

D. Housing (Recovery Support Function)

Coordinating Agency

Housing and Urban Development

Primary Agencies

Department of Homeland Security/Federal Emergency Management Agency, Department of Justice, Housing and Urban Development and Department of Agriculture.

Supporting Organizations

Corporation for National and Community Service, Department of Commerce, Department of Energy, Environmental Protection Agency, Health and Human Services, Small Business Administration, U.S. Access Board, Veterans Affairs, American Red Cross, National Organizations Active in Disasters

Mission

Address pre- and post-disaster housing issues and coordinate and facilitate the delivery of Federal resources and activities to assist local, State and Tribal governments in the rehabilitation and reconstruction of destroyed and damaged housing, whenever feasible, and development of other new accessible, permanent housing options.

Function

The core recovery capability for housing is the ability to implement housing solutions that effectively support the needs of the whole community and contribute to its sustainability and resilience. Like infrastructure and safety services, housing is a critical and often challenging component of disaster recovery. It is critical because local economies cannot recover from devastating disasters without adequate housing, especially affordable housing. It is challenging because many years' worth of housing repair, rehabilitation, reconstruction and new construction often need to occur at an accelerated pace as a result of a disaster. These conditions create design, construction, labor, materials, logistics, inspection and financing issues.

The Housing Recovery Support Function, through its member departments and agencies, works toward addressing disaster housing issues pre-disaster, focusing on solutions that are implementable, sustainable and resilient. As States and communities look to the Federal Government for assistance in housing both disaster survivors and others who choose to live in recovering communities, the Housing RSF coordinates and effectively integrates available housing-related resources, addresses conflicting policy and program issues and identifies gaps in service and assistance delivery.

Consistent with the National Disaster Housing Strategy (NDHS), the Department of Homeland Security (DHS)/Federal Emergency Management Agency (FEMA) maintains lead responsibility for sheltering and interim housing with interim housing support from Housing and Urban Development (HUD) as well as other primary agencies and support organizations. Sheltering falls under ESF #6 in the National Response Framework (NRF) where DHS/FEMA is the coordinating agency. Interim housing, as its name implies, is a transition to permanent housing and is dependent on the period of transition as responsibility moves from Emergency Support Function (ESF) #6 to the Housing Recovery Support Function. Addressing permanent housing, the third focus area of the NDHS, is under the Housing Recovery Support Function.

Pre-Disaster

- Works with local, State and Tribal governments, organizations and others in coordination with the National Disaster Housing Task Force, Joint Housing Solutions Group.
- Identifies strategies and options that address a broad range of disaster housing issues such as those dealing with planning, zoning, design, production, logistics, codes and financing.
- Builds accessibility, resilience, sustainability and mitigation measures into identified housing recovery strategies.

Post-Disaster

When activated by the FDRC, the primary and supporting departments and agencies deploy in support of the Housing RSF mission.

- Coordinates and leverages Federal housing-related resources to assist local, State and Tribal governments to address housing-related, disaster recovery needs.
- Encourages rapid and appropriate decisions regarding land use and housing location in the community or region.
- Identifies gaps and coordinates a resolution of conflicting policy and program issues.
- Maintains robust and accessible communications throughout the recovery process between the Federal Government and all other partners to ensure ongoing dialogue and information sharing.

Outcomes

Departments and agencies with expertise in long-term housing solutions work through this RSF and in conjunction with the National Disaster Housing Task Force so that:

- Housing resources that address local, State and Tribal disaster recovery housing needs are coordinated.
- Planning for current and post-disaster requirements are integrated into the organizations at the local and State level that perform land and community planning and building code administration.

- Local, State, Tribal and Federal programs, industry and construction options for addressing post-disaster housing needs are in place.
- Research results related to the disaster recovery housing area are shared.
- Interagency knowledge and expertise are shared with State-led housing task forces to address disaster housing issues.
- Pre- and post-disaster interaction and problem solving among Federal agencies and stakeholders with a focus on reconstructing permanent housing, including affordable and accessible housing that incorporates resilience, sustainability and mitigation concepts are facilitated.
- Timely construction of housing that complies with local, State and national model building codes, including accessibility standards, is facilitated.
- Loss of historic buildings and resources is minimized.

E. Infrastructure Systems (Recovery Support Function)

Coordinating Agency

United States Corps of Engineers

Primary Agencies

Department of Homeland Security (Federal Emergency Management Agency/ National Preparedness and Protection Directive), United States Corps of Engineers, Department of Energy and Department of Transportation.

Supporting Organizations

Department of Homeland Security, Department of Commerce, Department of Interior, Education Department, Environmental Protection Agency, Federal Communications Commission, General Services Administration, Health and Human Services, Department of Treasury and Department of Agriculture.

Mission

Facilitate the integration of the capabilities of the Federal Government to support local, State and Tribal governments and other infrastructure owners and operators in their efforts to achieve recovery goals relating to the public engineering of the Nation's infrastructure systems.

Function

The core recovery capability for infrastructure systems is the ability to efficiently restore the infrastructure systems and services to support a viable, sustainable community and improves resilience to and protection from future hazards. The Infrastructure Systems Recovery Support Function promotes a holistic approach to disaster recovery coordination, support, planning and implementation for infrastructure systems that serve the community. This includes single and multijurisdictional areas and regions.

The Infrastructure Systems Recovery Support Function Coordinating Agency conducts operations in accordance with its authorities and resources to provide vital public engineering services to strengthen our Nation's security and reduce risks from disasters. When appropriate, the Coordinating Agency, working together with FEMA, facilitates and promotes the efforts of the RSF primary and supporting agencies to ensure those agencies with the requisite authorities, expertise, and resources are positioned to provide assistance to and collaborate with public and private sector infrastructure partners to the extent authorized by law. The Infrastructure Systems Recovery Support Function Coordinating Agency does not directly undertake, however, any operational recovery or engineering activities outside the scope of its authorities and resources.

The Infrastructure Systems Recovery Support Function serves as a collaborative forum for Federal Government engagement with local, State, Tribal and private sector representatives to focus on public engineering services that can reduce risks from disasters and expedite recovery. The collaborative efforts of this RSF involve government and private sector partners with expertise in public engineering services, as appropriate, across the infrastructure sectors identified through the National Infrastructure Protection Plan (N I P P) Partnership Framework.

Therefore, the scope of this RSF includes, but is not limited to, the following infrastructure sectors and subsectors: energy, water, dams, communications, transportation systems, Agriculture (food production and delivery), government facilities, utilities, sanitation, engineering, flood control and other systems that directly support the physical infrastructure of communities; as well as physical facilities that support essential services, such as public safety, emergency services and public recreation.

Pre-Disaster

- Develops guidance and standard procedures for rapid activation of RSF capabilities to support community recovery.
- Identifies relevant statutory and/or regulatory programs, potential capabilities and/or limiting factors pertaining to recovery support for infrastructure systems.
- Provides a forum for interagency coordination, information sharing and exchange of effective practices.
- Supports planning, preparedness, education, training and outreach efforts to enhance capabilities for recovery.
- Works with partners to identify critical facilities and ensure considerations are made to reduce risk pre- and post-disaster.

Post-Disaster

- When activated by the Federal Disaster Recovery Coordinator, the primary and supporting departments and agencies deploy in support of the Infrastructure Systems RSF mission.
- Supports the recovery of infrastructure systems, dependent on the nature and scope of the disaster, and the specific authorities and programs within the jurisdiction of participating departments and agencies.
- Participates in the national-level coordination of damage and community needs assessments as appropriate to ensure infrastructure considerations integrate into the post-disaster public and private sector community planning process.
- Deploys Recovery Support Function resources, as required by the specific disaster situation and consistent with the specific authorities and programs of the participating departments and agencies, to the field to assist the affected community in developing an Infrastructure Systems Recovery action plan that:
- Avoids the redundant, counterproductive, or unauthorized use of limited capital resources necessary for infrastructure/recovery.
- Helps resolve conflicts, including those across jurisdictional lines, resulting from the competition for key resources essential to infrastructure systems recovery.
- Sets a firm schedule and sequenced time structure for future infrastructure recovery projects.
- Works with Recovery Support Function partners to leverage available financial and technical assistance, both from governmental and nongovernmental sources, in the execution of the community's Infrastructure Systems Recovery action plan.

- Promotes rebuilding infrastructure in a manner which will reduce vulnerability to future disasters impacts.
- Maintains robust and accessible communications throughout the recovery process between the Federal Government and all other partners to ensure ongoing dialogue and information sharing.

Outcomes

The Infrastructure Systems RSF provides the coordinating structures, framework and guidance to ensure:

- Resilience, sustainability and mitigation are incorporated as part of the design for infrastructure systems and as part of the community's capital planning process.
- Infrastructure systems are fully recovered in a timely and efficient manner to minimize the impact of service disruptions. The private sector critical infrastructure has the incentive and the means to support a unified community and national recovery effort.
- The capacity of all infrastructure systems is adequately matched to the community's current and projected demand on its built and virtual environment.

F. Natural And Cultural Resources (Recovery Support Function)

Coordinating Agency

Department of Interior

Primary Agencies

Department of Homeland Security/Federal Emergency Management Agency, Department of Interior and Environmental Protection Agency.

Supporting Organizations

Advisory Council on Historic Preservation, Corporation for National and Community Service Council on Environmental Quality, Department of Commerce, Institute of Museum and Library Services. Department of Interior, Library of Congress National Endowment for the Arts. National Endowment for the Humanities U.S. Army Corps of Engineers and Heritage Preservation.

Mission

Integrate Federal assets and capabilities to help State and Tribal governments and communities address long-term environmental and cultural resource recovery needs after large-scale and catastrophic incidents.

Function

The core recovery capability for natural and cultural resources is the ability to protect natural and cultural resources and historic properties through appropriate response and recovery actions to preserve, conserve, rehabilitate, and restore them consistent with post-disaster community priorities and in compliance with appropriate environmental and cultural resources laws. The Natural and Cultural Resources Recovery Support Function coordinates departments and agencies working together to provide information and assistance to communities seeking to preserve, protect, conserve, rehabilitate, recover and restore natural and cultural resources during recovery.

Relevant agencies and partners are those with expertise and programs including, but not limited to, specific natural and cultural resource issue identification, assessment and management (e.g., fish and wildlife, historic and traditional cultural properties, hydrology); natural and cultural resource planning; environmental planning and historic preservation compliance under Federal laws and Executive Orders (specific to programs that provide funding for disaster recovery); and community sustainability.

Pre-Disaster

- Identifies relevant Federal programs and incentives that have a role in supporting the preservation, protection, conservation, rehabilitation, recovery and restoration of natural and cultural resources during recovery.
- Develops a pre-disaster Natural and Cultural Resources RSF action plan to identify and communicate priority actions.
- Identifies and prioritizes gaps and inconsistencies within and between relevant Federal regulations, policies, program requirements and processes affecting natural and cultural resources that are used in disaster recovery, either separately or in combination with one another, and makes recommendations to the National Disaster Recovery Planning (NDRP) Division at FEMA Headquarters and specific Federal agencies.
- Works with private nonprofits and other nongovernmental organizations (N G Os) to leverage opportunities to encourage local, State and Tribal governments and institutions to develop emergency management plans that integrate natural and cultural resource issues.
- Promotes the principles of sustainable and disaster resistant communities through the protection of natural resources such as coastal barriers and zones, floodplains, wetlands and other natural resources critical to risk reduction.
- Assesses appropriate hazard mitigation strategies for the protection of cultural resources.

Post-Disaster

- When activated by the FDRC, the primary and supporting departments and agencies deploy in support of the Natural and Cultural Resources RSF mission.
- Works to leverage Federal resources and available programs to meet local community recovery needs.
- Identifies opportunities to leverage natural and cultural resource protection with hazard mitigation strategies.
- Addresses government policy and agency program issues, gaps and inconsistencies related to natural and cultural resource issues.
- Coordinates cross-jurisdictional or multistate and/or regional natural and cultural resource issues to ensure consistency of Federal support where needed.
- Encourages responsible agencies at all levels of government and their important private sector partners to support the local community's recovery plan and priorities by developing a Natural and Cultural Resources action plan that identifies how the agencies leverage resources and capabilities to meet the community's needs.
- Synchronizes the Natural and Cultural Resources action plan with other RSFs, as appropriate to support the broader vision of Federal support to disaster recovery.
- Helps communities and State and Tribal governments to leverage opportunities inherent in recovery to mitigate impacts to environmental or cultural resources.
- Promotes a systematic, interdisciplinary approach to understand the interdependencies and complex relationships of the natural and cultural environments.
- Maintains robust and accessible communications throughout the recovery process between the Federal Government and all other partners to ensure ongoing dialogue and information sharing.

Outcomes

With expertise drawn from Federal departments and agencies, the Natural and Cultural Resources RSF works so that:

- Considerations related to the management and protection of natural and cultural resources and historic properties (NCH) resources, community sustainability and compliance with environmental planning and historic preservation requirements are integrated into recovery.
- Local communities, States and Tribal governments are ready to address post-disaster natural and cultural resource recovery needs.
- Programs to support disaster recovery, coordination of technical assistance and capabilities and data sharing are coordinated.
- Natural and cultural assessments and studies needed post-disaster, including proposed solutions to environmental and historic preservation policy and process impediments, are developed.

(USAF/Senior Airman Christopher S Muncy/released)

Conclusion

As you read through these plans, it is important to remember that these ESFs are actions and authorities that the federal government are allowed to do in order to assist the people adversely affected during emergency situations. This is very different than the federal government declaring the authority to act in defiance of local government, to deny legal jurisdictions, or to suspend local sovereignties. It may seem odd to have all this talk about government mixed in with emergency response, but remember that in a disaster, the local government has the priority of lifesaving, stabilization, and protection of property and environment; the federal government's priority is to ensure the protection of our liberty and our form of government. The most important aspect of recognizing the power of the federal government's ability to influence our situation during a disaster is to understand that these are fellow Americans coming to our aid in a time of need.

Section II:
Mental Resiliency and
Making Your Choices

These next four chapters will ask you to make some serious determinations about where your head is when it comes to being realistic about your survival. This is important because any weaknesses in your thought process or indecision in the way you deal with adversity will become exaggerated during a disaster and may significantly hinder your ability to survive and protect your family.

This process is not to find fault. It is to help you find your strengths and identify areas where you can develop your ability to respond to high levels of stress. Remember that survival is in your head, in how you perceive and respond to stresses and threats. Take some time to identify your strengths and weaknesses and learn to work within your personal capabilities and limitations.

Personal Preparation

Before you can begin to prepare for a disaster, you should consider two questions that are specifically about you and your situation:

1) What can I do to prepare?
2) How much do I want to do to prepare?

Your answers to these questions will drive all of the choices and preparations you make for yourself and your family. There is no right or wrong answer. There is only your choice. Each choice comes with its own benefits and drawbacks. What follows is a discussion about different attitudes towards the possibility of a disaster and your choices on how to care for yourself in a disaster situation. It addresses what kind of plans different people may want to make and the scale and intensity of preparation and suggests appropriate levels of preparedness to provide a real chance of survival without undue stress on personal resources.

(FEMA photo/Andrea Booher)

An important aspect of this will be that your choices need to be flexible to meet changes with your situation. Things like geographic location nationally and even the location of your residence locally, your lifestyle, health considerations, dependent family members (including pets), and other aspects will also come into play. This will become evident as you consider the different levels of preparation in relation to your level of dependence on others for help.

Levels of Preparation (Choices We Make Before the Event)

The Spectrum of Preparation: Passengers, Planners, and Preparers

One of the major choices you will make is what level of preparation you will adopt for your lifestyle. The spectrum of preparation can range from living a life of preparation to ignoring the issue completely and letting the government worry about taking care of your needs. For the purposes of this discussion, we can separate levels of preparation into three general categories based on the level of dependence survivors will have on others (most likely the government) for rescue, relief, and assistance after a disaster. Those who will be highly dependent we will call Passengers, those who are moderately prepared but not completely independent we will call Planners, and those who desire to be as independent as possible from requiring any assistance we will call Preparers.

The chart below offers a graphic representation of the spectrum of preparation. One thing you may notice is that there is no part of the spectrum where you are completely dependent on or completely independent of government services. Taken to both extremes, as a Passenger, if you can still think and walk, you still have the capability to make a choice, and as a Preparer, no matter how much you want to separate yourself from government services, you will still be within the sphere of control of the government and benefit from its services even if you do not draw upon them directly.

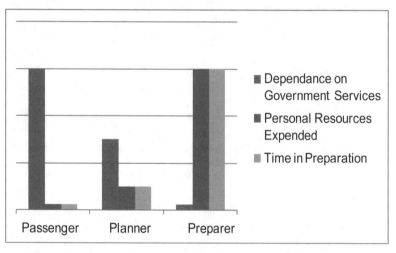

As a Planner, notice that the return of independence for the expenditure of personal resources and time is disproportionally large. A small amount of planning and preparation gets you a lot of independence and opportunity to make choices for yourself and your family. FEMA wants all individual citizens and families to be planners if they can be. FEMA knows that there will be many people who will need help, so anything you can plan and prepare to do for yourself is an advantage.

A discussion of Passengers, Planners, and Preparers will help you define the aspects of personal readiness you may wish to consider including in your plans. Understand that this decision is about how much control you want to have over your own situation and how you see your own risk (remember risk is a word used in planning). As a Passenger you may see risk in not having someone to help you. As a Preparer you may see risk in being dependent on others for help. As you read through these descriptions, think about which one seems the best suited for your needs.

Passengers

Passengers are people who are completely dependent on the plans and resources of others in times of disaster. Being a Passenger can be by circumstance or by choice, but in both cases the situation is the same. Your survival will be dependent on the plans made by emergency managers and the services provided by the government or by relief organizations, like the Red Cross, who work with them.

This is not necessarily a bad thing. The government puts significant effort into making plans to protect the population from the effects of disasters and aftermath. The issue to be considered is that there is a trade-off for depending upon the government. The easy part is that the government will provide for your needs with security, shelter, food, water, and transportation to a safer location if required. The difficult part is you will receive all of these things in minimal amounts and in a consistently slow manner. This is because when the government is providing for thousands of people, it will take time to get services to everyone who needs them. Remember that disasters, by definition, require more resources than are available. The designation of Passenger is designed for those who, for whatever reason, do not or cannot plan and prepare.

There are some situations that make it very difficult for people to plan, resource, and prepare for their own protection and sustainment before a disaster strikes. *Conditional circumstances* include people in dependent care, as in the case of hospital patients and people in assisted living who have special needs and will need help. *Situational circumstances* involve people who are in places where resources or distance make individual resource collection impractical. This is very true for people living in major metropolitan areas where finite resources like food, water, and transportation would be used up or overwhelmed almost immediately. They would have little choice but to participate in the government plan. This is not necessarily a question of wealth vs. poverty or age vs. youth. People become Passengers when they cannot avoid the effects of a disaster and need the government's help. The largest challenge the government has is convincing people that they can avoid becoming *completely dependent* Passengers by making plans and preparations to limit the amount of time they need to be a Passenger.

FEMA recommends that each family member have a three-day supply of food and water. Even this small amount of individual preparation represents a huge amount of time, transportation, and resources if that same amount of relief had to be brought to thousands of people in need.

If, for some reason, an able-bodied person chooses to be a Passenger just as an easy way to avoid their personal responsibility and puts the question of individual preparedness out of their mind, they may find that it was not the best idea. Being a Passenger does not make preparedness a non-issue for them before the disaster event. By choosing to *completely defer their responsibility*, they have made a choice to tap into the resources reserved for those who cannot take care of themselves. The difficulty comes when the disaster eventually happens and they are expected to agree with and follow the plans made for them by the emergency planners. If they let the government plan for them, the government will expect them to do two things:

1. To be quiet, remain calm, and be patient even when they find they are not happy with their situation.

2. To be cooperative and follow all instructions. This will likely include lots of waiting in potentially harsh, uncomfortable, but survivable situations. Note: if you saw the word "cooperative" and in your mind thought "submissive," you may not be a good candidate for the Passenger option.

Able-bodied Passengers may also find that when the Passenger population is triaged (categorized by need) by response personnel, those people who are Passengers by condition and have legitimate additional needs will have priority and will receive services before able-bodied situational Passengers.

The government knows there will be Passengers during and after a disaster. It spends a considerable amount of time making plans for the rescue, relief, and assistance of these individuals and significant amounts of money putting provisions and systems in place in anticipation of those needs. The government also knows that resources may not be available for all of the people who will need help. For this reason organizations like the Federal Emergency Management Agency (FEMA) and the Centers for Disease Control and Prevention (CDC) spend a good amount of time and energy in spreading the message of preparedness. Anything you can do for yourself is something they don't have to do for you. This will free up resources for those who are truly incapable of actively participating in their own rescue and relief.

There are times when you will need help. It is right and appropriate to seek shelter, food, water, and transportation when you need it from organizations designed to provide relief. It is wise to move to a safe place with the capacity to provide security after a disaster. Just understand that these services will be minimal and limited and your expectations of "customer service," privacy, and self-determination will have to be adjusted to meet the realities of the situation. If at all possible, you will want to give yourself options and not be trapped in a situation of long-term dependence.

When you make plans and preparations to avoid being — or limit the time you need to be — a Passenger, you are doing yourself and everyone else a favor. To accomplish this you will want to decide what kind of plans you need to make and how much preparation is required to make your plan work. If you do not want to be a Passenger, then you need to be a Planner.

Planners

Being a Planner is easy and relatively inexpensive. It involves using some of your own time and resources to get a few things ready just in case of a disaster. You may still need some help, but you give yourself the opportunity to be able to choose if and how long you may need to be a Passenger. The chances are good that you already have some of the planning skills you need or you may even be a Planner already. The keys are, first, to organize your thoughts and, second, to develop positive habits into simple plans and actions that will benefit you when you find yourself in need.

Remember the quote from Winston Churchill at the beginning of the book? He is talking about being a Planner and the importance of forethought (a plan), simple and effective action (gathering resources), and clear thinking (knowing what to do in an emergency). His warning is that not doing these things until the emergency is upon us threatens our self-preservation (survival).

Planners have discovered the golden rule of preparation and readiness: 20% preparation is the 80% solution. Most of us have concerns in life that occupy our thoughts more than planning for future disasters: kids, school, work, rent, family, and all those other things we want to do and need to do to get by in the world. Still those things worth living for are also worth protecting. Looking back at the spectrum of preparation chart, we see that the expenditure of resources and time in the Planners column provides a disproportionally large benefit of independence. A little time dedicated to planning and resources will significantly improve your options and readiness when a disaster occurs.

As was mentioned before, the government would like everyone in America to be as much of a Planner as they can be given their situation and available resources. Emergency managers want as many people as possible to be as ready and self-sufficient as they can be because the government already knows there will be shortages and time delays before relief resources can get to everyone who will need them after a disaster. This is not a deficiency on the part of government, but a reality of the scale and scope of disasters. Remember that even with 10,000 National Guard troops, vehicles, boats, and pre-positioned supplies on standby in the gulf coast states in preparation for Hurricane Katrina, it still took several days for relief to get to many people after the storm. The same was true in Super Storm Sandy in 2012. The storm itself did a lot of damage, but the nor'easter snow storm and cold weather that followed significantly slowed down power-recovery operations and disrupted deliveries of food and medicine. The people who had some extra food and medicine set aside and made arrangements for heat were much better off.

A Point of Clarification: For the purposes of our discussion, preparation as a lifestyle is not an attempt to escape society or avoid government, but rather a desire for self-sufficiency in times of disaster. Preparation should not be confused with extreme survivalist or anti-government sentiments. For our definition, a banker who lives in a high-rise condominium on Manhattan Island in New York City can be a Preparer just as effectively as a forest ranger living in the mountains of Colorado. America is a place where people are free to exercise their individual rights and liberties as long as they do not infringe upon the rights of others. Being ready to care for yourself and your family during a disaster and to avoid situations that require rescue, relief, and government assistance is well within those rights and is encouraged by both government officials and emergency managers.

Preparers

There are some people who feel that simple plans and emergency kits are not enough to keep them safe during a disaster. These people believe that disaster preparation is important enough to make it a part of their lifestyle. The line between being a Planner and being a Preparer is not an easily definable thing. The difference is less about how much money is spent than it is about how much time is spent realistically thinking about it. Preparation as a lifestyle seeks to independently provide several of the systems and service aspects of governance, regardless of the government's capacity to provide them. Some people just live away from the systems and services we take for granted in metropolitan, suburban, and established rural communities and by necessity have developed their own.

In some cases people have built aspects of self-reliance into their homes, more as a necessity of location than a preparation for disaster. In some parts of the United States, it is not uncommon to have a wood-burning fireplace and a storage area for dry wood, to keep several days or even weeks of food on hand, or having a generator available for when the power goes out. This is not what we mean by being a Preparer. Being a Preparer involves three major aspects:

1. Active planning: Developing and regularly refining detailed plans for disaster response.

2. Collecting and maintaining significant resources (both in importance and appropriate volume) that will allow for survival with little or no assistance.

3. Learning and practicing skills useful in disaster situations like first aid, field cooking, or driving routes to find the best roads for moving out of an area of effect. This could also include aspects of physical fitness and self-defense.

Just as there are different levels of preparedness among Planners, there are also different levels of preparation and skill sets among Preparers. Some Preparers have outdoor hobbies that equate to preparation skills, like hunting, fishing, and camping. Others enjoy the social aspects of organizations and clubs that practice preparation-applicable skills, like shortwave radio clubs and youth organizations like the Boy and Girl Scouts of America.

Depending on your situation and interests, you can choose to be a Passenger, a Planner, or a Preparer. The government knows that there will be people in all three categories and has made arrangements to assist and provide for everyone to the best of their capability. In the chapters on government plans, you saw the intent and level of detail within government preparation. This is important because as a citizen of the United States, you need to have confidence that our government is protecting our interests, especially in times of great distress.

One last aspect of the spectrum of preparation that is very important to recognize is that none of the methods addressed in this book release you from responsibility for yourself or make you completely independent from the government. In the end we cannot escape the paradoxical fact that we are both independent in our personal responsibility and connected in our social, cultural, and national relationships.

Personal Defense

In any conversation about disaster preparedness, it would be remiss not to address the issue of weapons. This point more than any other drives home the reality that your choices come with both responsibility and consequences. This issue also puts special emphasis on you, as a decision-maker, to make sure you plan and prepare correctly. In fact your whole plan should be addressed with the same seriousness because personal weapons are only one of the things that will get you hurt or killed if you do not give your choices due respect and consideration.

An aspect to consider is that during a major disaster the institutions of security — jails, prisons, and some kinds of mental institutions — may fail to confine danger- ous, confused, or violent members of their confined population. In addition, some members of society may feel that without police presence there is no incentive to obey laws that protect personal property and individual safety.

In a major disaster event there may be a period of time between the disaster event that disrupts rule of law and the reestablishment of security. This has been the case in multiple disaster situations in the United States. Two examples of where the loss of security was an issue were the lawlessness in the City of New Orleans in the aftermath of Hurricane Katrina in 2005 and the civil unrest experienced during the Rodney King riots in 1992. In both cases the citizenry was left unprotected by law enforcement for several days. Even when people called 911 for help, some people were told that they were on their own until order could be restored. During that time several incidences occurred where private citizens used legally owned personal weapons for their self-defense.

The Second Amendment of the Constitution of the United States guarantees the right of private citizens to keep and bear arms. There is much debate about the merits and shortfalls of our nation's private gun–ownership laws. We will not address that question here. The question is not *can* you own a gun; the issue is *should* you own a gun. If you think you may need to get a weapon for your self-defense and are considering acquiring one, then you need to ask yourself the following questions. They are presented in the first person because these questions are not hypotheti- cal or philosophical. They entail your actions and your responsibility. You must ask yourself "What will I do?"

1. *Given the situation I think I may be in, do I have a real need for a gun?* If you are planning to be a Passenger or a Planner who is looking at getting near people and relief supplies, then a personal weapon may just be a liability. If you believe you can get to a secure location, then you may be better off without a weapon. The security providers will not want weapons in their area and you may be asked to leave it be- hind if you want to travel on public transportation. This is not to say government will systematically disarm the public, but rather that there are places where guns may not be allowed, and you may have to choose between your gun and a ride out of the disaster area.

OK, so you think you need a personal firearm. Ask yourself this:

2. *Am I capable of taking a human life?* Understand that *willing to* is not the same as *capable of*. When you carry a firearm but have not mentally prepared yourself to take a life or have no true or ready intention of defending yourself and your family, then you are just carrying the weapon to the person who will use it to hurt you. This

is not a joke. You will point the weapon, your hand will shake, your eyes will drop to the floor, and then your attacker will walk over to you and take the weapon from your hand. They may hurt you, or worse yet, they may hurt your loved ones. Do not go down this road unless you have seriously considered the gravity of this situation. Remember that you're getting this weapon for self-defense in a disaster. This does not mean you must harden your heart or become cruel. It does mean you must consider the enormity and responsibility of the decision you are about to make. Take it seriously and consider well. Never carry a weapon you are not able and willing to use.

OK, you have the NEED and found the WILL to use a weapon. Ask yourself this:

3. *Can I legally carry a personal weapon where I live?* DO NOT purchase, possess, or carry a personal weapon in a city or state where it is illegal to do so. If you do, then you are a lawbreaker. Yes, criminals have guns and don't care about law and order. Do not add to the mess by becoming a lawbreaker yourself. If you end up having to use your weapon in a city or state where it is illegal to do so, then you are subject to prosecution under the law, maybe even for murder, even in cases of self-defense. If you feel you must own a firearm, then move to a place where it is legal to do so. This is part of your responsibility to the people you live around. If you choose to live in any community, rural or urban, you have consented to abide by the laws of that community. This is called the *social contract,* and it is taken very seriously by elected officials, the police, and the court system.

OK, you found you have the NEED and the WILL to use a weapon, and can do so LEGALLY. One last question:

4. *Can I now or am I willing to learn how to use a firearm so I do not cause unintentional harm to myself or others?* A firearm is not something you can put in a box and save for an emergency. It is a defensive weapon that requires maintenance, proficiency, and mental preparation for effective use. If you are going to own one, then you will want to become at least proficient with it, preferably an expert with it. This is not hard, but it does require a commitment of time and attention that is right and proper to expect. An untrained person with a weapon in their hands is a danger to themselves and anyone around them. Don't be that person. Here are some standards to help you develop and maintain a minimum desired level of proficiency.

Get the correct weapon for your needs. Remember that you are using this weapon for self-defense and avoid the urge to "gear up" with a high–round capacity, large-caliber weapon (sometimes called a "hand cannon"). Do some research and try firing a few different kinds of weapons until you find a style, size, and caliber that will meet your needs for ease of carry, access, and use.

Know your personal weapon: learn to use it safely and with technical proficiency. When a weapon is involved, safety is your first priority. This is about real familiarity with your weapon and proficiency at target practice. Invest in some dummy rounds and practice loading, unloading and clearing your weapon until you know how to do it correctly every time. Take shooting lessons and use the weapon until you can comfortably and consistently hit a 12-inch target at 30 feet/10 yards (about 10 paces) every time. If you're not willing to become a proficient marksman, then you're just dangerous.

It is important to use and get comfortable with having your weapon. If it is legal where you live, take the time to get a concealed-carry license. Then carry your weapon. If you are not familiar with the regular care, cleaning, carry, and safe handling of your weapon, you will be at a disadvantage when a disaster hits. The aftermath of disaster is not the time or place to start learning weapons safety and handling. You must be cognizant of, used to and comfortable with your weapon when you carry it.

Fire your weapon on a regular basis to maintain and improve your marksmanship skills. You should fire, at a minimum, 50 rounds through your weapon at least once every three months. The only way to get better at your weapons skill is to practice firing the weapon. No video games or informational technique CD lessons will give you the skills you need to handle and fire your weapon safely and accurately; spend the money on ammo, take the time to go to the range, and practice marksmanship with the weapon. Not just shooting, actually practicing.

Learn how to fight with your weapon. This is different than target practice or marksmanship. This is defensive weapons technique. A gunfight is nothing like target practice. Learn the difference and acquire both skills. You must first be a safe and proficient target shooter before you can learn to fight with a gun. There are classes for firearms self-defense in almost any city where they are legal to own.

Prepare yourself mentally to be an armed citizen. Learn to avoid confrontation and keep a cool head. An armed citizen has a legal and moral obligation to use their capability for defense in a responsible manner. This responsibility is greater than that of the unarmed citizen if only because of the terrible cost of using this power in a hasty, aggressive, or unwise manner. Make no mistake, this is a serious responsibility and you must respect it and govern your emotions accordingly.

By now you have figured out that this process is expensive, time-consuming, and potentially dangerous and requires a significant mental commitment as well as a higher level of emotional maturity. To have the power to not be a victim is a tempting thing, but the taking of a life, even in the most justified circumstances, stays with you forever. It is a thing that can cost much more than just money and time.

It may seem like this discussion is trying to scare you away from a personal weapon. That is not true. If you are willing to do what is necessary to be responsible and proficient, you are encouraged to consider this option (where it is legal and would be useful to you). It is your constitutional right, and you are encouraged to take full advantage of anything that can legally improve your chances for survival. Remember, once you have a gun, your goal is to never use it.

But if any of these very minimal recommendations seem too much, then leave the weapons to the police and National Guard personnel that will be doing everything in their power to get to you as quickly as they can to ensure your security. You can find ways to protect yourself without a gun. Get with a group of people and find safety in numbers. Hide someplace until you see police and military patrols. Villains may take your food and blankets. People may speak harshly to you and treat you in a disrespectful manner. But remember that survival is not a zero-sum game of you over all others. In a disaster, staying alive is all that is required to win, and finding ways to not fight is always a better option for you than fighting, regardless of whether you are armed or not. A personal weapon is no guarantee of safe passage or less frustration. Think about it and take the time to choose wisely.

Conclusion

The most important thing to take away from this discussion is that we have a choice in how we will prepare for and respond to disaster situations. Although natural or man-made disasters can quickly take the upper hand, we are not powerless to improve our chances for survival. With proper planning and awareness, we can be prepared, aware, and ready to take action to protect our lives, our loved ones, our property, our livelihoods, and our communities.

How to Make a Good Plan

Thinking About Plans and Making Plans

Most of the time you can recover from a bad plan and it is not a life-threatening situation. Sometimes a poor plan does nothing more than turn into a frustrating day and a good story. "There I was, up the creek without a paddle…" This is not true of disaster planning. Disaster planning requires you to get it right the first time in an unforgiving situation that is most likely dangerous. You will need a plan that you can depend upon. The government has made plans if you don't want to make one for yourself. Or you can make a plan for yourself. Your choice.

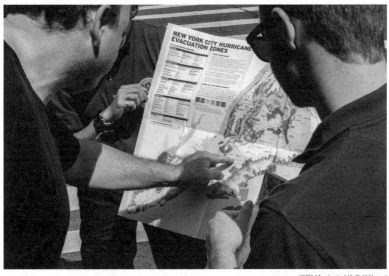

(FEMA photo/ K.C.Wilsey)

Read the next paragraph carefully.

If you want to have choices when disaster strikes, have a plan, keep it simple but effective, resource it, practice it, make it good enough to have confidence in it, and then commit to it. Using the techniques of simple and effective planning, you can choose your goals and make a plan for what methods you will use before, during, and after an event to meet the requirements of movement, sustainment, and communication. Before a disaster, you can then collect the items you will need immediately at the onset of a disaster, the resources you will need to sustain yourself during the disaster, and the documents and information required for rebuilding your life and livelihood after a disaster. This will give you options so your plans can stay flexible. Flexibility will let you make your own choices so you have the greatest chances of success in meeting your original goals.

The paragraph you have just read is what is called "Bottom Line Up Front." At the end of this chapter, you will see this paragraph again. When you get to that point, each of the italicized words should have a specific meaning in respect to time, intent, and action. Understand that the intent of this chapter is not only to inform, but also to teach a thinking skill, to provide a "thought framework" for how to make a plan. This is not the only way to make a plan, but it is simple and it works. If you learn how to do it well, it is very helpful. Learning about plans will address definitions and ways of thinking. It will ask you to separate issues and events and then respond to them appropriately. This will be easier said than done. This is because disaster planning is a thinking skill applied to an emotionally charged event.

This is important. The number-one reason plans fail is that people let their emotions cloud their reason, their ability to think clearly. This will almost always make it more difficult to successfully achieve a goal. Emotions are natural, and they will come out during a disaster. This does not mean emotions are bad. It means that emotions should not be the controlling factor in your decision-making. A disaster is a puzzle that requires you to think your way out if it. You will get tired, frustrated, angry, and sad and experience a sense of loss and fear of the unknown. Your goal will be to think clearly while you are feeling these emotions, to stay focused on your goals and adapt your methods to meet the changing situation.

At this point we need to separate some ideas and look at each one independently. We will separate the ideas of how to make a plan from how we will deal with our emotions during disaster. They are two different skill sets. The first set, making a simple and effective plan, will be addressed in this chapter. The second set, how to recognize and control our emotions during a disaster so that we don't get over-whelmed by them, will be addressed in the next chapter.

What follows are a series of short and simple lists that address the basic things that need to happen in the planning process. Some of the aspects will seem to repeat, but this is not exactly true. This is because the secret to making an effective plan is to think about the same subject in different ways depending upon when you think about it: before, during, or after. This idea of *before, during, and after* can be expressed as *goals, methods, and flexibility.*

As you progress through the lists, understand that these are not rules for you to memorize. There is no formula for success in survival, only the practiced skill of thinking with a clear and adaptive mind. The intent is to describe these different aspects by breaking them down into component parts in order to display the idea. None of the individual parts are that complex, but they must work together to be effective.

What Makes a Good Plan?

There is an idea about how things work, what makes them work, and what makes them fail: it is called Ockham's razor. Ockham is the name of the little European city where the idea came from, and the razor refers to a perfect point of balance, as if on the edge of a razor. Basically it states that for things to work their best, they should be as simple as they can be, but also as complex as they need to be in order to work properly. If something is too simple, it will lack the working parts it needs to func-tion effectively. If it is more complex than is required, then the additional complexity will slow the system down or cause it to fail completely. This applies perfectly to the process of making an effective plan.

In planning, the difficulty comes from confusing the difference between *what* you want to do (goals) and *how* you are doing it (methods). The ability to understand the difference between goals and methods has a huge impact on the success of a plan. Goals should be clear, concise, and well-defined to the point that they do not change. Methods should be flexible. Flexibility is so important that it gets its own part of the planning process as it relates to methods. This is not silly or simplistic; plans require you to think about them correctly or they don't work as expected. Many people make plans they think are good and have no idea why they go wrong.

Goals

Goals are your desired end state and are determined BEFORE you start making any plans. This exemplifies the proverb, "Be careful what you wish for, you just may get it." Be sure your goals are based on what you need and not on what you want. In the planning process, setting your goals starts when you decide to take action and ends when you begin to prepare. Your goals should not change even if your situations do change.

Methods

Methods are the ways and means you will use DURING your plan to achieve your goals. Methods can be described as actions and tools, what you want to do and what you need to do it. Methods include aspects of *movement, sustainment, and communication.* These are generalized categories of important things you will need in order to get out of a disaster situation, and we will address them in detail later in the chapter. Determining your methods starts once you have decided on your goals and continues through the collection of resources and knowledge required to meet your goals. It ends when you achieve your goals, which may well be after you escape the disaster.

An example of the difference between a goal and a method can be expressed in the following scenario. You are in New Orleans after Hurricane Katrina, and your goal is to move your family from a disaster-affected area to a safe area where there is security, shelter, clean food, and opportunity for work so you can provide for your family. You listen to the radio and learn that Houston, Texas, was not affected by the disaster and the government has made arrangements to assist families with life essentials and to relocate them to areas of economic opportunity. You also have family in Wichita, Kansas, who are willing and able to help you. The goal is reaching a safe area; the *method* is movement to Houston or Wichita. This is where flexibility comes into the picture.

Flexibility

Flexibility is the ability to adjust your methods AFTER you have started to execute your plan, or how to change your methods without changing the goals. The things you do to meet the requirements of *movement, sustainment, and communication* may change, but your goals should not change.

You can build flexibility into your plan by giving yourself some extra time and resources. Plan for events to be a little worse that you think they might be. This is true for both time and resources. If it takes three days for the county to plow the roads after a big snowstorm, then keep four or five days worth of food available. If the National Weather Center usually gives three days' notice of a developing hurricane, then make your plans to be able to move in one day. The extra 48 hours before or after may become important if the situation is worse than initial reports indicate.

An example of confusion of goals and methods can be expressed in the following scenario: a family has a goal of moving from a disaster-affected area to a safe area where there is security, shelter, and clean food & water. They travel by car to a FEMA relief center where there is security, shelter, food, and a public communications center. They have successfully met the requirements of *movement, sustainment, and communication.* Then, two months after the disaster, FEMA takes down the relief center. The family is out in the cold again because moving to a FEMA relief center was never a valid goal. It was a method, an important and necessary waypoint, but never a valid end state.

Keeping these concepts of goals, methods, and flexibility in mind, there are four things you will want to think about as you make your plans.

1. It is better to have a plan than to not have one. The simplest plan that seems like a waste of time to make because it's so easy that it just seems obvious is the plan that will save your life. Even the most rudimentary plans and preparations pay off in big ways. Do not confuse thinking about what you will do with having a complete plan. Thinking about what you will do is only the first step of a plan. Even the simplest plan still requires the addition of resources and rehearsal (practice).

2. Perfect is the enemy of good enough. The benefit of a plan must be weighed against the cost of time and resources spent in preparation. Taking action on a good plan is better than waiting for the perfect plan and never taking action. The action is the most important part of the plan and trying to completely work out every contingency will just slow you down with complex details. Remember Ockham's razor.

3. Prepare your plan and practice your plan. Gather the things you will need to make your plan work, and then check to make sure your tools and provisions are in order from time to time. Then think through it, walk through it, or drive through it to test your plan for faults and to become familiar with it. An un-resourced and unrehearsed plan will rapidly turn into a plan that fails.

4. Follow your plan. Do not make changes to your plan unless there is a good reason to do so, and learn how not to abandon your plan when you are forced to be flexible. If you have taken the time to decide on a goal, make a plan and prepare & rehearse your plan, then take advantage of the material and mental preparation you have invested in your survival. Once you decide on an identified goal and preparations to achieve that goal, stick to them. We will talk about how to adapt a plan (change the methods) without losing the goal as we get into the chapter.

Let's look at each of these points in detail and discuss the advantages of a simple, prepared, and practiced plan.

It is better to have a plan than to not have one. There is a reason for this. The reason is in the human mind; your brain likes order. It does not matter if you process information quickly or are the most disorganized person you know; your mind still works in the same general way. It follows patterns and categorizes data. A plan provides a pattern of response and a priority of effort. Your brain will like this and use it to your advantage when faced with an emergency.

During an emergency your brain will do two things. First it will try to digest a lot of information at once: what is the threat, what will you need, where should you go, what should you do first, and a myriad other questions. Trying to answer all those same questions at the same time will result in confusion. Trying to figure everything out all at once will, in many cases, result in failure. You will miss some vital detail, not have what you need, not go where you should, or do everything right but do it too slowly to benefit from taking the action. The trick is not to try to change your brain, but to help it do what it does naturally. Make your decisions early while you have the time to do what you need to do. Then when the emergency comes, you will have fewer decisions to make, and you can react more calmly and effectively to the situation.

The second thing your brain will do is categorize and prioritize things like threats, required actions, and emotions. A plan will categorize and prioritize your actions, providing your mind with a pattern to follow. This is a survival instinct. You will not notice it consciously at the time, but you can benefit from it. A very important benefit is you will not waste your time doing things that seem right but turn out to be a waste of time in an emergency. You will also be calmer, not less worried or appropriately concerned, but you will be more focused on the correct things to do. This is the difference between being effective and doing lots of stuff.

Slow is smooth, and smooth is fast. Think about this phrase. Running around trying to do 20 things at once takes too much time and may not complete the tasks you need to complete in order to survive. This is not the same as doing four things that

Baseline Considerations

Some may argue that, if you are going to change a plan anyway, why bother having a plan in the first place? The answer is simple: every plan will have some baseline similarities, common aspects that must be present in *any* plan. These are *movement, sustainment, and communication.* By being able to do these three things, you can meet the goal of almost any survival plan regardless of any changes you need to make along the way. Sometimes things go badly and your plan will go out the window, but even then your plan will still be of use to you. At the very least, a well thought-out plan gives you a known point from which to deviate.

Movement
The goal of movement is to travel away from hazards and threats to a place of safety and stability. The goal is more important than the method. Do not get too focused on one method of movement or discount another method because you don't like it. You can walk, drive in your car, ride a city bus, get into a railroad car provided by FEMA, or use a combination of transportation options as long as you get to safety and stability.

Sustainment
The goal of sustainment is to have shelter, water, and food. You will want to find these things in the order shown. A relatively healthy adult can generally live for up to three days without water and up to three weeks without food. This timeline is a little shorter if you are under the stress of a disaster, but they reduce dramatically when people are exposed to the elements. Shelter is a must. Clean water is imperative. There are many ways to purify water, which can be found in almost any survival book. If the situation of the disaster extends for more than two or three days, then clean food will be required to sustain your strength to last until rescue arrives. This may mean going to a relocation or relief center. Remember that you may need to sacrifice comfort and privacy, but comfort and privacy are not requirements for life. Quality of life comes after sustainment of life.

Communication
The goal of communication is to identify resources, safety, and stability in order to move toward them *and* to identify threats in order to avoid or escape from them. This can be as simple as using a whistle or a bright piece of cloth to get the attention of rescuers. It can be as complex as using a radio and a map to find passable roads, river-crossing points so you can keep moving, or identify areas of unrest and violence in order to avoid them. Communication involves both speaking and listening. It will also require you to think about what you hear and what the information you receive actually means.

Emergency managers and rescue personnel will give you information and instructions. These two things alone are not communication. Communication is more than just following instructions. The point of communication is to help you get the information you need to be able to make informed decisions. Listen to what people say, listen to the radio, pay attention to the information and instructions of emergency managers and rescue/relief personnel, and ask people about what they have learned, then make your own decisions.

An important note about information: a lot of the information you will receive following a disaster may only be good for a limited amount of time. This is especially true in a dynamic disaster situation where the disaster or aftermath is still developing. Some information that is initially correct will change without notice. Old information will still circulate, and rumors will be everywhere. You must sift through all of this data and act on what seems to you to be the most accurate and reliable. Information about resources and assistance from within the disaster area is especially susceptible to change.

you have identified as essential in a quick and concise manner and then getting someplace safe. In a disaster situation, calmness and deliberate action are important to your safety. Moving fast without a plan is hectic, unnerving, and incomplete. In the end, undefined speed takes more time than you can afford to use. Plans provide calmness, focus, and effective action. Moving calmly, deliberately (smoothly), and with a sense of purpose to complete the tasks identified in a plan takes less time. Slow is smooth, and smooth is fast.

Perfect is the enemy of good enough. This is where the idea of "20% preparation is the 80% solution" comes into play. When making your plans, accept the idea that no plan can answer every question or meet the needs of every situation. Don't try to plan for everything. More importantly, understand that even an exact plan leaves some room for flexibility. Flexibility and adaptation, the ability to adjust your plan to changes in situation, are key components to successful survival.

Charles Darwin was a naturalist in the mid-1800s who wrote extensively about his observations of nature. He made a very interesting observation about survival. He said, "It is not the strongest of the species that survive, nor the most intelligent, but the one most responsive to change." This holds true when making plans as well.

Prepare your plan and practice your plan. This premise is tied directly to the concept of time. This includes both *time to collect materials* and *time to learn things*. The point is that you can do things that are easy and effective now that will be difficult, expensive, or maybe even impossible after the disaster strikes. When making your plans, make sure you are focusing on the *capability* to move, sustain and communicate rather than on the *methods* used to do these things. Over-planning may take up valuable resources, including time, and under-planning will leave you with few, if any, survival options. Find the balance and remember to remain flexible in your plans.

Preparation

Preparation should be accomplished with a good amount of contemplation put into it by thinking about what you realistically need and what you can effectively use. One method of facilitating this process of thinking things through is to search for your tools and provisions. Time and money are both valuable resources, and to a certain extent they are interchangeable. When you have time, you can be more frugal with your money than when time is short. This same idea extends to how you collect your survival tools and supplies. An effective and frugal technique is to determine the tools and provisions you require for your plan and keep a list of these items with you. Over time, you can go to places where these items may be found (garage sales, auctions, clearance sales) and pick up a piece here and a piece there until, in time, you have built an emergency kit that could rival the most extensive and expensive kits on the market at a fraction of the cost. Many of the most important supplies and materials are inexpensive, readily available, and easy to store. This is the difference between cost and value. A whistle has a cost of under a dollar, but becomes very valuable when you need to signal for help. Some items may take a while to find if you don't want to pay full price. Balance the value of your time and your money. The main goal is to get what you need, to get as much as you can usefully store and transport (remember the goal of movement), and to acquire these things in time for them to be useful to you. Just as in your reaction to a disaster, thoughtful determination is more advantageous than a hasty rush.

Practice

Practicing the skills of survival is as important as having the materials you need. There are a few different aspects of this to consider. Three examples are offered here, but these are not all-inclusive. We will address rehearsals again in plan-making, but here are some examples of practice.

— If you buy a water-purification unit, then you need to practice how to use it. Your first attempt at assembly should not be the day you need water. Finding out you need a separate piece (batteries not included) after the stores are all empty will do you no good.

— If you travel your cleverly planned earthquake evacuation route and notice it takes you past a nuclear power-generating station, you may want to rethink that evacuation route.

— If your plan is to pack your survival items and be out of the house within three hours of a monitory evacuation order, you may want to make sure that 1. you know where everything is, 2. it all fits into the car, and 3. you can still fit your family in the car with everything you want to take.

Follow your plan. It may seem odd, but in an emergency many people just forget to act on their plans. This reinforces the importance of rehearsal, but more to the point, this addresses the mental state of people caught in a disaster. The ability to remain calm, keep your head, and think your way out of the emergency may literally save your life. This has a lot to do with the confidence you have in your plans. Did you just go through the motions to make yourself feel better, or did you make a real effort to make a workable plan? If you truly think about it and come to the conclusion that you have real confidence in your plans and are ready to act on them, you will have a much greater chance of actually benefiting from your efforts.

Making a Plan: Three Simple Steps

— Think about what you need to DO and need to HAVE on hand.

— COLLECT what you will need to make your plan work.

— KNOW what to do during an emergency.

1. Think about what you need to DO and need to HAVE on hand.

When we talk about what you want to do and what you need to have, it can get confusing in a hurry. So to keep things simple, think about your plans in these three general terms: Taking Cover (Immediate action), Planning to Stay (Bug in), and Planning to Move (Bug out).

Note: The "bug" reference is mid-century (WWII & Korea) military slang referring to a little bug getting out of the way of a large boot, or a smaller force evading a larger force. "Bug out" is generally used today as meaning to depart in a hurry. In survival terms, "bug in" implies the same avoidance of threat, but in a stationary location.

Take Cover! (Immediate Action): This is addressing those disasters that are quick-onset: earthquakes, tornadoes, thunderstorms, lightning, and other situations that require immediate action. In many cases immediate action involves getting to a physically safe place or modifying your behavior to avoid a dangerous situation. It may sound like we are starting at the end of the list (knowing what to do in an emergency), but it really just illustrates how the several parts of a plan are interrelated.

In this case, the first thing we want to do is to avoid the danger. Listen for advisories, watches, and warnings and react appropriately. In many cases we can avoid danger through our actions. It may sound simplistic, but not playing golf in a lighting storm and staying inside and hydrated when the temperature is over 100 degrees has a lot to do with staying safe. The government issues weather and temperature advisories to provide you with the information you need to stay safe. Listen to and react appropriately to those advisories.

There are times when you will need to move to a safe place. When this is the case, you will need to know where the safe place is and whether the safe place even exists. Ask yourself this question: do you have a safe place to go to, and do you have access to it? It is important not to make assumptions on this. You will want to make sure you can get to your safe place in the evenings or on weekends. Some public buildings with tornado shelters are only open during business hours. Keep this in mind when making your plans.

As for what you will want to have on hand, in many cases with quick-onset situations, you can get by with just a few items: a flashlight, a portable radio, a small first-aid kit, a bottle of water, and a few snacks can get you through an evening without power during a severe thunderstorm or tornado warning. The obvious exception to this is the earthquake or tornado that compromises your safe place.

The takeaway lesson of Take Cover is to know where your safe place is and to know it is accessible, then to get to it in a timely manner should the need arise. If you have the option of storing your emergency supplies in your safe place, it is a good thing to do. Just make sure you check your emergency items from time to time to make sure they are still useful and functioning for when you need them.

Planning to stay (Bug in): This is addressing longer-term considerations that are different from the immediate action of taking cover. There are times when the best thing you can do during an emergency is to stay in your home. As a general rule, bugging in is more dependent on preparation and supplies than it is on action plans. With some forethought you can make your home into a good place to be rather than a place where you are trapped. Staying put makes planning a little easier because it takes the *move* out of *move, sustain, and communicate*. The other side of the coin is that by not being able to move, you are limited to the preparation and supplies you have on-hand for the duration of the disaster. When thinking about bugging in, there are two general themes to consider: keeping yourself in and keeping things out. The difference between the two is that the first category addresses limitations of mobility and the second addresses hazards and threats outside the home.

From the "keeping yourself in" perspective, the disasters could be winter storms, extreme cold, extreme heat, or some other situation that limits the ability of services to get to you (water, power, fire rescue, etc.) and your ability to get to services (to the store or the hospital). In this case think of things you would do or need to have in a situation where the power is out and you do not have the option of going to get more supplies. Things to keep in mind are warmth, food and the ability to cook, clean water, sanitation, and communication when the power is out. There are ideas for helpful things you can do during a blizzard or snowstorm in the chapter on wintertime disasters.

From the "keeping things out" perspective, the disasters could be civil unrest, a pandemic illness, or some other situation that poses a threat to you through exposure to other people. The requirements of warmth, food and the ability to cook, clean water, sanitation, and communication are just as important, but the issues of security and social distancing also come into play. Social distancing is how to reduce personal interactions in order to reduce the risk of disease transmission. An in-depth discussion on social distancing is discussed in the Pandemic chapter of this book.

In both situations you can plan for several things. Public safety and utility services may be limited or interrupted. Food distribution, medical services, and fire & police rescue may also be interrupted or delayed. Also think about how long you may need to stay inside. Unless you are aware of specific situations where services will be interrupted for extended periods of time, seven to ten days is a good rule of thumb for planning.

Although transportation is a huge issue, it is not the only thing that affects Passengers, Planners, and Preparers. You can be a Passenger in a bug-in by being dependent on assistance from outside for food, water, medical assistance, prescription access, and heat/warmth. A Planner can limit outside dependence on these resources, and Preparers can arrange independent sourcing for most resource and services requirements.

Making Your Plan

With these general ideas about plans in mind, you can now start to think about your goals and the specifics of what methods it will take for your plan to successfully meet your goals. Remember that a plan involves information, resources, and actions. Making a good plan that you can have confidence in is not difficult or expensive if you take the time to think and act on your plan correctly. With the help of online resources and books, you can be prepared before a disaster to act during and after a disaster.

The following examples of goals and methods are just a few that demonstrate how people live normal lives that include preparation for disaster. Make note of the different types of goals and methods.

— In Kansas and Oklahoma, where seasonal tornadoes are common, people have a goal of surviving the storm. They use the methods of knowing the location and accessibility of the nearest storm shelter and keeping supplies like a working flashlight and a weather radio someplace where they can get to them quickly.

— In Montana and North Dakota, people live with heavy seasonal snowfall. They have a goal of sustaining themselves during times of limited mobility. The method they use is to maintain extra food, fuel, and other household items to hold them over for a few days of heavy winter snows that separate them from goods and services.

— In South Carolina and other states that are affected by hurricanes, people have the dual goals of protecting their property from damage and escaping the storm. Using the method of keeping special materials on-hand, they keep enough plywood and screws to board up their windows, knowing that when the storm warnings are announced through the media, time will be short and these materials will be hard to find. Using a method of movement by having a resourced and practiced evacuation plan, they can quickly collect the items they need and move to a safer location in a timely manner. In this case the time saved by being ready to meet the first goal of protection of property supports the short-timeline requirements of escaping the storm.

Hurricanes, tornadoes, blizzards, and earthquakes all have the potential to do great harm, but regular people have found ways to adapt to their regional situations. You can do this too. The level of readiness you want to prepare for is up to you and will, to a certain extent, be dependent on the probability and severity of the threats in your area. Here is a simple and effective three-step method of planning and action that can help you to develop a good plan and have the right materials available in case of an emergency.

Plan to move (Bug out): There may be times when you will have to leave your home and move to a safer place. Bugging out requires the full spectrum of planning: *movement, sustainment, and communication.* Examples of disasters that require you to move are hurricanes, volcanoes, tsunamis, and wildfires. These can be either quick- or slow-onset, depending on the nature of the disaster. We will cover details on each of these disaster types in the disaster section, but as a general rule, there are a few things to keep in mind.

Movement: the most important decision you can make is the decision to leave your comfort zone in order to save your life. Be prepared to make that choice. Disasters and disaster situations are not fair, and this is important to remember. When the disaster hits and you have failed to do what was required for your survival, there is no do-over. An experienced emergency manager once expressed this sentiment with the following advice: "Flee before the wrath of nature, for thou art small and biodegradable."

Early movement is a very good thing. The closer the disaster gets, the greater the possibility you will be unable to move. This is because people tend to wait until they *have* to move before they take any action. This is not advisable. Those who move early can avoid the mass exodus. If you wait, then you may be slowed down by the sheer numbers of people trying to move all at once. A Planner can completely avoid being a Passenger by taking advantage of an early move. Remember that strength and intelligence are not the deciding factors in survival. The adaptable are the most likely to survive.

Sustainment: shelter, warmth, water, and food are essential requirements. The most important aspect of sustainment is to think about what you will need before you need it. This is where your plan, survival kit, and provisions will become your lifeline. Having survival supplies is not the same as having well-thought-out plans and collecting the tools you need to survive. Take the time to truly contemplate on your sustainment needs and then plan accordingly.

Communication: listen to everything, but carefully examine everything you hear. Information is usually accurate when first announced, but becomes less accurate as time passes and may continue to be passed on well after it is no longer accurate. Rumors will most likely be inaccurate or irrational. You will have to determine the validity of what you hear when getting information from non-official sources. Keep a radio with you and stay up-to-date on what is going on. Your ability to anticipate future changes and requirements in order to adapt your plan will be dependent on your ability to get new and accurate information.

2. Collecting what you will need to make your plan work

When it comes to collecting what you need to make your plans work, there are two major aspects to keep in mind. First is to decide what you will realistically need, and second is to have access to it quickly when you need it. This is simple to understand and not so simple to do. It takes forethought, planning, and maintenance to do effectively. To collect what you need and to be able to get to it, think about your plans in three general areas: now, soon, and later. This can also be expressed as survival, sustainment, and rebuilding.

Immediate needs, now, survival: this category requires the fewest resources and the most discipline. It is the hardest part of readiness and the part that will give you the best opportunities to survive a disaster. It requires you to be mindful of your situation. When things go bad, they tend to go bad quickly, and not just from the event itself. The ability to perceive danger and act decisively with resources kept readily available is very useful. You should consider developing these talents or adapting your current talents to this effect. This includes self-defense. Self-defense is not just the question of weapon or no weapon. Regardless of that decision, you will want to refine the more important defense skills of situational awareness, conflict avoidance, inconspicuous action, and the fine art of getting out situations before they turn bad (whenever possible).

As an example of how quickly things can change, let's take a look at the commodity of gasoline on September 11, 2001. On the morning of September 11, gasoline was available nationwide for about $1.70 a gallon. Then at around 9 AM eastern time, the first plane hit the Twin Towers in New York City. Within a few hours, at least one national gas station chain had hiked their prices to over $5.00 a gallon and many independently owned stations did the same. The stations that did not hike prices were swamped with lines of cars blocking traffic all across the nation as people feared a gas shortage. People who had gas joined in the lines to top off their tanks based on the same fears. Within just a few hours, there was nationwide pandemonium. Although things looked bad at first, it was not long before people stopped to think about what was actually going on. Within a day or two, many of the stations that hiked their prices were charged with criminal price-gouging and prices stabilized quickly, but gas availability was low for a few days as the nation turned to ground transportation due to the grounding of all commercial aircraft. Admittedly, there was no way for the U.S. population to know that the attacks were going to take place (all conspiracy theories aside), but people who had gas were able to go about their business.

The point here is to illustrate how quickly things can change even when the disaster is not in our immediate area and how the perception of a shortage was what caused the shortage. When it comes to survival supplies, if you wait until you need it, you will not be able to get it.

When collecting the things you will need, keep a kit of simple essentials readily accessible. The Ready site at FEMA's www.ready.gov has excellent information on kit-building and plan-making for just about any situation from tornadoes to volcanoes. Make sure your kit includes communications. Portable, self-powered radios are a must for any emergency kit. Once you have your kit assembled, keep it where you can get to it and look at it at least twice a year and make sure the batteries are not corroded, tools are in good working condition, and supplies are still useable. That is the easy part. We'll go into more detail on this aspect in just a bit.

Now the hard part: you will need to keep your mind close at hand and be ready to use it. This will require you to develop survival habits. Some of the things you will want for your survival in an emergency are perishable. Not perishable like bread that will go moldy in a couple of days, but perishable in the sense that they are things you use every day. These things are common, easy to obtain, easy to use, and we don't think twice about using them up and then just getting more. They are mental awareness, gasoline, and cash. This may seem like an odd combination of things, but they are connected by a common thread: we take their availability for granted.

Mental awareness: When we feel nervous, we are more aware: we stop and listen; we take the time to look for and notice changes. Because most of us enjoy a safe and secure environment, we grow complacent and stop noticing the world around us. In fact we even go as far as to ignore the world around us. An example of this is texting and driving. The suggestion here is to swing the pendulum the other way in favor of awareness. Just as there is a fine line between genius and madness, there is a fine line between awareness and paranoia. No one advocates paranoia because it is a weakness of reason. Awareness, on the other hand, is the ability to perceive what is going on around you while still taking care of the details and responsibilities of your life. This includes the ability to recognize warning signs and make a timely decision to take action for your safety.

If you make a habit of knowing what is going on around you, then you will be miles ahead of the crowd when things go bad. Watch the news, listen to the weather, and know where your survival supplies are and if they are in good condition.

Gasoline and cash: The idea here is to think about those useful things that you have access to but don't actually have. Many of us live in a cash-free world of debit and credit cards; we drive by gas stations all day and don't think twice about driving our cars until there is nothing left in the tank but fumes; we keep little or no food in our homes because we eat on the go. What would you do if you could not get to these things even for just a few days? When the power goes out, debit cards don't work, banks close, and gas pumps will not function. A run on a grocery store can clean it out in an hour. Your assumption of availability is based on infrastructure working properly. In a disaster or even in response to a disaster someplace else, this accessibility can disappear very quickly.

With a little discipline and some good habits, you can take the edge off this scenario. The key is to not let yourself run completely out of the things you need and regularly use. Don't let your gas tank go under half full. Keep some cash of useable denominations ($5s, $10s, & $20s) in a safe and accessible place, as much as you think you may need to get by for a few days to a week. Keep a couple of days' worth of the food you like and eat in your cupboards, not as emergency stores but just not running yourself out of food in the home. Developing the habit of having a little something in reserve will serve you well in regular day-to-day life. It will also give you time and options in a disaster.

Things you will need Soon, Sustainment

This discussion is more about how to get what you need rather than what you need. The "what you need" lists for survival during a disaster is covered in the chapters on the different kinds of disasters. The issue most people will encounter is where and how to acquire all of the items they will need.

One option is survival kits that can be purchased online or from survival outfitters. These kits are very handy and very expensive. In looking at why they are expensive, you will find that it is not due to any specialized equipment or wonderful technology. The expense comes from just having everything you might need or find useful in one place already gathered for you. If you have the money and don't want to spend the time putting your own kit together, then this is an option, but it will still require you to think about what you need and how you will use it.

Another option is making a list of what you may need based on the recommendations of experts and then build the kit yourself. This is a slower option, but it is much less expensive and is just as effective. The Ready site at FEMA's www.ready. gov has excellent information on kit-building. This option also has the advantage of letting you think through your plans and get familiar with your equipment and supplies. Many of the items on the list are common and inexpensive. They can be found at reasonable prices at large retail stores. Some items like a signal mirror or an emergency whistle may not be found at the large retail stores, but can be found at outdoor sport, fishing, hunting and camping stores. Shop around and find a good price. Remember that by making a plan, you have given yourself time to shop for the best price while you prepare.

Make this a family affair. Get the kids and your spouse or significant other involved in finding the items you need. Building your kit together will help everyone participate in and know the plan. Just as with your immediate-needs items, ensure you keep your sustainment kits readily available. Readily available means you know exactly where it is and you can get to it quickly and easily. An emergency kit in a storage locker five miles from your house will be of little use to you in a disaster. These sustainment kits tend to be the size of a moving tote and don't take up much room. When you hear or see the warning signs of a disaster, know where your family and loved ones are and if you can keep them close. Take advantage of watches and other indicators of impending change by checking and updating your provisions where you can. This includes pulling out or putting on proper clothing, shoes, and coats.

Things you will need later, Rebuilding

When it comes to long-term items, think about important papers and other documentation. In a survival situation, you may think that the preservation of paper is silly, but it will save you much time and frustration later on if you consider life after the disaster. This is true regardless of whether you bug in or bug out. The items to consider are birth certificates, passports, deeds to vehicles and real estate, insurance policies, wills, trust papers, bank account records, and anything else that documents your identity, personal property or wealth, and legally binding agreements or instructions. In some cases the best place for these items is in a safety deposit box at the bank. You may not have access to them right away, but they will be safe in a vault. If you keep them at home, then invest in a home safe or other fire-resistant, lockable container. Also keep them centrally located so you know where they are and can get to them if you need to bug out.

With these items, also keep a current, laminated or water-resistant photo (within two years) of the members of your family or people that will be with you. They will help you communicate with people and authorities when you are searching for loved ones. If you don't have a passport, you may consider getting one for yourself and all the members of your family over the age of 10. It is a durable document that is recognized by state and federal agencies and will provide you with universally recognized identification.

3. Knowing what to do to during an emergency

Be ready. Practice your plan and be ready to change it as required to still meet your goals. Practicing your plan will provide you with two major advantages. First, it will help you identify any significant weaknesses in the plan, and second, it will save you from undue confusion if you find you ever end up needing to use it. This can be as simple as putting on a blindfold and finding your way out of your house to practicing escaping from a smoky house fire or as in-depth as driving your evacuation route and looking for appropriate alternate routes to use if the major roads are blocked.

An important part of practicing a plan is to have your family participate. To get an idea of how vital this is, have your family pack what they think they would need if you had to leave your home with only what they could carry or put in your car (with enough room to fit your family in too). It is better to have the discussion with your family about what is truly needed when you are not under the stress of a time restriction. Have the conversations about the things you want to preserve (a child's comforting toy and family photos) and the things you truly need (important legal documents and appropriate clothing for being outside) when you still have time to make special considerations or plans for your family.

Thinking about what to take with you and knowing where it is will save you valuable time. This may include organizing important papers and family documents into one location in your house or making hard, or emotional, decisions on what items you can realistically use or take with you. Also, do not to be too harsh in your selections. Interviews with survivors often include a lament from parents who leave a child's favored toy behind as "unnecessary" and too late realize the importance of the item to their child's mental comfort and ability to cope with significant change.

Children will not be the only ones affected by significant change. Disasters are scary and frustrating. The next chapter is a discussion about the reality of what to expect, things that will make you angry, and how to keep calm even when you're angry and frustrated.

(U.S. Army photo by Staff Sgt. Jim Greenhill/released)

Conclusion

Plans are about thinking and action. To be physically prepared and mentally ready to meet your goals, you should give yourself the time to make hard choices now in order to have time to make the right choices during a disaster. Take the time to think about potential disaster situations and develop and practice the ability to understand what is going on around you. Set goals, resource and practice a plan, and have confidence in your preparations and the government's ability to assist you. Then you will give yourself options. While others are trapped in their situation, you will have choices and be able to make realistic and informed decisions that will help you survive a disaster.

The next paragraph is the one from the beginning of the chapter. It should now have specific meaning and be a clear framework for how to develop a simple and effective plan.

If you want to have choices when disaster strikes, have a plan, keep it simple but effective, resource it, practice it, make it good enough to have confidence in it, and then commit to it. Using the techniques of simple and effective planning, you can choose your *goals* and make a plan for what *methods* you will use *before, during, and after* a disaster to meet the requirements of *movement, sustainment, and communication.* You can then collect the items you need *immediately* at the onset of a disaster, the resources you will need to sustain yourself during the disaster, and the documents and information required for *rebuilding* your life and livelihood after a disaster. This will give you options so your plans can stay *flexible. Flexibility* will let you make your own choices so you have the greatest chances of success in meeting your original *goals.*

Mental Resiliency in Disaster Situations

Plans are good, but they are only a reflection of this one irrefutable truth:

Survival is in Your Head

The most important aspect of survival is to stay calm and think clearly. To learn the methods of keeping a clear mind, we are going to discuss both why we think poorly and how poor thinking manifests. As we move through these ideas, look for the difference between awareness and perception. Awareness is the ability to collect correct information. Perception is the ability to maintain awareness without emotional distortion. This is vitally important. Fear is your enemy, and this chapter addresses how to deal with fear. We can't completely get rid of fear, and it is important that we do not. Fear is a kind of awareness, and we will need all of the awareness we can get in a disaster. We need it, but we have to control it. Fear is mastered with reason and countered with humor and humanity.

To address reason, we will discuss temperament, resistance, and emotional control. Understand that these are all aspects of your personality. Later, as we discuss humor and humanity, we will look at how to take the mastery of your emotions and turn it into mastery of your response to a disaster situation.

Reason

Rational thinking is as important of a skill as making fire when it comes to survival. If you are not thinking for yourself, then someone else will think for you. This is bad for two reasons: first, their decisions will be based on generalized information, and second, they may not bother to think for you at all and just let you fail. With that in mind, the question becomes how to keep your wits about you in a disaster situation.

Reason can be developed with the same methods we used for planning earlier in this book: before, during, and after. For the purposes of reason, this is expressed as *facts, awareness, and anticipation.* What do I know? What has or has not changed? And what may realistically happen in the future?

Having some reliable facts before a disaster lets us define how bad a situation may be in reality rather than based on fear or uninformed expectation. This is important because we do not want to spend time and energy responding to a threat beyond what is required and ignoring other threats that need to be addressed. Fearing a threat beyond its realistic effects is called dread. Dread is irrational and causes us to make mistakes. Facts help us keep threats in perspective. Think about a person who, dreading a snake, flees without looking where he is going and runs headlong into a tree. Fear of the effects of a poisonous snakebite is not bad, but respecting the snake's real abilities and moving calmly away from it beats dread and a panicked reaction every time.

Awareness during a disaster allows us to gather new facts. This is important because we know that disasters change our environment and expose us to hazards and threats. Being aware allows us to be effective in recognizing changes. Anticipation allows us to take the facts of the past and the awareness of the present to make reasonable predictions about the future and then take positive action. When you use reason in this way, you will find you are better able to respond to a disaster; you are more resilient. This resiliency does not come easy. Just like planning, reason is a learned skill and, like planning, it is simple to understand, but can be difficult to do well. The difficulty comes from a very powerful force: emotion.

Both emotion and reason are very personal things and are both vitally important to you in a disaster. Reason enables you to deal with the reality of the situation, and emotion, when it is under control, provides the hope, faith in yourself, and strength of willpower that will allow you to survive despite seemingly overwhelming odds. You will develop your own abilities of emotional strength and reason based upon your personality. Because disasters are stressful and invoke emotional responses, the emotional can overwhelm the rational. The trick becomes mastering your emotions and keeping them in the useful range so you can still have access to your rational mind.

The process of reason is a thinking game, and you can get good at it through practice. Keeping your emotions in check is a different matter. For the purposes of this discussion, there are three aspects that we will address.

- Individual temperament
- Resistance to reality
- Controlling your emotions (Anger management & controlling fear)

Understand that there are whole libraries dedicated to each of these subjects. The good news is that within all that psychological data, we can find some useful bits of personal realization that are basic, applicable, understandable, and in many cases universal to how humans think. It may make you a bit uncomfortable when you recognize yourself in some of these explanations, but disasters are all about being uncomfortable, so this fits right in. Deal with it now or deal with it later, your choice.

Nothing here will say if you are right or wrong, nor does it matter if your personal motivations are viewed as fair, selfish, or self-serving by others. This is about your survival. The intent is to help you identify and recognize your personality traits to help you control the ones that are less helpful and strengthen the ones that are more helpful to provide emotional strength during a disaster situation. The ancient temples of the Greeks had a motto carved over the door: "Know Thy Self." Think about who you are and play to your strengths. If you are not aggressive, then do not make an aggressive plan. If you are aggressive, then understand you may not have the patience to stand quietly in a line. Either way, develop your goals, plans, and methods accordingly.

Personality

Personality includes temperament, personal momentum, and how to make effective decisions even if you are not used to making them. This is a very broad subject, so we will want to narrow your scope a bit and talk about how people act on their motivations. How we act on our motivations is called temperament. Temperament has a little bit to do with what motivates you, but more to do with how you interact with others in getting what you want and need. For the purposes of making our plans for a disaster, we will limit the field even more and talk about how people interact with systems and call it System Temperament. The question of System Temperament becomes important to your plan because it ties directly into your choice of being a Passenger, a Planner, or a Preparer.

First a warning: Do not let physical appearance be your guide in this. The aspects of both physical and mental toughness come into play here. There are huge, strong men who are passive and as gentle as lambs and fragile elderly women who are pushy and aggressive. This is an exercise in self-recognition, not labeling. At the beginnings of each temperament description is the name of the temperament as described by the philosopher Aristotle. If you find that you wish to know more about the subject than is offered here, you may consider looking into his writings on the subject.

Steps for Making a Decision

If you are not used to making decisions, then use this simple method when you are not sure of what to do. It will help you make your choices.

Decide to participate in your own survival: this means taking the time to choose between right and right. Each day you must eat, wash, sleep, and move to the best place to be able to eat, wash, and sleep the next day. Learn what it takes to survive, and then move to the right place to do the things you need to do.

Ask questions and talk to people: think about whether you are in the right places and doing the right things. If you are unsure, then ask. If you are sure, then ask. Get more information and make sure you are doing the things that need to be done. Get the opinion of others and see if it sounds right to you. Then make your own choice. Asking will also allow you to get new information and network with others. Once again this is about participation.

Make your choices and act on them: ask yourself, "What is the best use of my time right now?" "What can I be doing to better my situation?" Remember that the situation will eventually force you to take some action. Disasters will put pressure on you to do the things required for you to survive. Let those pressures guide you rather than making them force you. Don't fight your participation in the disaster. You are there, you are not getting out any time soon, and ignoring the situation will just turn out badly. Within making choices, there are aspects of both thinking and feeling. You will want to use them both and you will want to use them for the right reasons at the right times. When you keep your mind calm with reason and you feel something is not right, listen to that feeling and act on it. You may find your "gut feelings" are very accurate. This is an important part of anticipation.

Feelings are an important part of gauging your situation and what is going on around you. This is a vital part of your situational awareness. But in order for you to be aware of your surroundings, you need to do your best to see that your ability to sense your surrounding is not masked by the physical demands of your body. To help you be aware, you will want to keep yourself as healthy as possible. This means thinking about want you need before your body tells you that you need it. Do not wait to sleep until you are too tired to stand. Do not wait to eat and drink until your stomach cramps and your mouth is bone-dry. Do not wait to use the restroom until you have to rush to the nearest commode.

By thinking about your physical needs and choosing to attend to them in a timely manner, you will let your feelings address things other than your immediate physical requirements. These "little things" are in fact very important decisions. Acting on your physical requirements before your body demands attention is a part of self-advocacy and participation in your own survival.

It does not matter if you are a Passenger, a Planner, or a Preparer, you will be responsible for yourself. Decide to participate, ask questions, then make your choices, and act on them.

System Temperaments

In the most general sense, there are four basic types of temperaments among people. These four temperaments are based on a variety of interacting personality traits: optimism vs. pessimism, quick response vs. slow response, social vs. loner, holding ideas vs. flexible thinking, relationship-oriented vs. task-oriented, desire for control vs. tolerance for being controlled, etc. These traits combine in general patterns of behavior that can indicate the types of motivations and perceptions most commonly seen within the people with these trait combinations. As individuals we would find ourselves somewhere between the four extremes of the definitions provided here. Most of us are some combination of these four temperaments. If you recognize yourself in one of these descriptions, understand that these are tendencies and not absolutes. The intent is for you to find a planning method that will work the best for your dominant temperament.

See facing page for a discussion of the four basic types of temperaments.

Contemplate your temperament. Talk it over with your friends and family because they may have valuable insights for you to think about. Your system temperament will not affect your goals, but will have everything to do with your methods.

Personal Momentum

When we talk about personal momentum, we are talking about being a self-advocate. Ben Franklin said, "God helps those who help themselves." This is very true in disaster situations. You will have to take action on your own behalf and on behalf of those who depend on you. This does not mean you need to take more than your share, but you will have to take part in the process: ask for help when you need it, get in line, and move when you are told to move. It is imperative that you not wait too long to do those things you need to do. Do not wait for someone to do it for you. You will not need to be overly aggressive or pushy; you just need to participate. In a disaster situation, you can and will get left behind if you don't move under your own steam or get someone's attention to help you survive if you have actual special needs. These would include, but would not be limited to, special medical needs such as injuries requiring dedicated medical attention, conditions requiring timed medications, or difficulty moving without a walker or wheel chair.

In many cases you will be caring for others: family members, friends, or just other people that need help. Your motivation for personal momentum may well be a desire to care for others. Understand that your choices will be dependent on if you are choosing for just yourself or if you are choosing for others who depend upon you. Also understand that sometimes your personal momentum will be the only thing that keeps others going. When they have eaten, then you can eat. When you keep watch, they can sleep. This is especially true for children. Be aware of this dynamic, and be willing to participate both with and for those who need you. Just as importantly, do not try to do everything yourself. Personal momentum can drain your strength if you don't take care of yourself while you are taking care of everyone else.

Resistance to Reality

It is important to understand that resistance is different than resiliency. Resiliency is the ability to keep hope and a positive attitude *despite the situation*. Resistance is the *refusal to recognize the situation*. One is courage in the face of danger, and the other is denial by self-delusion.

Disasters are very stressful in more ways than you might think, not only in the aspect of personal survival, but also in the aspect of radical change, loss of home and belongings, separation from friends and loved ones, and even death. The natural human response to stress and conflict is to try to control one's environment or get away from the situation. You may have heard of this as the "fight or flight" response.

System Temperaments

System People (Phlegmatic)

System people quietly work the process. Their motivation is to get access to everything the system offers and make full use of it. This is not bad. The system was made to be used, and System people are good at it. They are not particularly interested in interaction with other people and may prefer anonymity. They are more interested in their place, or ranking, within the system. As deep as they get into the system, they prefer to not be controlled by it, but rather prefer to maneuver within it. These are the people who can disappear in a system and live comfortably. They tend to be quiet and spend a lot of time figuring out how to get the most with the least effort and are optimistic about their chances for success. They are patient and can be slow to act, waiting for just the right time. Not a bad methodology for a Passenger.

Relationship People (Sanguine)

Relationship people are driven by their personal interaction with others. They survive on favors and special access. Their motivation is to get what they need from their "friends." They are less concerned about whether they are in control or being dominated as long as they get what they need. The system means little to them, as they will spend much time working out ways to bypass or ignore systems and are optimistic about the chances for success. They are quick to react and will jump to take advantage of opportunities, sometimes without regard for second- and third-order effects. Although they can use a system, they will be frustrated at the prospect of "becoming a number." They should consider being Planners within a group or smaller network of people, as this would meet their preference of personal interaction outside of a formalized system.

Independent Planner (Choleric)

Independent Planners are motivated by their own goals and tend to be pessimistic about anybody else's ability to assist them. Aggressive and independent in their plans and actions, they have a high desire to control their own situation and a low tolerance for being controlled. They are able to work for limited amounts of time within the system as long as it meets their needs and they can see a way out of the system. They are quick to react and may not care about the second- and third-order effects ("Damn the torpedoes! Full speed ahead!"). They make good friends and bad enemies... forever. For all of their independence, they understand the importance of networking and enjoy interaction as long as it does not interfere with their plans. Independent Planners should consider being Preparers and dedicating the resources required to meet their expectations for independence.

Loner (Melancholic)

Loners may find themselves at a disadvantage in disaster situations primarily due to their general pessimism towards both systems and people. They may distance themselves from the services and resources they need due to this general lack of trust. They have a low tolerance for being controlled, but also have a low desire to control their situation. They may be slow to react and take advantage of opportunities. If they dislike something or feel slighted by the system, they are slow to return and try again. They initially distrust the unknown and will avoid making decisions or interacting with others. If you recognize yourself in this description, then understand that "going off the grid" is difficult in disaster situations. Loners tend to be smart, independent, and capable, but the requirements of survival push them out of their comfort zone. Loners may see themselves as Planners or Preparers, but could end up being unsuccessful Passengers due to the weakness of their networking and relationships and tendency to distance themselves from the systems that can provide resources.

This can be a positive thing or a negative thing depending on the methods used for your escape from danger.

Some people find that stress motivates them to clear thought and positive action. Some people do not respond well to stress and will act in ways that are counterproductive to their survival. Because stress is cumulative, it can wear a person down over time to where they just do not want to acknowledge reality. When this happens, it will manifest in some predictable ways. Below are some examples of fight or flight responses that will not work well.

Unhelpful Fight Responses

The fight response manifests as aggression beyond the assertiveness of acting in your own behalf.

- Making demands that are unreasonable or beyond the available resources.
- Refusing to cooperate with authorities until unreasonable demands are met.
- Disrupting the rescue or support of others.
- Taking resources from others, self-justification (Blankets & food, opposed to looting).
- Inappropriate yelling or general aggressiveness towards family or strangers.
- Physically attacking others in frustration. This can include aggression towards friends and family.

Unhelpful Flight Responses

These behaviors may identify you as a person who is not in control. If you show this level of weakness, you may become a victim of another person's thoughtlessness or malice.

- "Checking out": Being completely unresponsive to your own needs. This can manifest as wandering aimlessly or sitting and staring into space.
- Panicked fear and hysteria (Different from belligerent disruption, but has the same effect).
- Denial: refusing to recognize facts that seem too difficult or frustrating to accept.

Realistic Expections

In both of these examples of fight or flight, there is a common theme: an unrealistic expectation of services or comfort. In both instances, the person stops trying to survive and, by surrendering to crushing depression or irrational anger, disrupts the survival efforts of others. One important way to avoid this pitfall is to have an appropriate set of expectations for what the situation may be like and what kind of help you can expect to receive. The importance of realistic expectations cannot be underestimated. Significant interruptions can occur during a disaster when people with unrealistic expectations interrupt the efforts of rescue and support personnel by making imposable demands for resources or assistance.

Let's take a look at some realistic expectations in disaster situations. These include, but are not limited to, the issues addressed here. Keep in mind that a person can make an issue of concern into an insurmountable obstacle. The goal here is not to convince you to just accept everything going on around you; that would be checking out. The intent is to help you frame the situation so you can respond in a positive manner to meet your needs. As with most issues involving emotion, the ideas are simple, the application can be difficult.

Loss of Comfort Level

In a disaster you will lose your comfort level. Understand this and do not let it be a controlling factor. You may have a lot to lose or just a little, but you will feel the loss: not only your real property, but also your "space." Being separated from your home and belongings can be a terrible stress. Not being able to sleep in your own bed or in having to sleep in a large room full of strangers will be stressful and uncomfortable. If the situation arises and you find yourself in a relief center, you will not have privacy at the same levels you are used to now. Understand that it is temporary. Use your dislike of the situation to motivate yourself and find constructive ways to better your situation with the goal of finding ways to return to your level of comfort. Remember that you have lost much, but not everything of importance; also accept that relief personnel will get you what you need, not what you want. Keep your expectations grounded by looking at the situation and thinking about what you have now, what you need now, what you will need soon, and the life you will want to return to after you survive the current situation.

Restriction of Personal Liberties

This is a significant issue for many people. People do not like being controlled, coerced, or told what they can and cannot do. This feeling becomes more intense as stressful situations escalate. The best way to describe the change you should expect is to provide the following train of thought. Every person has the right to live as they see fit as long as it does not infringe upon the rights of others. All of our actions affect others in some way, and this interaction becomes more pronounced in situations where resources are limited. Some of the choices that you were free to make without affecting others before a disaster strikes will directly impact on others during and after a disaster. Your expectations for freedom of movement, personal space, resource consumption, time for and place of expression of personal opinion, and many other things we take for granted as "personal liberty" may be limited, not by draconian authority, but by the situation and our closer interaction with others. Expect these changes and understand that personal choice is not being taken from you as much as it is temporarily limited by the situation.

Outrage Factors (real risk vs. emotional response or fear)

Disasters are not fair. You may encounter situations that are just wrong. Inequity and disproportionate risk will be evident all around you. You will see things that may be, literally, outrageous. Outrageous is defined as causing shock or indignation by exceeding the bounds of what is reasonable or expected. You will see things you did not expect to see. Expect this and do not let the shock of it put you off your game. Think about what you are seeing and adjust your actions accordingly. If you see a situation that is unfair and you can help by reporting it to authorities or doing something helpful yourself, then do so. If you see malice or serious criminal activity, then move away from it because it is a threat to your survival, then report it to authorities if you can. Some things that may cause you to have an emotional response are harm to children and animals, malice or indifference on the part of individuals, unintentional inequities in rescue efforts or services. The best you can do is to move away from the threats and inform authorities of issues you have encountered. The whole situation will be chaotic, and the response will seem disorganized. You will not be able to change any situation by losing control of your emotions.

Poor Communication (bad information)

Expect to have to confirm information. A lot of information has a limited "shelf life," the time in which it remains accurate. Understand that there is a difference between disaster communication and a promise. Emergency Managers will try to do everything in their power to get correct and timely information out to the public, but in some cases they will fail. These communication failures will be inconvenient and frustrating. Expect it to happen and do your best to protect yourself from it. When miscommunications like that happen, and they will, there is little chance that someone will be there to make it right for you. If you wait for food and it turns out to be the wrong location, don't waste more time getting emotional about it. You will be frustrated; just don't react in a counterproductive manner.

When relief agencies are the only game in town. There are a couple of things to keep in mind about realistic expectations of relief agencies. When relief agencies respond to a disaster, their intent is to get the minimum required resources to as many people as possible in the shortest amount of time. This means everyone gets a little, but no one gets a lot. Survival is not fair, convenient, comfortable, or an entitlement. No one will force you to take resources, and they will not try to make you do anything unreasonable. But if you want their help, you have to follow their rules. When you need help, ask for it and then get out of the road so they can help the next person. Ben Franklin is credited with the quote "God helps those who help themselves." By this he means proactive is better than reactive. Being proactive in a relief center involves cooperating with authorities and following instructions, which may include waiting your turn in a line, which may be very long. Once you receive goods and services, you should then depart as soon as you are able.

By keeping your expectations based on what is *planned for, possible, and probable,* rather than on an unrealistic or personal idea of what you *wish to happen,* you can avoid undue frustration and disappointment. When you take the time to think about what your situation may be like, you can develop more accurate and realistic expectations that will help you recognize and act upon the truth of your situation.

By accepting that survival is not comfortable, that the situation may limit your personal options for behavior and finally, that you are responsible for listening to information and thinking about what you hear, you will be able to move within a real environment and conduct yourself in a positive and helpful manner. Understand that while your goals involve *quality of life,* the goals of rescue and relief efforts are concerned only with *sustainment of life.* This will help you maintain an appropriate set of expectations.

Controlling Your Emotions

Anger management has been a punch line for a few years, but it is in fact a very useful tool. As with the other aspects of this book, anger will be broken down into its most basic aspects, and you will be provided with some simple tools to help you think and keep a cool head in a bad situation.

The first thing to understand about anger is that it is not a bad emotion. When you see malice, injustice, or anything else that makes you angry, you can use that to your advantage in your survival. You can use it to spur yourself to action. But anger must be controlled. Uncontrolled anger will expose you to danger in that it causes you to act without regard to your long-term well-being. People who do not control their anger tend to act first without thinking about the consequences of their actions or their defense.

There is a fine line between taking positive action and acting out. The first is justified, and the second is self-indulgence. As the same mind is making the determination, this can be a hard line to find. For the sake of definition, we will limit this discussion to anger based on the fear of loss, fear of the unknown, and reaction to risk. It could be the loss of control (your ability to make choices for yourself), the loss of resources (the things you need to sustain yourself), the uncertainty of facing a new situation that you believe you are unprepared to withstand, or being placed in a situation of great risk. In a disaster situation it is safe to say, "when you see anger, look for the fear." People who are afraid act out that fear in anger. This can be true of others as well as of you.

Every rational person will feel fear in a disaster; this is natural and important to survival because this fear will provide us with the desire to take action to remedy the perceived threat. This is our survival instinct. Fear and anger are good and will help you identify and act to avoid or mitigate threats. The question becomes *what should we fear and what is worth getting angry about?*

In a survival situation, there is only one thing that matters: your ability to act in your own best interests for your long-term survival. Although there are many things to be concerned about, (i.e. hazards and threats), not every concern will require you to take action. Not every situation will allow you to move or act freely. When a situation, or even a directive or instruction from relief personnel, keeps you from doing what you feel you need to do, it can become frustrating. Restrictions of this kind are even more frustrating when you are caring for others or traveling with your family. Your individual inconvenience (or even suffering) may be much easier to accept than the sight of your family under like circumstances. You must not let your frustration turn into counterproductive anger or rage. We will discuss outrage in just a bit.

The trick to controlling your anger is to control your fear. The way to control your fear is to be able to recognize when someone or something is actually restricting your ability to act in your own best interests. It is important to remember at this point we are taking about the *capacity* to take action and not the *method* of action. If someone says to ride on the train instead of in the car, you still get to move. If someone says you can't eat until tomorrow, you still get to eat. But when someone says you can never communicate with anyone else and have to do as they say, forever, then you have an issue. Note that *time* is not a factor until you get to "never" and "forever." Also do not confuse "we *don't* have any" with "you *can't* have any." There will be times when people want to help you, but just don't have the resources to do it. You can apply this same trio of *capacity, method, and time* to any aspect of movement, sustainment, and communication.

What should we fear, and what is worthy of our anger? To answer that question, it may be helpful to look at what it takes to emotionally turn a person from "frustrated" to "ready to revolt". Here is an important concept to keep in mind: the disaster is the "enemy" not the people who are telling you the bad news. People can sometimes transfer the frustration they feel during the challenges of survival onto the rescuers and responders who are trying to assist them. The requirements of rescue are not the same as tyranny and the authority of responders during a disaster is not despotism. The loss of services is not the same as denial of services. Upon examination of a frustrating situation, chances are good that the conditions for "ready to revolt" do not actually exist. There are very few situations, especially in a disaster situation, that would actually warrant action against the government in its attempts to assist the population.

What follows is a discussion on what it takes to purposely *make* people angry. Although it makes reference to revolution, the real intent is looking at what it takes to get people frustrated enough to act for, or against, their own interests. Do not limit your thinking to the idea of violence, but see how people, or even a situation, can trigger a fear response within you or others around you that may lead them to behave in a manner that is unproductive or even harmful to your situation. Look at what we truly fear when we think about losing control, and then think about how to master your thoughts and control your fear. Understand what is actually being lost vs. what is merely interrupted, and then subdue your emotions, use your capacity for reason and focus your actions on enhancing your chances for survival.

How manipulators make people angry and how to not let a situation manipulate you.

"The revolution is not an apple that falls when it is ripe. You have to make it fall." Che Guevara.

Ernesto "Che" Guevara was a communist revolutionary of the mid–20th century who was very insightful on the subject of what it took to make people frustrated enough to revolt. His premise was that in order for a people to be angry enough to act on that anger, they must believe they had been exposed to three conditions:

1. Real or perceived injustice,
2. Loss of voice or denial of voice, and
3. No hope for change.

The combination of these three things would cause people to become enraged and revolt against the "system." Mr. Guevara knowingly used the three tenets of revolution to force the conditions required for revolt. As you can tell from his quote, he also felt that these conditions needed to be forced or created, even within governments he felt were repressive. In many cases he would take one or two aspects that were real and then add the perception that the third aspect of the requirement was also true. If you look for absolutes, you will not find them. It is very hard to make all three of these things happen at the same time. In most cases at least one aspect of the trio is a false perception.

Because natural disasters can seemingly provide the initial situation of hopelessness and loss of communication (voice), disaster-response efforts must be extremely careful, or they can inadvertently complete the triad through a perceived denial of choice, which is a perception of injustice.

This is where the aspect of time becomes relevant.

Hopelessness during a disaster is not truly hopelessness, but is more likely to be the sorrow of loss and the fear of having to rebuild. In disasters it is not that things cannot change, but rather that they have changed too much or too quickly and the thought of rebuilding seems overwhelming.

Loss of voice may not truly be loss or denial of voice, but a temporary lack of access to methods of communication. Another aspect will be the fear that people, such as rescuers, are not listening to you. This can manifest when you feel you desperately need help with medical care or rescue-assistance and it seems like no one is listening to your calls for help. Calls for rescue may be delayed as other "higher priorities" are met. It is very hard to hear when your loved ones are hungry, trapped, or injured. Having to wait is not the same as being ignored.

Injustice may not truly be injustice, but rather the perception of injustice caused by unrealistic expectations. The most significant aspect of this is the idea of personal rights and liberties. It is not realistic to expect to have all of the rights (freedom of personal action) that you enjoy in a non-disaster situation during a disaster or its aftermath. This is not because your rights are lessened, but because your interactions are increased. Remember that a person's rights extend only until they interfere with another's rights. The closer the interactions the shorter range of individual rights. This does not include aspects of freedom like freedom of religion, civil equality, and due process of law, but it may put some limits on freedom of movement and speech. As an example, you may not be allowed to return to your home if authorities believe they will have to rescue you to get you back out alive or unharmed. Or you may not be allowed to voice your dissenting opinion while standing in a crowd of other survivors at a relief center if your speech disrupts the effective distribution of goods and services. Remember to carefully consider what seems to be not fair before you call it "injustice."

Outrage Factors, Perceived Risk vs. Real Risk and Using Outrage to Your Advantage

Another factor that will cause people to act or act out is how they respond to news and their perception of the risk that news represents. This will be of importance to you in a couple of ways, not the least of which will be in how you respond to new information that identifies risk and how others respond to that same information. Because this is dealing with human emotion, there is no concrete list or formula to guide you. Just read through the section and think about how you will receive information in a potentially high-stress environment.

To help us put these ideas into perspective, we can look at the writings of Dr. Peter Sandman, a leader in the field of risk communication and an expert on what he has termed "outrage factors."

At their most basic level, outrage factors are a balance between emotion and reason, partially about the news, but mostly about those components of a perceived risk that causes fear, anger, defensiveness, or frustration in people.

When you receive information, keep this important point in mind. Outrage factors are about balance: using the strengths of both emotion and reason to control what you can control and to not waste time on trying to change the things you can't control. There are a few aspects of outrage that you should keep in mind when considering how to maintain the balance between emotional feelings and rational awareness.

Before we look at how we see risk, let's define risk. Dr. Sandman defines risk as a combination of hazard (technical threat) and outrage (public concern). This is important because *what is* and *what is perceived* is not always in balance. Look at this again:

Risk = hazard (technical threat) + outrage (public concern).

Do you see where the importance of your being able to balance these factors is important? How is information communicated to you? How do you feel about the information you receive? How can you use the information and your feelings to make the best decisions during a disaster?

How is information communicated to you? Scientific risk vs. emotional risk. Government officials often rely on technically based information that does not consider the emotional response the public will have to that information. This means the way the government communicates risk and how we, as survivors and citizens, receive that message can be two completely different things. This is not a new idea. Government studies have shown that there has been virtually no similarity between the ranking of a threat or hazard by the general public and the ranking of those same hazards by technical experts. When Dr. Sandman is instructing risk communicators in the government, he says, "The ultimate job of risk communication is to try to produce a citizenry that has the knowledge, the power, and the will to assess its own risks rationally, decide which ones it wants to tolerate and which ones it wants to reduce or eliminate, and act accordingly." If the communicator fails to communicate successfully, the receiver (you) must be able to find the knowledge, power, and will on your own.

How do you feel about the information you receive? Recognize the validity and importance of your emotions. We discussed this before: anger is not necessarily a bad thing. Your concerns are valid and emotion can be an important indicator of our awareness that something is not quite right. But remember that this emotion may not be tied directly to a hazard or threat. This does not mean you are incorrect in feeling outrage, but keep in mind the difference between what *seems wrong* and what is *dangerous*. As we discuss some types of outrage factors, look for this difference and learn how to recognize it.

Mental Resiliency

Outrage Factors

Here are some of the issues that can cause an outrage response that were developed by Dr. Sandman and his fellow researchers. Do not limit yourself to this list in your contemplation of outrage factors. The factors that spark outrage will be different for different people, different cultures, and different disaster situations. As you read through these factors, think about what may be a factor for you and add to this list where it seems correct to you. You will find that several of these factors have very similar attributes. Look for the subtle differences.

1. Imposed or Voluntary? Do you choose your level of risk?
A voluntary risk is much more acceptable to people than a coerced risk. A voluntary or self-chosen risk may generate fear and concern, but not outrage. Consider the difference between being forced to get on a bus to an unknown destination or being asked to choose between two relief center destinations. The importance of having choices is critical and one of the most important aspects of how you will perceive your situation and level of control.

2. Industrial or Natural? Is the risk man-made or natural phenomenon?
This risk factor has a lot to do with the question of *why* there is a risk, specifically, who is to blame, or if there is blame, in the exposure to the risk. An example of this outrage factor is naturally occurring radon gas that collects in under-ventilated basements. While people are commonly aware of the hazards of asbestos insulation and leaded paints (man-made hazards), they are far less aware of naturally occurring radioactive gasses that are just as dangerous and arguably a greater risk to many people. The public's expectations of industry experts and of environmentalists are not the same. They will look to environmentalists to inform them of a situation, but will expect the industrialists to correct the situation.

3. Exotic or Familiar? Is the risk within our common frame of experience?
Risks that are outside of our common experience can cause significant concern simply because there is no point of common reference. When a risk comes from what people would consider as a strange or different source, the novelty of the introduction to the new experience could be enough to trigger outrage. This is different from merely being unfamiliar with the risk in a disaster situation. An exotic aspect could generate outrage even in non-emergency situations.

4. Memorable or forgettable? Is it a significant emotional event?
This is a straightforward aspect. A significant event — emotional (witnessing pain or suffering), physical (like an explosion), or a combination of both — will invoke a greater emotional response than a situation that lacks these aspects.

5. Dreaded or non-dreaded? Do we dread the risk?
Exposure to some risks invokes a greater emotional response than exposure to others. Exposure to water (drowning) may be a more acceptable hazard than exposure to fire (burning to death). This can also be situational where people will be reluctant to congregate in large groups during a pandemic or are concerned about the effects of exposure to radiation. The level of anxiety related to a threat or hazard will be proportional to the fear or dread of exposure.

6. Catastrophic or diffuse? What is the probability of exposure and effects?

This is an odd factor. It generates some non-linear thinking. This factor is important because it is a common occurrence that the potential effects of risk are often not the deciding factor in outrage. Let's look at two sets of scenarios.

Scenario #1: (a) A health risk guaranteed to kill 500 people a year in a city of 500,000. (b) A health risk with a ten-percent chance of wiping out a neighborhood of 50,000 in that city sometime in the next decade. Both of these have the same expected annual mortality of 500/500,000, or one in a thousand, but (b) is an enormously bigger outrage.

Scenario #2: (a) Over the last five years in the U.S., on average, 6,000 teenagers die each year in automobile crashes, by all accounts a national epidemic of death. This is an average of 18 a day, with summers and holidays having higher rates of fatalities. (b) Over the last 10 years of war in Iraq and Afghanistan, there have been about 6,500 deaths of U.S. Service members, with an average death toll of 54 a month, or about 2 a day. There were protests in the streets to "bring the troops home" and elected officials are removed from office by voters for failing to "end the wars," but there are no equivalent protest for a mortality rate of teenage drivers where the average annual death toll is just under the ten-year total for the combined casualties of the wars.

7. Unknown or familiar? Are we familiar enough with the risk to make an informed choice?

An unknown risk is a little different from an exotic risk in that with an unknown risk, it is not the risk itself that is strange, but the application or relationship to the particular situation that is the unknown. There is an expression that says, "The devil you know is better than the devil you don't." Untested or unfamiliar plans or options provoke more outrage than familiar risks. This has a lot to do with appropriate expectations. Understand that while an unknown risk can invoke outrage, appropriate information and communication, when provided correctly, has the potential to ease fear and outrage significantly, even when the risk remains the same.

8. Not controllable by individual or controllable by individual? Do you control the mitigation of your risk?

Many people feel safer driving than riding in the front passenger seat. When prevention and mitigation are in the individual's hands, the risk (though not the hazard) seems much lower than when they are in the hands of a government agency. There are times when you may want an agency with resources and personnel to be in control, but you will also want to be able to extract yourself from that situation if you desire. This may manifest as freedom of movement, the ability to exit a relief center, or even choosing the type of transportation you will use to move.

9. Unfair or fair? Is risk equitable in distribution?

People who must endure greater risks than their neighbors, without access to greater benefits, are naturally outraged — especially if the rationale for the greater risk looks more like politics than science. An example of this can be seen in the aftermath of Hurricane Katrina, where the claim was made that race was a determining factor in deciding what parts of the city would receive the most protection and rescue resources.

10. Ethically unacceptable or ethically acceptable? Is the choice moral?

Are the choices made in the mitigation of risk morally acceptable? The old adage of "women and children first" is a good example of this. The importance of maintaining our humanity when our survival is threatened is imperative. People will accept triage and priorities of assistance, but will not accept the abandonment of the old or injured, undue risk of harm to children, or other actions of seeming indifference or immoral behavior.

Continued on next page

Mental Resiliency

Outrage Factors (Cont.)

11. Source not trusted or trusted? Is the assister trustworthy?

Does the agency come across as trustworthy or dishonest, concerned or arrogant, compassionate or draconian? Does the agency communicate with survivors about what's going on, and what is the plan for assistance? Do agency representatives listen and respond to survivor concerns? This has everything to do with "Do you trust your government?" When FEMA offers thousands of people transportation by railcar in order to get them out of an unsupportable major metropolitan area and moved to relief centers, the population must not see "a prison car to a holding area." This is very important because the population (and you) must understand that there is no malice intended in the discomfort and austerity incumbent with the government plans to provide for the relief of the maximum number of people.

12. Unresponsive process or responsive? Are your needs being met?

Remember the discussion about Che Guevara and how he used the lack of voice to get people to revolt? This is a similar aspect. When you feel you are being ignored and your needs are not being met, you are much more likely to feel outrage. In a disaster situation where, by definition, there are not enough resources to meet everyone's needs, you can see where this may become an issue among survivors.

13. Affecting children and the unborn or not affecting them? Are children being harmed?

This is another very straightforward outrage factor. There are very few outrage factors that will have the emotional impact that this will have or invoke action as quickly or as intensely. Consider the situation and try to find out if the factors causing the harm are actually under anyone's control.

14. Are there any outrage factors that you can identify as important to you that are not on the list provided?

Write it in here and keep it in mind as a consideration of how you perceive and respond to risks. Outrage Factor: _____.

By considering these, and your own, outrage factors before a disaster strikes and examining your reaction to risk, you can give yourselves the opportunity to recognize your outrage early and use it to your advantage. If you find yourself outraged, ask yourself this question: "Why am I outraged?" The strength of emotional determination is an absolute requirement of survival, and the capacity for reason in the face of disaster is a precious commodity. Building emotional resiliency and rational strength will allow you to balance your response to risk. This will allow you to effectively respond to the real hazards and threats you will encounter.

How can you use the information and your feelings to make the best decisions during a disaster?

This means using information to its best effect. As we will see in the outrage factors below, outrage is based on both legitimate self-interest and valid psychological needs. Remember that belief trumps reality in the mind and the fight-or-flight response can be initiated by the perception of unacceptable risk regardless of severity, or even existence, of an actual risk. By learning to use your emotions as effective tools to help you recognize the root of your outrage, you can use these same emotions to help you decide upon the best course of action for your survival needs. As was noted before, these descriptions are not a formula, but rather a way of looking at things so you can decide what risks you choose to tolerate and which ones you want to reduce or eliminate and then act accordingly.

- When you find yourself outraged, ask yourself this question: Why am I outraged?
- This is very important! Ask yourself the following questions:
- Did I set myself up to be in this situation?
- Did I take the time to make choices when I had the chance?
- What positive thing can I do now to change my situation before I get angry?

If you have taken no action to help yourself or prepare in any substantive way prior to the disaster, can you be so bold as to declare you are outraged by the situation you find yourself in after the disaster has struck? Keeping this in mind, read through the questions below. This idea of your level of acceptance of the situation will be critical to your ability to deal with the frustrations of a disaster. This is not to say that these are not real and justifiable outrage factors. It only means you should ask yourself if the fix to your outrage should be directed internally or externally. Did you do this to yourself? Is someone else doing it to you? Or is it just the nature of the disaster?

Keeping these things in mind, a thoughtful person would be able to see what is happening clearly and realize the importance time plays in the duration of a disaster and have an opportunity to control the anger and anxiety that accompanies both justified and unjustified fear. Disasters can temporarily separate us from security, communication, and rule of law, but it is vitally important to know the difference between temporary separation and true loss.

You WILL be concerned or even frightened during a disaster. The power of the disaster and the devastation it causes WILL cause you to experience the pain of loss and separation. You WILL feel the situation is out of your control, and you WILL be frustrated by the difficulties of survival during a disaster. *The only thing you can control is your reaction to all this fear and loss.* The ability to maintain control of your emotions and think, to keep your wits about you, will be the major contributing factor in your ability to survive. Control your fear and you will control your anger. Control your fear and your chances for survival go up exponentially.

The last skill we will address in anger management is to cultivate the ability to recognize when others have lost control of their fear and succumb to anger. The adage "desperate people do desperate things" is very true. Your ability to keep your wits about you and recognize when others are losing theirs will be a significant advantage to your survival. This is true of individuals as well as crowds. Your ability to be aware of your surroundings will be dependent upon your having a realistic set of expectations for what will happen during and after a disaster. Keep your fears in check and let your emotions work for you instead of against you. Understanding outrage factors and how they will affect you, other people, and groups of people around you. Survival is in your head.

Mental Resiliency

Reason, Humor, and Humanity

Why thinking about a Zombie Apocalypse is helpful

There is a group of Planners and Preparers in California who formed a club called the "Zombie Squad." They gather socially and watch zombie movies and then talk about, research, and practice the skills they believe would help them in a "zombie apocalypse." It is socially fun and just a little bit silly. Regardless of the probability (or improbability) of the threat, the skills involved in personal readiness and response are based on serious and realistic skills that are applicable to real disaster scenarios. It turns out that being ready for a zombie apocalypse is some of the best preparedness training found anywhere in the country. Why would that be the case?

There is a lot to think about in this chapter. The thing most likely to keep you from preparing for a disaster may be the very idea of a disaster: a situation that is just too terrible to think about. The question of how to do all of the things required for survival is a legitimate concern. How will you face this specter and overcome the threats that loom like impenetrable walls between you and survival? What methods could the average person use to explore the ideas of temperament and control of emotion? Where do you start? As odd as it may sound, the best place to start is to look at your worst possible fears and deconstruct those fears and issues you may encounter with reason, humor, and humanity. We have discussed the tool of reason, but have not discussed its application. Now we will put reason in context with strength of humor and humanity.

This next section may seem like a discussion on planning, but it is not. It is about perspective, positive attitude, the strength of social connections, and how you *choose* to perceive your fear.

The way to master emotional terror, *fear*, and anger is to counter each of these elements with their opposites: overwhelming emotion with reason, fear with humor, and anger with humanity. *Reason* to make the threat understood rather than unknown, humor to dispel the non-rational and fearful aspects of the threat, and *humanity* to provide a moral compass to guide your actions.

Reason is the ability to think clearly and to use the information we have to make good decisions. Good decisions include not only thinking correctly, but also speaking correctly and acting correctly. It means thinking, speaking, and acting with our emotions under our control. The ability to know what we need to accomplish is good, but if we cannot communicate our ideas or enrage others with thoughtless, hurtful, and uncompassionate words, we will not be able to act on those ideas. Reason helps us to avoid conflict with both friends and strangers. The less time and energy you spend in conflict with other humans, the more you have available for survival within the disaster environment.

Humor is helpful in preparation and vital to survival. In humor we find hope. Humor includes a personal sense of acceptance of just how ridiculous the struggle for life can be and the equally important acceptance of the challenge of survival. To destroy the Specter of Fear, which is a very real mental monster, one must laugh at it. This sense of the ridiculous is where the zombie apocalypse comes into play.

A zombie apocalypse represents the worst possible disaster. Not only in terms of loss of infrastructure and security, but also in the most devastating possible loss: that of our humanity. The victims are left completely on their own. No power, no food or water, and no essential or public services in a biological threat environment complete with antagonists (the undead). Realistically the idea of a zombie apocalypse is ridiculous. It is a fantasy disaster scenario, but the elements of disaster within it are very real, and in that fact we find its strength and importance. Looking at aspects of disaster through the lens of the ridiculous actually gives us hope that we can overcome its very real challenges. It allows us to look at a situation and discuss

Tools for Keeping Your Head

Use Reason to Inform Yourself

- **Facts** - What do I know?
- **Awareness** - What has or has not changed?
- **Anticipation** - What may realistically happen in the future?

Use Your Individual Temperament to Help Guide Your Actions

- Play to your **strengths** & be aware of your **weaknesses**
- **Temperament** – Know your likes and dislikes so you can make appropriate decisions for your temperament: Passenger, Planner or Preparer
- **Personal Momentum** – Self Advocate & Take actions to help your situation
- **Effective Decisions** - "What is the best use of my time right now?" AND "What can I be doing to better my situation?"

Avoid Resistance to Reality

- **Resiliency** is the ability to keep hope and a positive attitude despite the situation.
- **Resistance** is the *refusal to recognize the situation.*

Control your Emotions and Use Them to Your Advantage (Anger Management & Controlling Fear)

- Remember **Fight or Flight** response and avoid unhelpful reactions
- **Keep your expectations realistic**
- **Outrage Factors:** Real risk vs. Emotional response or Fear
- What makes you **"Ready to Revolt!"** Don't mistake the people responding to a disaster as the cause of restrictions and frustrations in a disaster.

Reason, Humor, and Humanity: Powerful tools to help keep a level headed

Survival Is In Your Head

Mental Resiliency

options and plans without necessarily committing ourselves mentally to the pain and sorrow of the disaster.

Humor in preparation is important also. The mental weight of preparation for disaster can be a heavy load. By finding humor, positive social interaction, and recreational enjoyment in the preparation process, you can take a worrisome subject and make it far more palatable. This does not mean you should take the situation lightly, but rather make the preparation less frightening by not allowing it to be worse than it already is: the tornado shelter can be your gopher hole; the survival box can be your emergency picnic basket. The preparations and rehearsals can be a chance to get the family together. The events are exactly the same, but the fear is replaced with respect for the strength of nature, an understanding of appropriate response and the knowledge that we will not be alone when the time comes.

There are some groups in the United States that use the worst-case scenario of the zombie apocalypse as a planning guide for their disaster preparations. The idea being that if they practice survival skills (equip, prepare, and rehearse) with their friends (network), they can band together (resources) to survive an otherwise complete social breakdown in a biological/viral pandemic or high-security-threat environment, then they can pretty much survive anything. By adding friendly and social networking into the mix by watching zombie movies to facilitate the discussion of plans, collection of supplies for survival needs, and practice of the survival skills in social camping settings, they complete two important tasks. First they meet the needs of movement, sustainment, and communication. Second, they demystify the fear of a real disaster by learning how to respond to an unreal and ridiculously difficult apocalypse. The strength of this fun and social practice is in the development of friendship and commitment to others. This brings us to our third point of humanity.

Humanity is vital to survival. In any disaster, remaining human is the ultimate goal. If we lose this aspect of ourselves during a disaster, then even if we live through it, we do not survive. There is no recovery for those who abandon humanity to expedite their own survival. Do not confuse humanity with weakness, and do not confuse necessity with cruelty. Be firm, be compassionate, be understanding; then do what you need to do to survive. But before you tell yourself, "I had no choice," to justify some cruel or selfish action, think about the message of this book and how to give yourself choices.

Conclusion

You have read several things that are important to remember. First and foremost, survival is a mindset. A positive attitude and positive action are the tools of a survivor. Think about how survival in a disaster has a lot to do with the success of our interactions with other people, even when different people go about it in different ways. Knowing about temperaments in ourselves and others helps us recognize the motivations that drive us and the methods we use to meet our goals, both positive and negative.

You have read that self-delusion and fatalism is a trap that is hard to escape; being willing to see the reality of a situation for what it is and being realistic in our expectations are key components to our ability to make smart and effective choices; and finally that the number-one obstacle to our well-being is the danger of succumbing to our fears and letting anger do our thinking for us. By knowing what will make us anxious and frustrated during a disaster, we can guard against irrational fear. By recognizing outrage factors, we can anticipate emotional failure and distance ourselves from people or groups who will surrender their free will to the self-fulfilling destruction of fear, anger, and hopelessness. By using the strength of reason, humor, and humanity, we can learn to master our minds and our emotions in order to control our reactions and responses to disaster; in this way we give ourselves choices.

My Choices Worksheets (Know Thyself)

In this chapter you will be asked to make some determinations about yourself and your situation that will become your baseline for the development of your survival goals, plans, and methods. The questions are simple, but they may not be easy to answer at first. These choices are important and require you to think about them, make the choice, and then commit to the choice through your plans and actions. Don't look for a "correct book answer" because there isn't one. The right answer will be the one you come up with for yourself, and there is a distinct advantage to taking the process seriously. Use your reason, your feelings, and your personal preferences. It is important to think about each question independently of the other considerations. Then, at the end of the chapter, you will gather your assessments and choices together, and it will give you a clearer understanding of what methods may work best for your choices.

These baseline choices will affect all the other choices you will make in the future. Before you begin framing your plans, you need to look at your situation and yourself. Looking at your situation allows you to identify known and potential disaster risks (remember how the idea of risk is used in the planning and in the difference between a hazard and threat). Looking at yourself will help you take actions that fit your personality and temperament so that you will make plans that are realistic for you *and that you will be comfortable using.* The charts below are to help you get an idea of what motivates you. Again, there are no absolutes and there is no right or wrong answer. It may seem silly to put all of this in a chart, but doing so will allow you to see patterns of your own thinking, which will be helpful to you.

The real purpose of these mental gymnastics is to get you thinking about what is important to you and how you will plan and take action. There are only three questions, but these three questions are the ones that everyone will be required to answer: *you will encounter* hazards and threats, *you will respond* in accordance with your personality and temperament, and *you will be part of a plan,* yours or someone else's. The difference between you and most other people is that you are making your choices before the disaster. By doing so, you are significantly improving your chances of survival.

The three choices are:

Choice 1: What threats are you willing to live with?

This question has several aspects, including probability of encounter, willingness to encounter, and options for avoidance. A review of the disaster-data chapters will help you fill in this chart and make your choices. Work Chart #1 will help you go through the process of comparing the different aspects of disasters and determining if there is a particular disaster type that you feel strongly about avoiding. This essentially comes down to you deciding if you are a person who prefers the common threat of tornadoes with the understanding that if you stay aware you can escape, a person who lives on the side of a volcano who bets the mountain will not blow up in your lifetime, or someplace in between.

Because some disasters cannot be avoided, you will be asked to address:

Choice 2: To what level are you willing to be dependent on others for assistance after a disaster?

This is different from your level of preparation. This is about how you will conduct yourself within your plan. Remember that the way a System person conducts himself as a Passenger is similar to how an individual Planner conducts himself as a Preparer. Both have a plan for how they will get access to resources, but they look at the questions, and even definitions, of "independence," "dependence," and "control" in very different ways.

Recognize how your personality type and personal motivations manifest themselves. Use this knowledge and play to your strengths to use them to your advantage. This is not about good or bad, right or wrong, strong or weak; this is about finding the best methods for you to use for your survival. With this recognition you will be able to begin your planning process by deciding:

Choice 3: What level of planning and preparation will you need to be as ready as you believe you should be?

As with the other choices you have made, this is not an absolute conclusion. This is to help you decide when you want help and what level of assistance you think you may need or be willing to accept. When will you need to be a Planner and when will you need to be a Passenger? Are you comfortable with working within the framework of government disaster response, or do you want to make a lifestyle decision and move away from reliance on services or assistance and commit to being a Preparer?

With these three choices made, you can start deciding on your goals, identifying the methods that will work best for you and begin your preparations.

Worksheets

Over the next several pages are a series of three worksheets to help you evaluate your choices. Once you've completed your three worksheets, place the results of your assessments and choices into the template on the facing page "Know Thyself - Your Conclusions & Choices."

Know Thyself - Your Conclusions & Choices

Once you have have completed your three choices worksheets, place the results of your assessments and choices into the simple template provided here. Then look at the patterns of your thoughts and choices and see if they make sense to you given what you have learned while reading this book. Make adjustments accordingly if you see an area that does not seem quite right to you. Take the time to find the reason(s) your gut told you to reexamine your initial assessment.

Disaster-situation avoidance: Remember this is not a list of disasters, but of the aspects of disaster.

The disaster situation I most want to avoid is: _____
_____.

Temperament:
I am primarily a(n) _____ *temperament*
and secondarily a(n) _____*temperament.*

My level of comfort with dependence on the resources and assistance of others is _____.

The method of my personal preparation will be:
_____.

Conclusion

You have completed your initial thought process for the planning of your survival in the event of a major disaster. You have made important choices that will put you on the path to having a real plan that will help you meet your goals using methods before, during, and after a disaster to meet the requirements of movement, sustainment, and communication. You have examined yourself and your temperament in order to give yourself the best chance to make plans that will work for you and to control your emotions in order to survive in dangerous and stressful conditions. You have a good idea of your level of comfort in respect to your level of dependence on emergency-response and assistance plans.

You are armed with new skills in how to make plans and how to develop appropriate expectations of the level of assistance you may find in a disaster. You know how to see yourself and how to see what is going on around you in respect to how people react to their fear during a disaster. You now have a clear idea of what you want to do in order to survive. You are now ready to control the one and only thing you can control in a disaster: yourself.

Worksheet 1

What threats are you willing to live with?

As a quick review, look at the Big Eight disaster descriptions and think about your preference of avoidance. Do not just see the list of disasters, but think in terms of the different aspects of disasters.

1. What will happen — Known Effects and Measurements
2. Where will it happen — Areas of Known Probabilities
3. How big will it be — Area of Effect
4. How long will it last — Duration of Effect
5. How much reaction time will I have — Quick or Slow Onset
6. What will be left — Destruction of Infrastructure
7. Who can help me — Disruptions of Services
8. What comes next — Aftermath

For each disaster type, there are five questions. Look at each one and determine how it affects you. Then see if the effects are acceptable to you. Risk exposure, frequency, and level are all factual aspects; acceptance risk is purely up to you. If you want to live alone on the side of an active volcano to avoid floods, tsunamis, and civil disturbances, at least you have made an informed personal choice.

Factual Data

Risk Exposure
Are you in an area of effect? (Yes/No)

Risk Frequency
How often does the threat occur?

(Very Rarely, Rarely, Every X # of years, Annual, Seasonally, X # of times a year)

Risk Level
What is the risk level to you during the disaster? (High, Medium, Low)

Your Opinion and Ideas

Acceptable Risk
This is solely up to you. (Yes/No)

Action
Is there something you do or can do to negate or lessen the risk?

Example Chart #1:

As an example, we have a fictional person. He was in Hurricanes Andrew and Katrina and did not like it. He now lives in a small city in the Central States. There are no coastlines or volcanoes nearby, but a fault line runs within 300 miles. There is a nuclear power-generating station within 50 miles. There are seasonal winter storms that close roads, limit emergency services, and cause power outages as well as seasonal spring severe thunderstorms and regular potential for powerful tornadoes in the spring and fall. He is a Planner and keeps some basic supplies and helpful tools readily available. He has considered where he wants to live in geographic terms of event probability, physical location, and population density. He prefers to avoid hurricanes and large cities.

Natural Disaster	Risk Exposure	Risk Frequency	Risk Level	Acceptable Risk?	Action
Hurricane	Yes	Annual	High	No	Live Inland
Earthquakes	Yes	Ea. 100 Yrs	Low	Yes	Emergency Kit
Wildfire	Yes	Annual	Low	Yes	Be Aware
Floods	Yes	50–100 yrs	Low	Yes	Live on a Hill
Volcanoes	No	---	---	---	N/A
Tsunamis	No	---	---	---	N/A
Tornado	Yes	3–5 X a Year	High	Yes	Have Shelter
Blizzard or Ice Storm	Yes	Seasonally	Low	Yes	Extra Supplies
Pandemic	Yes	Very Rare	High	Yes	Be Aware
Man-Made Disasters					
Nuclear Event	Yes	Very Rare	High	Yes	Live upwind
Civil Disorder	Yes	Rare	Low	Yes	No Metro living
Chemical Spill	Yes	Very Rare	Moderate	Yes	Be Aware
Action Plan	Live in a rural community in the Midwest				

Now fill out Work Chart #1 for yourself and see if you need to make any significant choices about where or how you live. Remember the point is not to avoid all risk, because you can't. Think about your lifestyle and determine what disasters you may encounter. Then use this information to make your choices, plans, and preparations.

Natural Disaster	Risk Exposure	Risk Frequency	Risk Level	Acceptable Risk?	Action
Hurricane					
Earthquakes					
Wildfire					
Floods					
Volcanoes					
Tsunamis					
Tornado					
Blizzard or Ice Storm					
Pandemic					
Man-Made Disasters					
Nuclear Event					
Civil Disorder					
Chemical Spill					
Action Plan					

My Choices Worksheets

Worksheet 2

To what level are you willing to be dependent on others for assistance after a disaster?

People are different in how they respond to life and life's challenges. Some people work alone, and others prefer to move in a crowd. Regardless of whether you want to take care of yourself or receive assistance from others, you will want to make that decision based on a solid understanding of who you are. Your survival will depend upon your ability to move effectively within the level of assistance you have chosen to put into your plan.

There is no right or wrong answer to this question. It is about you and your personality. Neither is this an exercise in labeling. We are all motivated by all four of these influences, but to different degrees. You have had an opportunity to read about the temperaments. Keeping these aspects in mind, write your temperaments in the order of the strength you see them in yourself. Be honest and you will get a more helpful result. If you find Loner in first or second position, you will want to decide which of the other three methods you will use when you find you must deal with other people. Don't try to change yourself, just adapt to the situation and learn to be effective around others until you can get out on your own again.

Temperament Types

System People (Phlegmatic)
System people quietly work the process.

Relationship People (Sanguine)
Relationship people are driven by interaction with other individuals.

Independent Planner (Choleric)
Independent Planners are motivated to develop their own plans and willing to work within networks for information and materials.

Loner (Melancholic)
Loners may distance themselves from the services and resources provided by society and government by making arrangements to provide services and resources through their own preparations and skills.

Example Chart #2

Temperament	Note strengths or required adaptations
Independent Planner	Makes strong plans and can survive without assistance for several days
System	Willing to work with the system for resources and information
Loner	May avoid contacts longer than is prudent
Relationship	Not as strong at networking, must be more willing to work with others

Example of a temperament assessment: Our example person in Example Chart #2 is a small-business owner who is used to working alone. This person plays on a softball team and goes to church, but tends to keep to himself about his private life, finances, and work. Our example person would want to be cognizant that in the event of a disaster, he will need to be a little more open to working with people.

Work Chart #2

Place the four temperaments in precedence for your personality in Work Chart #2.

Temperament	Note strengths or required adaptations

Figure 7, Work Chart #2.

The next step is to look at where you placed your temperaments. Remember that there is no right or wrong; this is who you are. The goal is to find your place in the spectrum of dependence through self-recognition. Once you find where your balance point is, you can recognize if you have a strong preference or situation that leads you towards system-dependence or social-separation. Do you see any areas where you recognize a temperament that may keep you from information or resources during a disaster situation? If you do, then think about what you can do to avoid being system-dependent or socially separated. Just as our example person has found that in order to get to the information and sustainment supplies he needs, he will have to adapt to work outside of his personal comfort zone to engage with others. Figuring these things out before a disaster will be much easier than trying to learn them under stress.

Write down two things that you can do, in relation to your personality and temperament, that could help you in your ability to *move, sustain, and communicate* more effectively. What can you do to give yourself more opportunities for making your own choices? This may look like what you just did in the "Note strengths or required adaptations" portion of the temperament worksheet, but the intent is to get you to write down and commit to your survival-adaptation challenges.

1. _____

2. _____

Now that you have an idea of how you will personally respond and where you may need to challenge yourself to be a better survivor, you are now ready to make a choice on what level of preparation may work best for you.

My Choices Worksheets

Worksheet 3

What level of planning and preparation will you need to be as ready as you believe you should be?

You may want to go back and reread Chapter Two and contemplate the ideas presented there. Quick descriptions of Preparer, Planner, and Passenger are provided again here, but remember your temperament and your situation. It is very possible you will find that you need to work within more than one definition. Remember to be realistic with yourself and that these are just methods for you to use to reach your goals. Be firm in your goals and flexible in your plans.

Preparer
Preparers arrange for much of what they need in the way of infrastructure, systems, and supplies. This is a lifestyle choice and includes not only the creation of infrastructure and the collection of resources, but also the acquisition of personal skills through dedicated training. This is a life of constant vigilance in maintaining systems, resources, and skills. Some believe preparation costs too much thought, time, and money, while others gain great personal satisfaction from the preparation way of life. This is a personal choice.

Planner
Planners are ready and resilient, aware and prepared. They have collected exactly what they need for their immediate needs and have those supplies located where they can get to them fast. They know how to get access to movement, sustainment, and communication. They will be the masters of not being caught in the disaster in the first place. And if they do get caught in one, they will be the people moving calmly and purposely through the chaos with a flashlight, a first-aid kit, and a plan for how to get out and survive. They desire a balance between relying on themselves and using the government's disaster-response framework to the best advantage.

Passenger
Passengers know and accept that they are at a distinct personal disadvantage in a disaster. Special needs or a situation has them in a place where they know they will need significant or collective assistance to meet the needs of movement, sustainment, and communication. They understand that other people will be in the same situation with them. Their plan is to accept the assistance offered by local, state, and federal agencies and cooperate with those organizations that provide disaster relief until such time as they are moved to a location where the infrastructure and resources for life are available by independent means. Passengers' individual planning includes the clothes on their back, sensible shoes on their feet, and a small bag they can carry. This makes them available for movement to a place of organized security and sustainment within the systems and networks of the disaster response framework.

Safety in Numbers (Be Part of the Team)

Circles of Preparedness

Your level of preparation can be enhanced by those around you. In a disaster situation it is really true that collective efforts are more successful than individual ones. The strength of each individual adds to the greater strength of the whole, with the sum of the whole being greater than the sum of the individual parts. So what are the circles of preparedness?

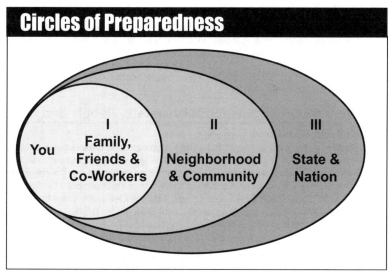

Circles of Preparedness

You

I
Family, Friends & Co-Workers

II
Neighborhood & Community

III
State & Nation

The first thing you will notice is that these categories can and do overlap. Second is that you are not separate from family, friends and co-workers. When disasters happen, the people you are with at the time become your survival team. Let's look at what you can do to build your team and, if you chose to, help your community be better prepared by examining circles one and two. Having covered Federal Response in chapter 3, State and Nation response is explained but there are some new federal approaches to community preparedness that will be of interest. Understand that many of the resources that you will use in circles one and two are provided by the federal government through FEMA preparedness programs and delivered at the local level. Do not think of these circles as separate areas of influence but rather as interlocking aspects of a continuum of effort.

References:

http://www.ready.gov

http://www.citizencorps.fema.gov/downloads/pdf/ready/citizen_prep_review_issue_6.pdf

All for One and One for All

Up to this point the discussion has been focused primarily on your individual preference, choices and personal readiness. It is true that your understanding of your personal goals and your control over your emotions will always be the primary base for success in your ability to survive a disaster and successfully recover your life afterwards.

It is also true that in a disaster the chances are high that you will be surrounded by people, some whom you know and others that you will not. Remember the definition of disaster; it is when the disruption of infrastructure and services is greater than the capacity of a community to respond to the needs of the population. This means that disasters are about effects on people; hundreds and often thousands, maybe even millions. It just so happens that your understanding of your personal goals and your control over your emotions will also always be the primary base for success in your interactions with others during a disaster and will be key to recovering the lives of your family and community afterwards.

Although there is valuable information provided in this chapter, what is provided here just scratches the surface of the resources available to communities in web based information and real emergency instruction available in your community. You are highly encouraged to seek these resources yourself and find the information, methods, and most importantly, the human connections that will be required for success in your disaster preparations.

What FEMA knows about Disasters, People and Preparedness

There is a direct link between community readiness and personal survival. FEMA knows that within any community, the more people who participate in individual awareness, household readiness and community preparedness, the correspondingly greater chance for individual survival. It may seem simplistic but it has proven to be true. The issue FEMA finds is that people think they are ready when they are not. Thinking about a plan and even understanding readiness is not the same as having a prepared, resourced and practiced plan. This is why FEMA has provided www.ready.gov and a wide variety of printed publications with similar information.

Much of what you will need to get started on your personal plan is at the Ready.gov site and it is well worth a visit. The site expands to a variety of different sources and sites that provide excellent information.

www.ready.gov/be-informed

www.ready.gov/make –a-plan

www.ready.gov/build-a-kit

www.ready.gov/get-involved

www.ready.gov/business

www.ready.gov/kids

I. The First Circle: Family, Friends & Co-Workers

The first circle includes those people who are close to you. This can be family, friends and co-workers depending on your life situation. The average person spends about a quarter of their time at work, another quarter of their time out and about in

FEMA Information and Children

Reference: http://www.citizencorps.fema.gov/downloads/pdf/ready/citizen_prep_review_issue_6.pdf

Children can be active and positive participants in disaster preparedness. They can and need to be included in the process of preparation. Studies have found that diversification of disaster education significantly improved children's understand and level of mental preparation. Specifically that participation in more than one disaster education program increased a child's understanding of disaster related information. It is also important to make sure these different programs were age appropriate.

Keep your child's age in mind when reading FEMA information. FEMA uses specific references to describe different ages of children but not all material provided by FEMA is generated by FEMA. Make sure you are using information appropriate for the ages of your children.

"Kids" is a general term that encompasses all ages from toddler to 24 years of age. A study of disaster related material for children showed the terms "youth" and "children" are used interchangeably and included research on children between the ages of 7 and 18. It is in this age group that children can be active participants in their survival but are still susceptible to the unique vulnerabilities of youth. Children should not be treated the same as adults when it comes to disaster preparedness and education.

As a general rule FEMA information uses the following age distinctions:

- **Infants and young children** (0 to 4 year-olds).
- **Youth** (5 to 14 year-olds)
- **Adolescents and young adults** (15 to 24 year-olds)

Parents should be aware of these variations in age descriptions and be careful to ensure they are using age appropriate materials for their children.

The Parents section of http://www.ready.gov/kids has helpful and applicable tips for how to interact with your child on disasters and disaster preparation. The site uses different words for different ages of children.

the world engaged in errands, recreation and collective social gatherings like going to church and other forms of being with friends. Finally we spend about half of our time at home. Understand that this is an average and each person will have different percentages based upon their life situation. The take away point is to think about who you spend your time with, or even just in proximity of, because these will be the people that you will be with in a disaster.

Important Note: According to FEMA, research on preparedness shows that people who believe themselves "prepared" for disasters often are not as prepared as they believe. Forty percent of survey respondents did not have household plans, 80 percent had not conducted home evacuation drills, and nearly 60 percent did not know their community's evacuation routes.

Nearly 20 percent of survey respondents reported having a disability that would affect their capacity to respond to an emergency situation, but only one out of four of them had made arrangements specific to their disability to help them respond safely in the event of an emergency. Remember that even Passengers need a plan.

Children and Disasters

Reference: http://www.ready.gov/kids

FEMA Says: Children compose a special population known as "vulnerable groups": those that are more prone to damage, loss, suffering, injury, and death in the event of a disaster. Though a variety of factors can influence exactly how vulnerable a child can be when faced with a potential risk, studies indicate three types of vulnerability that children in particular experience during disasters:

1. Psychological vulnerability: In terms of developmental/cognitive differences, children can become very vulnerable in the event of a disaster. Because they may be non-communicative or they may feel anxiety during the disaster, children may be too afraid or unwilling to share information at a disaster site, which could prove to be detrimental when a child is trying to articulate distress or if someone is trying to establish the child's identity. Being non-communicative can also make it difficult for children to describe symptoms or localize pain, in the event that they are physically harmed. Children may also lack self-preservation skills, which could prevent them from knowing when to flee from danger. The shock of disasters can also cause other developmental effects, such as sudden changes in behavior (e.g., an outgoing child is suddenly shy) or regression (e.g., going back to thumb sucking). This is not "weakness" on the part of the child but rather a result of the disruption of the cognitive developmental process.

A serious traumatic event such as a natural or man-made disaster can greatly impact the mental health of children; most studies focus on post-traumatic stress disorder (PTSD) or similar conditions. Studies found growing evidence that shows the adverse effects of disasters on children, claiming that 30 to 50 percent of those children are likely to develop PTSD symptoms that will persist for long periods of time.

2. Physical vulnerability: Purely on the basis of anatomic and physiological differences, children are prone to become ill more quickly when exposed to hazards due to their smaller size and higher breathing rate; they require different dosages of antibiotics; they may need different-sized emergency equipment; they do not possess the fully functioning motor skills to escape a disaster site; and they require more food and drink. Additionally, children's skeletons are more pliable, making them more susceptible to fractures; their heads are a heavier portion of the body, making head injuries more common; their skin is thinner than adults, making them more vulnerable to toxic agents; and they breathe more times per minute than adults, making them more vulnerable to air toxins.

Being Aware and Prepared

What can you do to help the people with you in your first circle be aware and pre-pared? Remembering that 20 percent preparation is the 80 percent answer; a little preparation goes a long way and you can help them be aware and prepared.

1. Communication is Key: Present disasters in a realistic light; as dangerous but survivable. A solid understanding of disaster types and their effects (see chapter 9) is helpful to finding the balance to turn disinterest or fear of the unknown in to healthy respect for the forces of nature and the confidence that comes with awareness and preparation.

2. Learn Together: Learn how to survive a disaster as a family or group with each member learning at a level appropriate for age and ability. Practice your skills together. This can be a camping trip, a route rehearsal family road trip or an in office rehearsal; the goal is to learn how to work together, travel together and, most importantly, communicate with each other.

3. Choose a Role: Let the strengths and interests of each individual bring a needed skill to the team. When someone has an interest in a subject let them go into depth on that skill set. It can be a trained skill, hobby or a profession. Cross level these skills within your team. Everyone should know a little about each area, learning from the person with the interest and drive to be proficient on the subject matter.

A. Move Skills

- Map reading and movement skills (routes into and out of the city/neighborhood/region)
- Mechanical (cars, bikes, boats, snowmobiles – whatever is in your plan)
- Transportation options (Reliable and imaginative ways to move)

B. Sustainment Skills

- Medical skills (First aid training to Emergency Medical Technician or nurse certification)
- Pathogen Control (Understanding pathogens - transmission threats, protection methods)
- Cooking skills (Food safety and safe food preparation in disaster situations)
- Shelter building (Overhead cover and off the ground, use of specialty tools)
- Fire making (Building and controlling fires: both require know-how and practice)
- Self-defense (Conflict avoidance, or as a last resort martial arts & weapons skills)
- Improvisation (How to make things you need from what you have at hand)

C. Communication Skills

Shortwave radio skills (Listening skills, requires a receiver and lots of practice)

Armature "Ham" radio operation (VHF/UHF radio - equipment, skills & license)

Citizens Band radio operation (equipment, license required in some states)

In looking at skill sets it is important not to focus too much on who does what or who "owns" a skill. That is an incorrect way to apply this idea. The goal is to draw upon the mental resources of those who are with you and add your knowledge to theirs. Survival requires cooperation and there is no place for power plays or information control through withholding skills. The stronger each person becomes the greater the strength of the group as a whole.

A 2008 study found that different types of disasters affect the physical vulnerability of different age groups. These scholars found that in the United States, infants and young children 0 to 4 year-olds are most likely to die of exposure to extreme heat, 5 to 14 year-olds are most likely to die in storms and flood events, and adolescents and young adults 15 to 24 year-olds are most likely to die of excessive cold.

3. Educational vulnerability: destruction caused by a disaster can negatively impact children's academic performance, as it causes children to miss school and delay their progress. A 2008 study found that children may experience up to 11 school changes over a 3-month period following a storm, with the average being three moves per child. These disruptions on education can case children to lose

What can you do to help your children be aware and prepared?

As stated earlier, survival skills need to be age and ability appropriate. This is especially true for children. Disasters can leave children and teens feeling frightened, confused and insecure. A child's response to the stress of disaster can be quite varied. It's important to not only recognize these reactions, but also help children cope with their emotions. Controlling yours will help them control theirs.

The Parents section of http://www.ready.gov/kids has helpful and applicable tips for how to interact with your child on disasters and disaster preparation. The site uses different words for different ages of children.

In the short term (before and during the disaster):

- **You are their biggest influence.** When you can manage your own feelings, you can make disasters less traumatic for your kids. Even though children are developmentally different from adults, it has been found that their reactions generally reflect those of their parents. Children, for the most part, take cues from their parents when it comes to distress and danger and will react on the basis of their observations regarding safety. Thus, it is vitally important for parents to remain calm and to be adequately prepared during a disaster, as children who perceive greater levels of parental distress were also seen to cope less effectively. Parents should also make it a point to discuss their emotions with their children before, during, and after a disaster, to reduce their child's anxiety levels.

- **Encourage dialogue.** Listen to your kids. Ask them about their feelings. Validate their concerns. The quality of interactions among family members can determine a child's adjustment to a major disaster. A 2001 study found that healthy family cohesion and truthful communication was a mitigating factor in helping children process and recover from traumatic experiences.

- **Answer questions.** Give just the amount of information you feel your child needs. Clarify misunderstandings about hazards, threats and danger. When children receive education about risks and hazards, it is important for them to fully understand the extent and reality of those risks in an age appropriate way. A child's realistic perceptions will lead to the child's comprehension and perhaps to positive behavioral investment in their survival, such as preparing a disaster kit or looking up shelter locations.

One strategy that has proven to be ineffective is the use of scare tactics. Studies found that the use of exaggerated dangers, false information, or biased presentations could lead the child to disbelieve the message and even discredit the messenger. In 2001 researchers discovered that when parents used exaggerated messages to try to provide truthful information to youth, this approach could backfire, especially when the child is exposed to other forms of information and advice. Relating the true dangers of a disaster combined with a positive survival attitude and actions for preparations to mitigate the dangers provides the best opportunity to deal with the stress of a disaster.

- **Be calm, be reassuring.** Discuss concrete plans for safety. Have children and teens contribute to the family's recovery plan as well as the disaster plan. Children need structure and a chance to focus their energies as much as adults. Give them that opportunity within their capabilities.

- **Shut off the TV!** News coverage of disasters is designed to create drama to hold the attention of viewers and revenue for the broadcaster. This will result in confusion and anxiety for your child. Repeated images may lead younger kids to believe the event is recurring. If your children do watch TV or use the Internet, be with them to talk and answer questions.

- **Find support.** Whether you turn to friends, family, community organizations or faith-based institutions, building support networks can help you cope, which will in turn help your children cope. Remember that your children are feeling the same emotions you are and may express those emotions exactly as they see you express them or in different ways than you. Either way your children will need to deal with those emotions just as you will.

Longer term effects on children (After the disaster)

For many children, reactions to disasters are brief. But some children can be at risk for more enduring psychological distress. Three risk factors that can cause a longer-lasting response are:

- Direct exposure to the disaster such as being evacuated, observing injuries of others, or experiencing injury. Experiences in a disaster that represent disruption and loss can bring on these long-lasting feeling of fear or insecurity. Understand that a child's view of the world and felling of safety are focused on consistency of family and within the home.

- Loss/grief relating to the death or serious injury of family or friends. Direct exposure to or even knowledge of death and injury can leave long lasting effects.

- On-going stress from secondary effects, such as temporary housing, loss of social networks, loss of personal property, or parent's unemployment. The insecurity of a disaster is not limited to the event itself and can be felt long after the disaster is over when the situation continues to be unstable or transient.

The same techniques parents can use during a disaster work effectively after the disaster as well. Special emphasis should be placed on keeping a positive and compassionate attitude, answering questions, talking about your own feelings and finding support.

Age Appropriate Awareness / Teaching children about readiness

A big part of putting your child's mind at ease and building mental resiliency is to offer specific actions for preparation in the form of activates. FEMA has a great site for children with teaching games and great basic information on all types of disasters, http://www.ready.gov/kids. The site provides information for children, parents and educators.

The Kids section at http://www.ready.gov/kids has four main areas;

Make a plan, Build a kit, Know the facts and Get involved.

Because the information in those areas is the much the same as is offered in this book (but in a "kid friendly" format) it will not be repeated here. The site is a very good resource for both you and your children to use. The Know the Facts link has information on 15 different types of disasters and events with tips for before, during and after the event. It is a children's version of chapter 9 of this book. Each disaster link has excellent tips on do's and don'ts. Of interest are the information links for blackouts, house fires and space weather. Although these are not specifically disasters these events are all either common or probable enough to include in your resiliency plans.

Learning games for young children

As with any life skill we can begin teaching them at a very early age with games to provide children valuable skills that they can develop into maturity over time. The Red Cross Pillowcase Project is an excellent example of this kind of learning tool. It is designed for 5 to 7 year olds to help them to understand what a survival kit is for and how to make one.

The goals of The Pillowcase Project are to:

1. Help students become familiar with the types of disasters that affect our local area including thunderstorms, tornadoes, fires and floods.

2. Inform students and, by extension, families about the importance of creating a disaster preparedness kit and plan.

The kits are rudimentary but representative of important considerations. Note the methods of imitation provided for the child. When building the kit they gather:

- A pillowcase to hold their supplies
- A mini first aid-kit;
- A glow stick;
- An activity book; and
- Crayons to start their own personalized disaster preparedness plan!

Read more about the Pillowcase Project on the American Red Cross Website, or at http://preparecenter.org/activities/pillowcase-project-preparing-students-disasters.

A Child's Disaster Plan: Who should I contact? AND Where should I go?

Communication with children during a disaster is much more accessible than in the past. Children have (or can get access to) cell phones and smart phones with relative ease. It is not inappropriate to teach them to, and expect them to be able to, communicate directly with parents and let them know their current situation. Parents can then provide instructions and prove information important to their child. Children should memorize or have access to family contact information and should have simple, easy to follow instructions on what to do in case of a disaster. A child's plan should be simple and effective.

Who should I contact? (Modify this list to meet your needs): Remember that after a disaster cell service may be disrupted or overtaxed with calls. Texts often have a better chance of getting through.

- Home number
- Parent's number: (One or both as the case may be)
- Cell phone
- Work phone
- Sibling's cell
- Trusted neighbor's home phone and cell
- Out of state point of contact if possible (in case communications with parents are disrupted   within the disaster area of effect)

Where should I go? The question of "should your child move?" comes into play here.

  • If at school, church or another venue where adults can see to their care until you arrive, it is prudent to have your child stay where they are.

  • If your child is away from the house but not in a controlled environment then have a plan for where to meet. Pick a spot with these considerations in mind:

  • Just outside of your house: Where will you meet up with your family if you have to get out of your house quickly? Also identity and practice two (if possible) escape routes from each room of your home with your children.

  • In your neighborhood: Use a familiar, well-known and easy to find land mark such as neighbor's house or big tree.

  • Out of your neighborhood: If the neighborhood is evacuated and you are not at home, again, find locations that are familiar, well-known and easy to find such as the library or house of worship.

Friends and family outside the home

The plans you make with your children work just as well as a basic plan with your friends and extended family. Who should I contact? AND Where should I go? These plans will modify a bit as your adult friends will have better access to communications and transportation. This allows you to extend the distance of potential meeting places to outside of the disaster effects area. An example of this is families taking separate means of transportation from New Orleans and reuniting in Texas after Hurricanes Katrina and Rita.

Coordinating with a mutual friend who lives outside of the area of effect to be a team member can be helpful as well. The "away" point of contact can serve as a messaging center and information hub. Being outside the areas of effect they will have more consistent communications to include access to current news coverage.

You are encouraged to seek the full potential of any plans you make with your friends. Coordination with friends, many of whom may have similar hobbies and interests as yours family, can augment and enhance your groups move, sustain and communicate skill sets significantly. Some groups have gone as far as to develop, resource and practice coordinated/joined disaster plans and make social events out of disaster preparedness rehearsals. The Zombie Squad mentioned earlier is an excellent example of this kind of social disaster preparedness preparation.

How many people should be in your group? Your needs and associations will dictate this to a curtain extent but the optimal number seems to be about a dozen people. The military knows this and for the last two thousand years the average size of an infantry squad has been twelve Soldiers. It takes about a dozen people to keep 24 hour watch and do all the other things required to survive in conflict; move, fight, communicate, cook, eat, wash, sleep, etc. This does not mean you must find a dozen people. Your team size will depend upon your plan. The point to take away is that cooperative groups are beneficial to individual survival in dangerous situations.

II. The Second Circle: Neighborhood & Community

The second circle is your neighborhood and community. For all intents and purposes this includes Tribal Government as well because although Tribal government has connections at the State and Federal level their disaster preparation and response operates more like a community or county.

Volunteer

You may feel you have more to offer than just a family plan. If you are so inclined you can have a significant impact on your community by volunteering within your community to assist with disaster preparation education. It is to your benefit to get as many people as possible into a state of readiness as you can. Preparing others can take a lot of time and effort but can be very satisfying personally as well as strengthening to your own plans. The extent to which you wish to engage in this process is dependent upon several factors. First is your temperament, second is the size and proximity of your family/friends (same house, same community or far away) and third is the community you live in. Volunteering is a very personal thing so let your conscience be your guide and do what feels right for your situation.

Volunteer opportunities are varied and can fit any temperament. As you find your place within your community preparation efforts you will discover that your own plans will change and refine as you learn more and your preparation skills will become more practiced and effective. The best way to learn a skill is to become proficient enough to teach it.

Neighborhood

If you want to keep your efforts more local consider neighborhood programs. This can be through your church or community center. Cities often hold an annual disaster preparedness days or similar activities. In many cases these activities are presented within neighborhood venues, often focusing on environmental issues like winter cold or disease control. Many of the same skills used in severe weather situations can be applied to disaster survival.

Your city or county emergency management coordinator is a good place to start for a point of contact. The name of the office may be a little different in your community; i.e. disaster management or emergency coordination office but they are the same function. FEMA has a program called "Faithful Readiness" where they provide Webinars (Web based seminars). This is an effort in 2014 to get communities ready at the grass roots level for a National Preparedness Month/National Preparation. The efforts are local but the goals are national. City and county events are scheduled regularly and usually correspond with seasonal preparations like winter readiness in the fall or tornado/thunderstorm season in the spring.

City and County

Just as with your neighborhood efforts, the city or county emergency management coordinator is a good place to start for a point of contact. The only real difference between the neighborhood/city events and the county efforts will be who provides personnel and resources for the event. Because all disasters are local, all response, education and community outreach will initially generate at the local level, sometimes with the assistance of state offices that have received federal materials or funding. Like the Incident Command System, the national disaster response effort is coordinated for similar levels and types of preparedness. At this level you may hear about a program called Citizen Corps.

Citizen Corps

The mission of Citizen Corps is to harness the power of every individual through education, training, and volunteer service to make communities safer, stronger, and better prepared to respond to the threats of terrorism, crime, public health issues, and disasters of all kinds.

The goals of Citizen Corps is to preparing the public for local risks with targeted outreach, engaging voluntary organizations to help augment resources for public safety, preparedness and response capabilities and finally to Integrating whole community representatives with emergency managers to ensure disaster preparedness and response planning represents the whole community and integrates nontraditional resources

Following the tragic events that occurred on September 11, 2001, state and local government officials have increased opportunities for citizens to become an integral part of protecting the homeland and supporting the local first responders. Officials agree that the formula for ensuring a more secure and safer homeland consists of preparedness, training, and citizen involvement in supporting first responders. In January 2002, the President of the United States launched Citizen Corps, to capture the spirit of service that emerged throughout our communities following the terrorist attacks.

Citizen Corps was created to help coordinate volunteer activities that will make our communities safer, stronger, and better prepared to respond to any emergency situation. It provides opportunities for people to participate in a range of measures to make their families, their homes, and their communities safer from the threats of crime, terrorism, and disasters of all kinds.

Citizen Corps programs build on the successful efforts that are in place in many communities around the country to prevent crime and respond to emergencies. Programs that started through local innovation are the foundation for Citizen Corps and this national approach to citizen participation in community safety.

Citizen Corps is coordinated nationally by the Department of Homeland Security's Federal Emergency Management Agency. In this capacity, FEMA works closely with other federal entities, state and local governments, first responders and emergency managers, the volunteer community, and the Corporation for National & Community Service.

Citizen Corps resources

Citizen Corps has many valuable resources including that are directly applicable to your personal plan as well as local issues during and after a disaster. These include FEMA Independent Study Courses, Neighbors helping Neighbors programs, Community Preparedness tools and youth programs just to name a few.

At initial levels of volunteer involvement with Citizen Corps there are significant resources to include printed materials and on-line content. At higher levels of involvement you can organize events and even request grants to assist you in your local efforts. You can learn more at http://www.ready.gov/publications under the "Get Involved" tab.

FEMA Says: At http://www.ready.gov/about-citizen-corps

III. The Third Circle: State & Nation

The third circle is state and national government. As mentioned at the beginning of this chapter the federal government response is addressed in chapter 3. In terms of disaster preparedness their efforts have been shifting in response to resent events. These shifts are outlined in the 2014 National Preparedness Report (NPR).

The NPR is an annual status report on the nation's progress toward reaching the National Preparedness Goal of a secure and resilient nation established in the Presidential Policy Directive 8: National Preparedness.

The NPR identifies areas of sustainment and progress made across 31 core capabilities towards building a secure and resilient nation while identifying opportunities for improvement. Key overarching findings from the 2014 NPR include:

- **Embracing a new approach to disaster recovery:** Major events, such as Hurricane Sandy and the severe 2012-2013 drought, have served as catalysts for change in national preparedness programs, drawing clearer links between post-disaster recovery and pre-disaster mitigation activities.

- **Launching major national initiatives:** The Federal Government has initiated several national-level policy and planning initiatives that bring unity of effort to preparedness areas, including critical infrastructure security and resilience, cybersecurity, recovery capabilities, and climate change.
- **Managing resource uncertainties:** Budget uncertainties have created preparedness challenges at state and local levels of government, resulting in increased ingenuity, emphasis on preparedness innovations, and whole community engagement.
- **Partnering with tribal nations:** Tribal partners are now more systematically integrated into preparedness activities. However, opportunities remain for Federal agencies and tribal nations to increase engagement and expand training opportunities on relevant policies.

For a copy of the full report go to: www.fema.gov/national-preparedness-report. As this NPR indicates, as a nation we can continue to become better prepared. Note the "Budget uncertainties" concerns. The federal government, as well as the states, has discovered the staggering cost of rescue, response and recovery. Quite wisely they have committed to spending smaller amounts of money "up front" to ensure readiness, safety and savings in recovery of areas affected by disasters.

FEMA says: One way to do this is by registering for the America's PrepareAthon! campaign and participating on September 30, 2014—National PrepareAthon! Day. Learn more about America's PrepareAthon! at www.ready.gov/prepare.

Watch for similar events in 2015 and beyond, with community, county and state events that tie into national readiness goals. Having a better understanding of the process you should now see how these standardized and combined efforts tie into neighborhood and community readiness utilizing a desired national standard of readiness for American homes.

Conclusion

The connection between your readiness in respect to that of your community, state and nation is a direct link. Your plans are affected by the plans of others individuals, groups and even the Federal Response Framework. Understanding how these plans interact will help you form your plans to tie into or avoid these other plans as you feel is appropriate. But remember that your plans will meet with major resistance if you design them to conflict with the federal, state, tribal, community or neighborhood goals. Remember that regardless of the situation, your liberty does not allow you to infringe upon the liberty of others. Plan appropriately and accordingly; them help others do the same within the limits of your temperament.

No matter what your plans may include you can make them stronger by working with your friends and neighbors within your community but tapping into the strengths and skills of your family and those around you to best utilize the knowledge and resources provided by the federal government for the sole purpose of enhancing your disaster preparedness plans.

Survival Kit Basics

Survival kits should NOT be a collection of tools and supplies *you think you may need,* but rather a collection of tools and supplies *you will have a purpose for* in a disaster situation. The difference is in the time you put into thinking about and acting on a real plan. Survival kits consist of the simplest items, and when you're done collecting them, you will look at your kit and think, "Is this everything I need to survive?" The key to a useful survival kit is *thinking about what you will have a purpose for* and how it will be used based on your plan. Remember that survival is a mindset, and it is important to understand that just having a kit will not save you. You will save yourself by using the tools effectively.

This may seem like semantics, but it is not. You can pay thousands of dollars for premade survival kits that claim to have "everything you need to survive," but a survival kit alone will not save you; thinking about your survival and preparing tools and supplies for your plan is what will help you the most. Your survival kit must meet *your* needs. Make it yourself and make it your own. This does not mean that a premade kit will not help if you have determined it meets your needs. But you will want to choose what you want your kit to do for you.

The FEMA website at www.ready.gov/basic-disaster-supplies-kit will give you good advice on different items for different kinds of disasters. Remember that these are suggestions to help you plan. The FEMA list may not meet all of your needs, so think through your plan and let the FEMA recommendations help you make choices.

Survival kits consist of three basic categories: what you will wear, what you will carry, and what you will consume. This idea of clothing, tools, and consumable supplies is important in terms of durability and how long you expect to have or use them. There are suggestions in this chapter that list the components of and purpose for some items to consider.

Survival kits can come in any size. The only limitations are your load capacity and your imagination. Some examples are provided here for reference. Your kit will have the items you need for your plan. The vehicle kit and the shoulder kit shown here are updated and alternate from winter kits to summer kits in the spring and fall so the kits match the season. The pocket kit is used regularly.

Large Vehicle kit

Clothing, shovel, axe, sleeping bags, shelter material, rain gear, shelf stable rations, large first aid kit, communications electronics, room for quick gather items and much more. This long term kit is ready to "bug in" or "bug out" on short notice.

Medium "Shoulder Carry" Kit

You can fit a surprising amount rials into a small shoulder kit or back pack. Remember not to over load this type of kit because it will get heavy very quickly. Designed for short duration situations, it is primarily first aid, weather gear and signaling materials (mirror, signal panel, whistle and lights to facilitate rescue). This kit is in a vehicle in a plastic travel box.

Pocket Survival Kit

Just the basics: fire, a knife and a flash light in a repurposed leather phone case. The tools you need for your plan are all that is required. You may not need anything fancy, complicated or expensive to meet your needs.

Conclusion

It cannot be stressed enough that this kit is for you and your family. Make it your own. Your needs will be specific to your geographic location, north or south, urban or rural. Don't just buy "survival stuff" and put it in the closet. Think about your needs and update your supplies to keep them current and ready to use. Check your kit in the spring and fall and make clothing changes for the summer and winter months. It helps to have a schedule and then check your supplies on certain dates. Days such as daylight savings time change days and the spring and autumn equinoxes are good times for changing seasonal items in your kit. Some people like to use birthdays or holiday weekends; use whatever dates work for you. Remember to consider the type of disaster event you are most likely to encounter and plan accordingly.

Clothing

Selection of correct clothing can solve many issues of safety and exposure to hazards. Knowing what you want to wear during the disaster becomes important. Your clothing should be durable and full-length to cover your arms and legs. Think about temperature and use layers rather than one heavy garment. Well-chosen clothing will be to keep you warm and protect you from sun, wind, and biting insects. You will want light, loose (not baggy) clothes that you can use to regulate your temperature. You will also want to have more than one set of clothes and several sets of extra socks and undergarments. This simple list provides ideas for your clothing choices.

Sensible Shoes
You will want a sturdy, closed-toe shoe. They will need to be comfortable and light. Although leather or canvas is preferable, avoid shoes that are too heavy. Keep a few extra pairs of socks on hand also. Hiking shoes are a good option.

Pants
Full-length pants are a must. Denim, canvas, ripstop, or some other durable material is preferable. You may want to consider a pair of work pants. Painter's pants and farm jeans are durable and have useable pockets. Cargo pockets should be high on the thigh. You will not want items banging on your knees as you try to walk. If you get heavier pants, make sure you break them in.

Shirt(s)
This is where layering is important. A tee shirt and a long-sleeve shirt to wear over it is a good option. This will allow you to limit exposure to the elements and regulate your temperature. Avoid tight-fitting clothes. This is true of any fabric, from cotton to man-made moisture-wicking materials. Any fabric that clings to your body will hold the salts and oils left behind by evaporation against your skin. These will irritate your skin and cause rashes and sores if worn for extended periods of time.

Hat
A hat to keep the sun off your head during the daytime and keep your head warm in the evening will provide basic protection that you will need and appreciate.

Light Jacket or Coat
You will want outer garments to keep you warm and dry. Think about temperature range (how hot and how cold) and plan accordingly. Keep a pair of durable gloves in one pocket and some warm gloves in the other. Speaking of pockets, choose a jacket with some carry and storage options.

Underwear and Socks
These two items will help you stay clean. Any infantryman will tell you that fresh socks are a must. Keeping your feet clean and dry will allow you to preserve your mobility. Change your socks every day or after your feet get soaked. The same is true of undergarments. Keeping clean (at least well-rinsed) dry cloth as your first layer of clothing will go a long way towards preventing sores and rashes that could become infected.

Tools (Survival Kit Bag)

These are the items that will help you to move, sustain, and communicate. It is a surprisingly short list of very basic and handy items. You will want to add to this list as you need to, but keep the weight you have to carry to a minimum.

Rightsize your Tool Bag

Here are a few things to think about when making your kit and collecting your tools:

Don't pack the kitchen sink. This is a survival pack, not a vacation bag. Keep it as simple as possible. Remember your methods of movement, sustainment, and communication, and select items that meet those needs.

The tool kit is separate from the supplies. A survival kit is a set of tools, and you will want to keep it small enough to carry in a shoulder bag or small backpack. Assume you may have to move, and keep weight in mind. You can fit an amazing amount of truly handy tools into a small lightweight bag.

A Note on Tools: Many survival experts recommend having more than one of the items in your kit that are vital to your plan, just in case the one you have stops working. The rule for tools is, "Two is one and one is none." You will have to balance this idea with your weight and space limitations. Consider this option for mechanical tools like turn-handle can openers, flashlights, and portable radios.

Movement Tools

Sturdy Bag. A good bag that is easy to carry is the best way to tote your tools. It should be of significant construction; durable; made of canvas, leather, or heavy nylon; have shoulder straps; be water-resistant if not waterproof; and be able to carry all your tools with some room left over for consumable supplies.

Map. A map of the city or local area with roads, rivers, and rail lines on it is a basic requirement. Take the time to mark the location of hospitals.

Prescription Glasses. If you need glasses but prefer contacts, keep a pair of prescription glasses in your kit. You will not want to wear contacts after a disaster for several reasons. First, disasters tend to put a lot of debris into the air that can irritate your eyes. Concrete dust, smoke from fires, building insulation, and other fine airborne debris will be a problem, and you will not be able to keep your contacts from collecting this dust. Secondly, you will not want to touch your eyes with unclean fingers, and chances will be good that in a disaster situation you will not have access to extra water for eye-care needs.

Sunglasses and Clear Safety Glasses. After a disaster there will be a lot of debris floating in the air. Dust, building insulation, smoke, and other particulates will get in your eyes. Having some basic eye protection will be helpful. Protect the glasses in a case that clips to your belt or your tool bag.

Dust Masks. Just as with your eye protection, having some basic breathing protection will allow you to move through areas that may otherwise limit your movement.

Watertight Document Container. When the situation forces you to move, you will want to take your important documents with you. If you do not have a safety deposit box in a bank vault, then you will want to secure birth certificates; passports; deeds to vehicles, buildings, and land; or any other documents that are proof of identity or ownership. In most cases you can fit these documents in a one-gallon heavy resealable freezer bag. It does not have to be fancy or complicated; it just has to keep your documents dry and be easy to carry.

Sustainment Tools

Flashlight. A battery-powered or hand-crank flashlight is a must and can also be used for signaling at night. Have extra batteries if you use them.

Wrench or Pliers. To turn off utilities like gas lines.

Multi-tool. This will provide you with a small knife and some very basic tools that you will need. Take some time to learn how to use it effectively and without hurting yourself.

Manual Can Opener. There are several types, so find one that you can manage easily. The good old-fashioned mechanical can opener is easy to use and can open several cans without hurting your fingers. Keep one with your tools and another with your food. This tool is important enough to have more than one on hand. There is a survival saying: "Two is one and one is none."

First-Aid Kit. The basic necessity of being able to deal with cuts and burns, stop bleeding, and sanitize and cover a wound cannot be overemphasized. This kit should include over-the-counter medications for basic pain relief, antihistamines, or any other needs that have to be identified. First-aid basics such as adhesive bandages, sterile dressings, wrapping bandages, antibiotic ointments, eye-wash solution, and other necessities like scissors and tweezers should be included and kept up to date. The intent is to clean and cover any wound and provide basic pain relief. See the complete list of recommend first-aid items at the end of this chapter.

Plastic Bags. Plastic baggies to keep important things dry: garbage bags can be used for shelter, rain gear, water-collection, and carrying supplies, and sheet plastic can be used for shelter. They are all very light and take up very little room.

Duct Tape. There are whole books dedicated to the useful applications of duct tape. FEMA and the CDC recommend it to help seal windows and doors when you want to make an airtight seal, but that is just the beginning of the utility of this important tool.

Sanitary Kit. Keeping yourself clean is important. Moist towelettes, garbage bags, and twist ties will help keep you clean and reduce the spread of disease.

Fire-starting Tools. WARNING, if you are not used to working with fire, then don't start one. Fire is tricky to work with and can hurt you fast. If you decide to carry a lighter or fire-starting kit, then make sure you know how to control and completely extinguish the fire you start. Although fire is an important tool, it can also be a real hazard, not only from burning but also from the smoke of materials you may burn. Many wood and paper products have chemicals in them that are highly toxic to humans when burned. FEMA recommends you not start a fire at all, but if you feel you must, then learn how to do it right in order to avoid hurting yourself or others.

Communication Tools

Radio and NOAA Weather Radio. A battery-powered or hand-crank radio that can receive both regular broadcast and NOAA weather date information. Have extra batteries if you use them.

Whistle. This essential communication tool is good for getting the attention of rescuers who are within hearing distance or to signal for help to someone you cannot see due to darkness or a physical barrier.

Mirror. To signal for help when you are far from rescuers. This is good for getting the attention of rescuers who are out of hearing distance. It is helpful if you want to signal for help to someone in an aircraft or in a high-noise environment. You will want to learn how to use the mirror signal effectively.

Phone Charger. An auto adapter or solar charger is a must for keeping your phone charged. The initial loss of phone communications may last a few days, but you will want to be able to use your phone if the wireless service is restored.

Consumable Supplies

The basic kit should have at least a three-day supply of food and water for each person as well as hygiene items and prescription medications.

Water: One gallon per day for each person. This covers both drinking and sanitation.

Food: At least three days of non-perishable food for each person. You don't have to have "survival food"; canned and dried foods work just as well. Avoid high sugar or salt content as these can cause dehydration. Learn how to make food last by eating smaller meals throughout the day.

Sanitary items: This includes toilet paper, feminine products, diapers, and other single-use disposable hygiene items.

Prescription medications: You may not be able to have extra of these to store with your survival kit, but you must remember to take them with you. If you do have extra, learn how to store them so they are well preserved and still useful to you when you need them. This is also true for dental appliances, hearing aids, and other medical appliances.

Rightsize your supplies and know where they are located: as a general rule you should be able to fit what you need for one person in a standard 20-inch x 15-inch plastic tote. They seal well enough for storage in the home when you keep them in a cool and dry place. Keep what you need on hand, and remember that if space is a premium in your house, a small amount of supplies is far better than none at all.

FEMA recommends that you store your supplies in a cool dry place and check them every six months.

At Home

Your disaster supply kit should contain essential food, water, and supplies for at least three days. Keep this kit in a designated place and have it ready in case you have to leave your home quickly. Make sure all family members know where the kit is kept. Additionally, you may want to consider having supplies for sheltering for up to two weeks.

At Work

You need to be prepared to shelter at work for at least 24 hours. Make sure you have food and water and other necessities like medicines in your kit. Also, be sure to have comfortable walking shoes at your workplace in case an evacuation requires walking long distances. Your kit should also be in one container and ready to grab and go in case you are evacuated from your workplace.

Vehicle

In case you are stranded, keep a kit of emergency supplies in your car. This kit should include jumper cables; flashlights and extra batteries; first-aid kit and necessary medications in case you are away from home for a prolonged time; food items containing protein such as nuts and energy bars; canned fruit and a portable can opener; water for each person and pet in your car; an AM/FM radio to listen to traffic reports and emergency messages; cat litter or sand for better tire traction; a shovel; an ice scraper; warm clothes; gloves; a hat; sturdy boots; a jacket; and an extra change of clothes, blankets, or sleeping bags.

Also consider: Be prepared for an emergency by starting your day with a full tank of gas and a fully charged cell phone. Keep a phone charger in the car along with flares or a reflective triangle. If you find yourself stranded, be safe and stay in your car, put on your flashers, call for help, and wait until it arrives. If you have a small child, consider keeping extra baby formula and diapers.

Section III:
Things You Need to Know About Disasters

Natural Disasters

This chapter provides a description of different types of natural disasters. The conversation starts out very general and gets more specific as each description progresses. This is done on purpose because your preparations will be based on the generalities of the type of event. Your actual survive activities during a disaster will be based on the specific situation with that particular event. This combination of general preparation and specific action is not a contradiction but rather an important method of thinking. When you understand the generalities of a disaster type it helps you anticipate so you can take specific actions to increase your chances of survival. You will not be able to do everything to protect yourself, your loved ones and your property, so you will need to prioritize and be able to choose the right things to survive.

(Shutterstock)

Natural Disasters

Each Disaster type includes discussion on the following subjects:

General Description

General description provides a short introduction of the nature and general scope of the disaster type. This gives a general overview of what you may encounter.

Disaster Charts

As part of the disaster description a "Disaster Chart" is included. The Disaster Chart is a visual representation of the "Big 8" questions described in Chapter 2 and explained in greater detail later in the disaster type discussion. It is designed to give a generalized view of the effects of a disaster type. This is helpful because every disaster has aspects that are destructive, dangerous and unpredictable. That said, natural events that have the potential to cause disasters also tend to have predictable patterns of behavior.

Each type of event has some element that will allow you to avoid or reduce the impact of its effects if you take the time to be aware and prepared. To assist in expressing this idea visually, each disaster description has been provided with a "Disaster Chart". This is not high science. The Charts are subjectively based on observation and experience. They are designed to serve as a way to express an idea.

Disaster Chart (Total Points)							
Effects	**Least**						**Worst**
Areas of Known Occurrence	Known	1	2	3	4	5	Unknown
Scales and Measurement	Before	1	2	3	4	5	After
Quick or Slow Onset	Days	1	2	3	4	5	Minutes
Area of Effect	Local	1	2	3	4	5	States
Duration of Effects	Hours	1	2	3	4	5	Months
Destruction of Infrastructure	Minor	1	2	3	4	5	Total
Disruption of Services	Minor	1	2	3	4	5	Total
Aftermath	Minor	1	2	3	4	5	Disaster

The number system provided in the Disaster Chart accompanying each disaster type is not a grade to say which disaster is the worst; they are all bad. The purpose is to express the aspect of each disaster type that can be used to anticipate, prepare for, and avoid its effects. The worst disaster would have a score of 40: unpredictable, rapid onset, long lasting, with wide spread destruction, disruption and aftermath. The point to take away here is that there is no disaster

(Natural Disasters)
A. Hurricanes

General Description

Hurricanes are huge storms that can be hundreds of miles across. They build up at sea and transfer the energy from the warm water of the ocean into high winds and raging seas. When these storms make landfall, or even pass nearby the coast, they bring high winds, torrential rains, and surging sea water.

Hurricane (29)								
Effects	**Least**							**Worst**
Areas of Known Occurrence	Known	1	**2**	3	4	5	Unknown
Scales and Measurement	Before	1	2	**3**	4	5	After
Quick or Slow Onset	Days	**1**	2	3	4	5	Minutes
Area of Effect	Local	1	2	3	4	**5**	States
Duration of Effects	Hours	1	2	3	**4**	5	Months
Destruction of Infrastructure	Minor	1	2	3	4	**5**	Total
Disruption of Services	Minor	1	2	3	4	**5**	Total
Aftermath	Minor	1	2	3	4	**5**	Disaster

Major Threat

Hurricanes are a triple threat: they kill with wind (the debris it carries), water from the storm surge or rain flooding, and aftermath. There is very little you can do to change your situation once you get caught in a hurricane. The winds will do the most damage and set conditions for aftermath. Wind damage is not directly related to wind speed, and all hurricane-force winds (74 MPH or more) can carry deadly projectiles. The storm surge is a wall of sea water 50 to 100 miles long resulting from the wind pushing the ocean in front of the storm. Storm surge presents the greatest immediate threat to your life, but a typical hurricane of any category will also drop between 6 and 12 inches of rain, causing significant flooding. This flooding is the primary cause of fatalities after a hurricane. If you do survive the storm, then you will face the aftermath, which may be even worse. In addition, be aware that as the hurricane dissipates over land, it has the potential to spawn tornadoes.

Survival Strategy

Use the predictability and slow-onset time to your advantage: be long gone before the hurricane arrives. If you like living by the ocean, then you should be aware of the weather, be prepared to board up your house, and be ready to evacuate. Give yourself 48 hours to move and you can avoid the storm completely. You risk some property loss to wind, water, or looting, but risk to personal safety can be effectively avoided.

> *Government Information Websites:*
>
> *National Oceanic and Atmospheric Administration (NOAA) — http://www.noaa.gov/*
>
> *National Weather Service (NWS) — http://www.weather.gov/*
>
> *Federal Emergency Management Administration (FEMA) — http://www.ready.gov/*
>
> *Centers for Disease Control and Prevention (CDC) — http://www.cdc.gov/*

A. The BIG EIGHT:

1. Areas of Known Occurrence, Possibility

Several hurricane-force storms occur per year during an established annual season within historically known areas of effect. Major hurricanes strike the U.S. on an average of every three years, but do not occur on a regular schedule. Up to three major storms have struck in a single year, but between 1992 and 2004 there were no major hurricanes. The annual hurricane prediction gives the best idea of what is in store for that year.

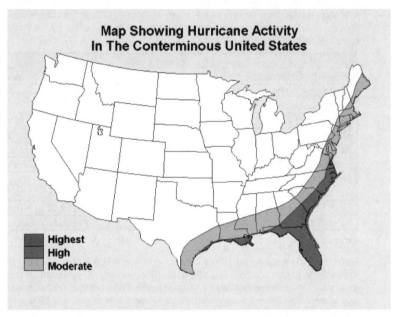

Map Showing Hurricane Activity In The Conterminous United States

Highest
High
Moderate

Hurricanes are seasonally active primarily in the Eastern United States along the Atlantic coast and to a lesser extent along the coast of the Southern United States in the Gulf of Mexico. See the Location Chart. They can have devastating effects more than a hundred miles inland of the coast of the Atlantic.

2. Scales and Measurement, Predictability

Effective measuring before the event allows for accurate prediction of time, place, and severity. Hurricanes are large and destructive, but they are also very slow. They take a long time to develop and move with reasonable predictability.

Hurricanes are measured during the storm and can be accurately measured prior to the hurricane making landfall. The National Weather Service is an agency of the National Oceanic and Atmosphere Administration (NOAA) and is responsible for making weather predictions as well as issuing watches and warnings.

NOAA says, "The Saffir-Simpson Hurricane Wind Scale is a 1 to 5 rating based on a hurricane's sustained wind speed. This scale estimates potential property damage. Hurricanes reaching Category 3 and higher are considered major hurricanes because of their potential for significant loss of life and damage. Category 1 and 2 storms are still dangerous, however, and require preventative measures. In the western North Pacific, the term 'super typhoon' is used for tropical cyclones with sustained winds exceeding 150 mph."

Scales and Measurement (Hurricanes)

NOAA outlines the anticipated effects of hurricanes with the following descriptions.

Category 1
A Category 1 hurricane has sustained winds of 74–95 mph, 64–82 kt, 119–153 km/h. *It has very dangerous winds and will produce some damage*: well-constructed frame homes could have damage to roofs, shingles, vinyl siding, and gutters. Large branches of trees will snap, and shallowly rooted trees may be toppled.

Category 2
A Category 2 hurricane has sustained winds of 96–110 mph, 83–95 kt, 154–177 km/h. *It has extremely dangerous winds that will cause extensive damage*: well-constructed frame homes could sustain major roof and siding damage. Many shallowly rooted trees will be snapped or uprooted and block numerous roads.

Category 3
A Category 3 hurricane is considered a major storm and has sustained winds of 111–129 mph, 96–112 kt, 178–208 km/h. *Devastating damage will occur*: well-built framed homes may incur major damage or removal of roof decking and gable ends. Many trees will be snapped or uprooted, blocking numerous roads.

Category 4
A Category 4 hurricane is considered a major storm and has sustained winds of 130–156 mph, 113–136 kt, 209–251 km/h. *Catastrophic damage will occur*: well-built framed homes can sustain severe damage with loss of most of the roof structure or some exterior walls. Most trees will be snapped or uprooted and power poles downed. Fallen trees and power poles will isolate residential areas.

Category 5
A Category 5 hurricane is considered a major storm and has sustained winds of 157 mph or higher, 137 kt or higher, 252 km/h or higher. *Catastrophic damage will occur*: a high percentage of framed homes will be destroyed with total roof failure and wall collapse. Fallen trees and power poles will isolate residential areas.

There are minor changes made to the wind scale from time to time. A one-mile-per-hour change in scale was made in 2012. This was for record-keeping purposes and has nothing to do with the actual damage potential of a hurricane. Do not disregard a warning based solely on category identification, and remember the storm surge when making your decisions on response and evacuation.

Hurricanes

A note on names: hurricanes, cyclones, and typhoons are all have the same dynamics. They have different names based on where they take place in the world. In the Atlantic and Northeast Pacific, the term "hurricane" is used. The same type of disturbance in the Northwest Pacific is called a "typhoon," and "cyclones" occur in the South Pacific and Indian Ocean. For all intents and purposes of preparation and response, they are the same storm.

3. Quick or Slow Onset

Slow, usually several days' warning. Where weather tracking is available, it provides several days of warning of intensity and location of landfall.

4. Area of Effect

Because hurricanes are very large, they can affect hundreds of miles of coast, spanning whole states and even multiple states. This can place significant distance between survivors and rescue/relief personnel.

5. Duration of Effects

3 to 10 days of heavy rain including 2 to 3 days of intense hurricane wind effects, weeks of flood effects, and aftermath.

6. Destruction of Infrastructure

Ranges from minimal structural damage to complete annihilation. Even moderate wind damage tends to affect power, which affects everything else. Hurricanes bring rain for several days after the event, which compounds roof damage and shelter considerations. Road networks and transportation are affected, but road damage and flooding causes limitation or delay of access to resources like food and water.

7. Disruption of Services

Services usually suffer delays and disruptions for days or weeks. Lack of medical, security, food-delivery, and fresh-water access are all associated with hurricane disruption. The large areas of damage associated with hurricanes stress services even when actual destruction does not occur.

8. Aftermath

Hurricane aftermath has a direct correlation to both the severity of destruction and the area of effect. Hurricanes tend to have significant aftermath based on two factors: 1) severity of destruction affecting the ability to provide services and 2) area of effect, which impacts how long it takes to get resources and services to where they are needed. The descriptions offered here are generalized and intended to offer an expectation of what may remain after a hurricane. These are not absolutes. The reality of the situation will be dependent on the actual effects of any storm.

Patterns of Mortality and Injury

As a general rule, deaths and injuries in disasters tend to go up when associated with high winds or water. High winds result in more injuries than deaths, and high water tends to result in more deaths than injuries. In as much as hurricanes result in both high winds and high water (from both storm surge and rain flooding), hurricanes have a high probability of causing both deaths and injuries.

Government Response

Help will come as rapidly as possible with thousands of responders and huge amounts of relief supplies by ground, rail, sea, and air. This will be a full-spectrum response from all government levels that are still capable of providing any services.

Aftermath (Hurricanes)

Category 1 Aftermath: Extensive damage to power lines and poles likely will result in power outages that could last a few hours to several days. Commercial and government infrastructure will be damaged. Access to resources such as food and water may be delayed until stores can reopen. Repairs to your home may be required. Essential government services like police and fire will be busy but available. Stability services such as sanitation and mail service may be delayed for a few days. Security will be maintained by local authority, and rule of law will be readily available.

Category 2 Aftermath: Near-total power loss is expected with outages that could last from several days to weeks. Infrastructure will be damaged and services will be interrupted for several days and may be limited for several weeks. Commercial and government infrastructure will be damaged. Access to resources such as food and water may be delayed or limited until some stores can open again. Repairs to shelter may be required. Essential government services like police and fire will be limited. Stability services such as sanitation and mail service may be delayed for a few days. Security will be maintained by local authority, and rule of law will be readily available.

Category 3 Aftermath: Electricity and water will be unavailable for several days to weeks after the storm passes. Infrastructure will be damaged to the point where outside resources will be required to provide any services. Services that do arrive will be limited for several weeks and may take months to restore at the local level. Resources such as food, water, and shelter may be very limited. Essential government services such as police and fire response will be limited or delayed in response if available at all. Stability services such as sanitation and mail service will be suspended for weeks. Security may be lost in some areas for several days, and rule of law will not be readily available. A major federal response will be required in addition to the assistance of neighboring states not also devastated by the event (remember that Hurricane Katrina was a "strong" category 3 hurricane; it was the widespread scope of the damage that added to the intensity of the aftermath).

Category 4 Aftermath: Power outages will last weeks to possibly months. Most of the area will be uninhabitable for weeks or months. Infrastructure will be devastated to the point that outside resources will be required to rescue and relocate survivors. Whole communities will cease to exist and will not return. Resources such as food, water, and shelter will not be available until it is brought in. No government services, essential or otherwise, will be available. Security will be lost for a limited period of time in some areas until restored with the assistance of the National Guard or activated federal military forces. Rule of law will not be readily available. Those not killed by the storm or drowned in the storm surge and flooding will face hunger, exposure to the elements, lawlessness, and infection from injuries and exposure to diseases.

Category 5 Aftermath: Power outages will last for weeks to possibly months. Most of the area will be uninhabitable for weeks or months. Infrastructure will be annihilated to the point that outside resources will be required to rescue and relocate survivors. Whole communities will cease to exist and will not return. Resources such as food, water, and shelter will not be available until it is brought in. No government services, essential or otherwise, will be available. Security will be lost for a limited period of time in some areas until restored with the assistance of the National Guard or activated federal military forces, and rule of law will not be readily available. Those not killed by the storm or drowned in the storm surge will face hunger, exposure to lawlessness, and infection from injuries and exposure to diseases. This is the same description as a category 4 hurricane. This is a designation for record-keeping purposes only and represents the difference between devastation and annihilation. If you're trapped in this level of aftermath, your risk of death or injury goes from highly probable to certain.

B. Outlooks, Watches, Warnings, & Advisories

Remember that these alerts and bulletins are designed to inform and instruct in order to cause the public to change their behavior or take specific action for their safety. Be aware of these communications.

Weather Alerts: The National Weather Service and its pendant offices communicate alerts in the form of *outlooks, advisories, watches, and warnings* to the public. They provide real-time notification of weather events that threaten local areas.

Emergency Management Bulletins: Emergency-management agencies will broadcast *emergency-management bulletins* in the case of disasters or special events when officials need to communicate public-safety information or special instructions to the public. In many cases both weather alerts and emergency-management bulletins will be broadcast during a disaster situation.

Outlook: Indicates the potential for significant weather events up to seven days in advance with a forecaster confidence around 30%.

Watch: Indicates that conditions are favorable for the particular weather event in and near the watch area, which may pose a risk to life and property. Watches are issued up to 48 hours in advance with forecaster confidence around 50%.

Warning/Advisory: Indicates that a particular weather event is imminent or occurring. **Advisories** are issued if the weather event will lead to nuisance conditions, while **Warnings** are issued for significant weather events that will pose a risk to life and property. Warnings and advisories are issued up to 48 hours in advance with forecaster confidence of at least 80%.

Alert Notifications

Alert notifications will come in the form the following reports. This list includes reports you are most likely to hear during a hurricane, but this is not an all-inclusive list. Be careful to listen for emergency communications and take information as you can get it. Remember that official government emergency communications may be more reliable than unofficial sources. The alerts you will want to listen for are:

Hurricane Alerts
Hurricane alerts are issued for locations in or near an area threatened by a tropical storm or a hurricane.

- **Hurricane Warning:** Issued when sustained winds of 64 knots (74 mph) or higher associated with a hurricane are occurring or expected in a specified coastal area generally within 24 hours. A hurricane warning can remain in effect when dangerously high water or a combination of dangerously high water and exceptionally high waves continue, even though winds may be less than hurricane force.
- **Hurricane Watch:** Alerts residents along coastal areas that a hurricane may become a threat, generally within 36 hours.
- **Hurricane Wind Warning:** Issued for inland counties when sustained winds of 74 mph or greater associated with a hurricane are occurring or expected within 24 hours.
- **Hurricane Wind Watch:** Issued for inland counties when sustained winds of 74 mph or greater associated with a hurricane are possible within 36 hours.
- **Tropical Storm Warning:** Issued when sustained winds of 34–63 knots (39–73 mph) associated with a tropical storm are occurring or expected in a specified coastal area, generally within 24 hours.
- **Tropical Storm Watch:** Alerts residents along coastal areas that a tropical storm may become a threat, generally within 36 hours.

- **Tropical Storm Wind Warning:** Issued for inland counties when sustained winds of 39–73 mph associated with a tropical storm are occurring or expected within 24 hours.
- **Tropical Storm Wind Watch:** Issued for inland counties when sustained winds of 39–73 mph associated with a tropical storm are possible within 36 hours.
- **Tropical Weather Statement:** Provides general updates related to a tropical storm or hurricane event.
- **Typhoon Watch/Warning:** Similar to Hurricane Watch/Warning, except issued for interests in the Western Pacific Ocean.

Marine Alerts

Marine Alerts are issued when a variety of weather conditions threaten boating interests or coastal living.

- **Special Marine Warning:** Issued for hazardous weather conditions (thunderstorms over water, thunderstorms that will move over water, cold air funnels over water, squall lines, or waterspouts) usually of short duration (two hours or less) and producing sustained winds or frequent gusts of 34 knots or more.
- **Marine Weather Statement:** Issued to provide follow-up information on Special Marine Warnings; describe short-duration, non-severe, but potentially hazardous conditions that may make small-craft handling difficult; provide information for a variety of conditions not covered by warnings or routine forecasts (e.g., low-water conditions, dense fog, etc.); or discuss increasing or decreasing winds and to convey details on possible later warnings.
- **Lake Wind Advisory:** Indicates that winds of 20–25 mph or gusts of 30–39 mph are expected, causing a rough chop on area lakes. Small boats may be especially prone to be capsizing.
- **Gale Warning:** Issued when sustained surface winds or frequent gusts of 34–47 knots (39–54 mph) are occurring or likely to occur and not directly associated with a tropical cyclone. Conditions will be hazardous to commercial vessels and extremely hazardous to small craft.
- **Gale Watch:** Issued when surface winds or frequent gusts of 34–47 knots (39–54 mph) may become possible.
- **Hazardous Seas Warning:** Indicates waves with extreme steepness are imminent or occurring. Shallow waters are likely to be very dangerous to navigate.
- **Hazardous Seas Watch:** Indicates waves with extreme steepness may become possible.
- **High Surf Warning:** Issued when breaking wave action results in an especially heightened threat to life and property within the surf zone. High-surf criteria vary by region.
- **High Surf Advisory:** Issued when breaking wave action poses a threat to life and property within the surf zone. High-surf criteria vary by region.

Special Weather Alerts

Special Weather Alerts correspond to a broad range of weather events not related to precipitation such as dense fog, high winds, extreme heat, extreme cold, or conditions conducive to wildfires.

- **Emergency Management Bulletins:** These are issued by local government emergency-management agencies to inform the public of the nature and area of effect of a disaster. These bulletins will include important information on current conditions and identified hazards, probability of additional events, road closures, location of relief centers, special instructions, and other appropriate information.

The predictive nature of hurricanes allows the government to act before the event to preposition supplies and personnel for rapid response to the disaster. For details on the plans for your area, contact your local city or county emergency management office, who will have the response plans.

Primary efforts will include the federal response of FEMA, national relief non-governmental organizations like the Red Cross, and, if requested, the active-duty military. The state effort will consist of state-level and National Guard elements. This will include responding communities from outside the area of effect as well as assistance from neighboring states based upon mutual support agreements called Emergency Mutual Aid Compacts (EMAC). These are agreements rather than contracts, allowing nearby states to provide as much as they can. It is a good system. Local response will be limited and delayed due to the damage of the storm, but will establish jurisdictional control as soon as they are able. State and federal resources will be provided to local government to assist them. Private industry will also arrive as soon as the area is opened to public access, most notably to bring utilities back online, but also to reopen businesses. All of this will include elements to provide the immediately essential services of rescue, medical, security (police and fire), transportation, sustainment (food, water, & shelter), and communication.

After rescue is complete and security is well established, the priorities will be for electricity, water, U.S. postal services, and other services that are all vital to recovery and stability. Rule of law provided by state agencies and nearby communities will be returned to local authority as soon as possible. This will be dependent on the infrastructure of police stations, legal offices, courtrooms and jails.

Dependent on the severity of the storm and the geographic area of effects, it may take several days for rescue to arrive. This may seem like a long time, but remember they have to travel to you and find you. The better you can mark your location, the quicker you will be rescued.

C. Personal Plans and Readiness

Hurricanes are a wind and water disaster. They bring not only high winds and storm surges, but the additional extremes of tornadoes on the outer edges of the hurricane and floods resulting from heavy rains. You will want to take these things into consideration when making your plans to preserve your home and property.

The best option for preservation of life is evacuation. Reliable transportation and early movement are imperatives. Include wet-weather gear and watertight storage containers in your survival kit. Even evacuation to a safe location may still require you to deal with rain and flooding on roads. Having extra gas in a gas can (preferably stored on the outside of the vehicle) is a good idea as fuel may be in short supply during an evacuation order.

(Natural Disasters)
B. Earthquakes

General Description

Earthquakes are the result of movement in the earth's crust that releases large amounts of energy that shake the affected areas violently. They affect buildings, roads, and infrastructure, both buried as well as overhead such as water, gas, and power lines. Earthquakes are the very definition of a disaster. They are rare in their frequency, little- to no-warning, rapid-onset, and very destructive. An earthquake can undo in a minute what it has taken us whole lifetimes to create. As with the volcano scenario, people who live in earthquake zones do so at their own peril in the hopes that the "big one" will not strike in their lifetime.

Earthquakes (32)							
Effects	**Least**						**Worst**
Areas of Known Occurrence	Known	**1**	2	3	4	5	Unknown
Scales and Measurement	Before	1	2	3	4	**5**	After
Quick or Slow Onset	Days	1	2	3	4	**5**	Minutes
Area of Effect	Local	1	2	3	**4**	5	States
Duration of Effects	Hours	1	2	3	**4**	5	Months
Destruction of Infrastructure	Minor	1	2	3	**4**	5	Total
Disruption of Services	Minor	1	2	3	**4**	5	Total
Aftermath	Minor	1	2	3	4	**5**	Disaster

Major Threat

Everything, the sheer scale of the destruction releases a dizzying array of natural and man-made hazards and threats that the survivor must navigate to escape the surreal pandemonium of a major earthquake and its aftermath.

Survival Strategy

Readiness and resiliency. Surviving a major earthquake takes real skill: not just knowing what to do, but being ready to do what is necessary in a disaster situation. All the things we take for granted will not just be gone, but will change. Buildings will not be welcome shelters, but rather dangerous traps ready to collapse. The ground will not be firm, but will split and become soft with water or motion. The air we breathe will be filled with the gases and chemicals we are no longer able to contain. People will be driven to desperation, and desperation is not a good thing. You will need all of your self-control to stay as aware as you can be in order to move to a place of resources and security. Resiliency becomes a major factor in this size of an event and your ability to persevere through constant hardship and multiple setbacks is paramount to your survival. Understand that many of the major fault lines in the U.S. are directly under large cities and will affect huge numbers of the population. This is especially true of the West Coast in the land of sunshine between the mountains and the sea.

> **Government Information Websites:**
> *Federal Emergency Management Administration (FEMA) — http://www.ready.gov/*

Earthquakes

A. The BIG EIGHT:

1. Areas of Known Occurrence, Possibility

High to the point of absolute assurance. Life on earth is dependent upon the re-generative nature of the planet. This includes tectonic-plate movement and violent surface renewal. It always happens eventually, and when it does, the changes are significant. Earthquake zones and fault lines are well documented by the United States Geological Survey (USGS). Major earthquake zones are located in South Carolina, along the New Madrid Fault Line that follows the borders of Tennessee, Arkansas, Missouri, Illinois, and Kentucky along the Mississippi River and all over the Western U.S., ranging from the Rocky Mountains to the California coast. The good news is that the probability of a major earthquake is low (relatively). Fortunately this renewal takes place slowly in human terms, and although the Earth's crust is constantly shifting with earthquakes taking place in several different locations around the world at any time of the day or night, major seismic events that devastate human habitation are not common in North America.

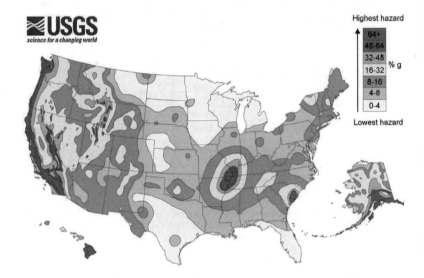

2. Scales of Measurement, Predictability

Very Low, fault location can be found with high accuracy using historical records and modern seismic equipment. Earthquake warning systems exist, but offer no advance warning because the earthquake must start before it can be identified for warning. No part of the U.S. has a widespread public earthquake warning system in place as of 2012. Earthquake measurements are taken during the event by seismic activity–recording stations and are recorded and analyzed after the event. There are two primary scales used to describe the release of energy during an earthquake. They are the Richter scale and the Modified Mercalli Scale. They differ in that the Richter Scale measures the total amount of energy released and the Modified Mercalli scale measures effects on different locations during the event.

See folllwing pages for discussion of the scales of measurement for earthquakes (the Richter Magnitude Scale and the The Modified Mercalli Scale of Earthquake Intensity).

3. Quick or Slow Onset

The effects of earthquakes are virtually instantaneous.

4. Area of Effect

Not all earthquakes have a measureable effect in their area of effect. Few significant effects are experienced until magnitude reaches a strong rating of 6.0 or higher. At that point, an area of about 100 miles across (50 miles from the epicenter) will be affected.

5. Duration of Effects

Although the initial quake may not last more than a few minutes, the aftershocks can go on for hours or days.

6. Destruction of Infrastructure

Roads will crack and some will become impassable. Elevated highways and bridges may collapse or be closed until safety inspections can be completed. Rail lines will be significantly damaged, and rail services will be cut off for a significant length of time. Buildings will be damaged and no longer fit for shelter or services. Overhead electrical lines will topple, and ground-based infrastructure like fiber-optic cable lines, water pipes, and gas lines will break. Communications infrastructure will be knocked out of service. What remains will be limited and quickly overwhelmed. This will delay rescue efforts. Although infrastructure will not be completely destroyed, it will require significant repair, taking months or even years to complete.

7. Disruption of Services

Disruption of services will come in the form of loss of communications and capability. This will cause a cascading demand that overwhelms the remaining capacity. The number of injuries and emergency calls will quickly overwhelm emergency medical, fire, and police first responders. Hospital emergency capability will be swamped with walk-in injuries. This will limit or delay response to fires and criminal activity. Fires and looting will cause a loss of security, which will result in suspension of mail, sanitation, and other standard services. Commerce will be hindered by power outages in both electrical and gas supply and by transportation limitations from damaged roads, rails, and ports, both sea and air. Lack of water service and employee absenteeism due to injuries and other inconveniences resulting from loss of infrastructure will be a contributing factor. This will affect commercial services including healthcare providers, food and gasoline distribution, transportation providers, and many other essential services provided by the private sector. The large number of survivors will consume resources faster than they can be replenished.

8. Aftermath

The aftermath of an earthquake will be heavily influenced by population density. The larger-magnitude earthquake events in California tend to range in the Strong scale of 6.0 to 6.9 with some reaching up into the low-7 magnitudes. These events cause significant property damage and injure many people rather than killing them. There are historical incidences in which over a hundred people lost their lives, but even these numbers are small in relation to the total population. There have been several 7.0-or-greater events, the most notable of which is the great quake of 1906. That 7.8-magnitude event caused massive amounts of property damage, and the combination of the quake, collapsing buildings and fires killed over 3000 people. Thousands more

Scales and Measurements (Earthquakes)

Richter Magnitude Scale

The Richter scale gives a rating for the entire event called magnitude. Magnitude is expressed in numbers from 1 to 10, with 1 being the least effect and 10 being the greatest effect. As a rule, lower-magnitude earthquakes happen with greater frequency and higher-magnitude earthquakes have greater effects.

The following is a list of the magnitude descriptions, earthquake effects, and frequency of occurrence as described by the Richter magnitude scale:

Less than 2.0: Micro
These earthquakes are not felt. They happen continually around the planet.

2.0–2.9: Minor
Generally not felt, but recorded. There are an estimated 1,300,000 earthquakes of this magnitude per year around the world.

3.0–3.9: Minor
Often felt, but rarely causes damage. There are an estimated 130,000 earthquakes of this magnitude per year around the world.

4.0–4.9: Light
Noticeable shaking of indoor items, rattling noises. Significant damage unlikely.

There are an estimated 13,000 earthquakes of this magnitude per year around the world.

5.0–5.9: Moderate
Can cause major damage to poorly constructed buildings over small regions. At most, slight damage to well-designed buildings. There is an average of 1,319 earthquakes of this magnitude per year around the world.

6.0–6.9: Strong
Can be destructive in areas up to about 160 kilometers (99 mi) across in populated areas. There is an average of 134 earthquakes of this magnitude per year.

7.0–7.9: Major
Can cause serious damage over larger areas. There is an average of 15 earthquakes of this magnitude per year around the world.

8.0–8.9: Great
Can cause serious damage in areas several hundred kilometers across. There is an average of one earthquake of this magnitude per year somewhere in the world.

9.0–9.9: Devastating
Affects areas several thousand kilometers across. This magnitude of quake only happens on an average of once every ten years.

10.0+: Massive
The planet buster. An earthquake of this magnitude has never been recorded. It would cause widespread devastation across very large areas; extremely rare (Unknown/May not be possible).

The Modified Mercalli Scale of Earthquake Intensity

According to FEMA information, the Modified Mercalli scale measures how much energy is felt at any given location affected by the quake and assigns different intensity values rather than magnitudes. The intensity scale differs from the Richter magnitude scale in that the effects of any one earthquake vary greatly from place to place.

Intensity ratings are expressed as Roman numerals between I at the low end and XII at the high end. Ratings of earthquake effects are based on the following relatively subjective scale of descriptions:

I. People do not feel any Earth movement.

II. A few people might notice movement if they are at rest or on the upper floors of tall buildings.

III. Many people indoors feel movement. Hanging objects swing back and forth. People outdoors might not realize that an earthquake is occurring.

IV. Most people indoors feel movement. Hanging objects swing. Dishes, windows, and doors rattle. The earthquake feels like a heavy truck hitting the walls. A few people outdoors may feel movement. Parked cars rock.

V. Almost everyone feels movement. Sleeping people are awakened. Doors swing open or closed. Dishes are broken. Pictures on the wall move. Small objects move or are turned over. Trees might shake. Liquids might spill out of open containers.

VI. Everyone feels movement. People have trouble walking. Objects fall from shelves. Pictures fall off walls. Furniture moves. Plaster in walls might crack. Trees and bushes shake. Damage is slight in poorly built buildings. No structural damage.

VII. People have difficulty standing. Drivers feel their cars shaking. Some furniture breaks. Loose bricks fall from buildings. Damage is slight to moderate in well-built buildings; considerable in poorly built buildings.

VIII. Drivers have trouble steering. Houses that are not secured to their foundations might shift on their foundations. Tall structures such as towers and chimneys might twist and fall. Well-built buildings suffer slight damage. Poorly built structures suffer severe damage. Tree branches break. Hillsides might crack if the ground is wet. Water levels in wells might change.

IX. Well-built buildings suffer considerable damage. Houses that are not secured to their foundations move off their foundations. Some underground pipes are broken. The ground cracks. Reservoirs suffer serious damage.

X. Most buildings and their foundations are destroyed. Some bridges are destroyed. Dams are seriously damaged. Large landslides occur. Water is thrown on the banks of canals, rivers, lakes. The ground cracks in large areas. Railroad tracks are bent slightly.

XI. Most buildings collapse. Some bridges are destroyed. Large cracks appear in the ground. Underground pipelines are destroyed. Railroad tracks are badly bent.

XII. Almost everything is destroyed. Objects are thrown into the air. The ground moves in waves or ripples. Large amounts of rock may move.

Earthquakes

were injured. Aftershocks will be a major concern as they will disrupt rescue efforts and damage hastily built, temporary-response infrastructure.

There is some scientific speculation that the West Coast area is not capable of producing a Great earthquake 8.0 in magnitude. This supposed inability to produce "the big one" is of little consolation when the real danger of an earthquake is in the aftermath.

To put things in perspective, when Army General Fredrick Funston came to the aid of San Francisco in 1906, he requested tents and food for 200,000 survivors. The 2010 census tells us there are over 6,000,000 people in the counties around the San Francisco Bay and another 16,000,000 between Los Angeles and San Diego. After Hurricane Katrina, there were 100,000 people left in New Orleans. With over 10,000 National Guard troops standing ready with supplies, it took three days to get into the city and get the people out or properly supplied. Another 14,000 National Guard personnel and over 3,000 federalized active-duty troops took almost a week to restore security, order, and rule of law. That was with most roads passable and rail systems functional to within 50 miles of the city.

Patterns of Mortality and Injury

The earthquake will injure many and kill fewer initially. The negative results of aftermath will present the significant threats and hazards and be multiplied by aftershocks. As a general rule, the closer you are to population centers and man-made infrastructure, the more threats and hazards you will potentially encounter.

Government Response

Help will come as rapidly as possible with thousands of responders and huge amounts of relief supplies by ground, rail, sea, and air. This will be a full-spectrum response from all government levels that are still capable of providing any services. The unpredictable nature of earthquakes makes them difficult to specifically prepare for in terms of gathered supplies and ready-standing response personnel. This does not keep anyone from making plans; it just adds some time to get things moving when the time to respond arrives. For details on the plans for your area, contact your local city or county emergency management office, who will have the response plans.

Primary efforts will include the federal response of FEMA, the active-duty military and national relief non-governmental organizations like the Red Cross. The state effort will consist of state-level and National Guard elements. This will include responding communities from outside the area of effect as well as assistance from neighboring states based upon mutual-support agreements called Emergency Mutual Aid Compacts (EMAC). These are agreements rather than contracts allowing nearby states to provide as much as they can. It is a good system. Local response will be limited and delayed due to the damage from the earthquake, but will establish jurisdictional control as soon as they are able. State and federal resources will be provided to local government to assist them. Private industry will arrive as soon as the area is opened to public access, most notably to bring utilities back online, but also to reopen businesses. All of this will include elements to provide the immediately essential services of rescue, medical services, security (police and fire), transportation, sustainment (food, water, & shelter), and communication.

After rescue is complete and security is well established, the priorities will be for electricity, water, U.S. postal services, and other services that are all vital to recovery and stability. Rule of law will be returned to local authority as soon as possible. This will be dependent on the infrastructure of police stations, legal offices, courtrooms, and jails.

B. Outlooks, Watches, Warnings, & Advisories

Remember that these alerts and bulletins are designed to inform and instruct in order to cause the public to change their behavior or take specific action for their safety. Be aware of these communications.

Weather Alerts

The National Weather Service and its pendant offices communicate alerts in the form of *outlooks, advisories, watches, and warnings* to the public. They provide real-time notification of weather events that threaten local areas.

Emergency Management Bulletins

Emergency management agencies will broadcast *emergency management bulletins* in the case of disasters or special events when officials need to communicate public-safety information or special instructions to the public. In many cases, both weather alerts and emergency management bulletins will be broadcast during a disaster situation.

Outlook

Indicates the potential for significant weather events up to seven days in advance with a forecaster confidence around 30%.

Watch

Indicates that conditions are favorable for the particular weather event in and near the watch area, which may pose a risk to life and property. Watches are issued up to 48 hours in advance with forecaster confidence around 50%.

Warning/Advisory

Indicates that a particular weather event is imminent or occurring. **Advisories** are issued if the weather event will lead to nuisance conditions, while **warnings** are issued for significant weather events that will pose a risk to life and property. Warnings and advisories are issued up to 48 hours in advance with forecaster confidence of at least 80%.

Alert Notifications

Alert notifications will come in the form the following reports. This list includes reports you are most likely to hear during an earthquake, but this is not an all-inclusive list. Be careful to listen for emergency communications and take information as you can get it. Remember that official government emergency communications may be more reliable than unofficial sources. The alerts you will want to listen for are:

Emergency Management Bulletins

These are issued by local government emergency-management agencies to inform the public of the strength and area of effect of an earthquake. These bulletins will include important information on current conditions and identified hazards, probability and severity of aftershocks, road closures, location of relief centers, special instructions, and other appropriate information.

Dependent on the severity of the earthquake(s) and the geographic area of effects, it may take several days for ground rescue to arrive. This may seem like a long time, but remember they have to travel to you and find you. Once roads are reopened, the situation will improve rapidly.

(Shutterstock)

C. Personal Plans and Readiness

Earthquakes are one of the most destructive events imaginable due to the area of the damage and the level of destruction. Services are not just interrupted. The infrastructure required to provide those services is destroyed. The remaining infrastructure is fragile at best and immediately strained to its remaining capacity. Take this into consideration when making your plans and preparations.

You will need to move, sustain, and communicate in full measures and potentially for extended periods of time. Because you may well be away from your home when the earthquake strikes, you will want to have emergency kits in your car and at work. These smaller kits should be able to sustain you for 24 hours and be designed to help you move to your residence so you can rendezvous with your family and collect your full survival kit.

(Natural Disasters)
C. Wildfires

Chap 10

General Description

A wildfire is an uncontrolled fire within grassland, forest, or scrub-brush terrain. The fire's origin can be arson, carelessness, or natural. Wildfires build quickly and are hard to control at the outset. They pose a serious risk to life and property. The main components of fire are fuel, air, and an ignition source. The same is true of wildfire, but emphasis is placed on fire's natural counter element of water. Lack of moisture in the ground, vegetation, and air make wildfires more likely.

Wildfires (23)							
Effects	**Least**						**Worst**
Areas of Known Occurrence	Known	1	2	3	**4**	5	Unknown
Scales of Measurement	Before	1	2	3	4	**5**	After
Quick or Slow Onset	Days	1	2	**3**	4	5	Minutes
Area of Effect	Local	1	**2**	3	4	5	States
Duration of Effects	Hours	1	2	**3**	4	5	Months
Destruction of Infrastructure	Minor	1	**2**	3	4	5	Total
Disruption of Services	Minor	1	**2**	3	4	5	Total
Aftermath	Minor	1	**2**	3	4	5	Disaster

Weather conditions such as high temperatures and low relative humidity dry out fuels that feed the wildfire. This can create a situation where fuel will more readily ignite and burn more intensely. Wind is also a significant factor. The greater a wind, the faster a fire will spread and the more intensely it will burn. Wildfires tend to burn quickly and completely, consuming homes down to the foundation.

Major Threat

Wildfire threatens in a variety of ways. Other than the obvious threat of burning, there are the threats of smoke and speed. Smoke can disorient and incapacitate quickly. Even the most familiar locations and routes can become alien when shrouded by smoke. This effect is made worse by smoke inhalation, which causes cough, shortness of breath, hoarseness, headache, and mental confusion. Smoke can also be as hot as fire, causing burns to the nose, mouth, face, and lungs. Speed is another factor. Under the right conditions, which are not uncommon in a wildfire, the fire can spread faster than a human can run. Wind and upward incline are the two greatest factors in fire speed.

Survival Strategy

Move quickly away from the fire, the fire's path, and any potential fuel. Due to the uncertain behavior of wildfire, it is best to get out of its way as quickly as possible. This should include avoiding locations where you can escape the flames but still be harmed by heat and smoke.

Wildfires

> *Government Information Websites:*
>
> *National Weather Service (NWS) — http://www.weather.gov/*
> *Federal Emergency Management Administration (FEMA) — http://www.ready.gov/*

The BIG EIGHT

1. Areas of Known Occurrence, Possibility

Although wildfires are most common in the arid states west of the Mississippi, any location with vegetation as fuel can be affected by wildfire. This is directly tied to moisture. As the level of moisture in the ground, air, and vegetation decreases, the likelihood of wildfire increases. This is especially true in times of drought, where vegetation dies off and dries out and even areas where wildfires do not usually occur can become susceptible. This is directly tied to your proximity to fuel. If you live in or near a grassland, forest, or scrubland, you could be affected by a wildfire.

2. Scales of Measurement, Predictability

Wildfires are measured after the fact in acres burned and damage to property. This measurement method is of no use at all in prediction. Awareness of fire warnings and weather conditions is the best method to give you warning of wildfire potential. Wildfires are virtually unpredictable because the conditions for fire are always present to some degree. The greatest modifiers are the amount of moisture on the ground, in the vegetation, and in the air. This level of unpredictability extends into the event itself. A wildfire can look like it is dying out and then unexpectedly flare back to life.

3. Quick or Slow Onset

Wildfires are quick-onset and move rapidly.

4. Area of Effect

Wildfires can burn thousands of acres and transition to urbanized areas within natural-growth areas with little difficulty.

5. Duration of Effects

Although wildfires can burn for months, the areas burned by them are affected depending on the speed of the fire and the amount of fuel. A wildfire can burn through an area in a matter of hours or take a matter of days.

6. Destruction of Infrastructure

Wildfires are extremely destructive and tend to consume structures completely within their area of effect. Anything on the surface may be consumed, but buried services will be less interrupted. This means you may lose power but not water service. You can use this to your advantage in your preparations.

7. Disruption of Services

Due to the Incident Command System and community mutual support agreements, fire response trends to be good within its capacity. Essential services like police and fire will be on hand, but stressed. After a wildfire, public services will be delayed for up to several days while infrastructure is replaced or repaired and service personnel return to their jobs.

8. Aftermath

Because, in most cases, services are interrupted rather than infrastructure destroyed, the potential for aftermath is limited. Recovery takes time, but can begin relatively soon after the area is cleared for public return. There are some incidences of looting, but police are aware of this, and looters depart prior to police (and homeowners) returning.

Wildfire Safety Tips

Lots of information is available on line for wild fire safety. Most sites concentrate on how to protect your home and landscape to reduce the availability of fuel for fires. Remember that once a wild fire warning is issued the best course of action is to follow your disaster plan, collect your essentials (if you have time) and evacuate immediately.

(Shutterstock)

For tips on how to protect your home look into these and other wild fire safety websites:

FireAdapted.org
Fire adapted communities has a site FireAdapted.org which is a good site with lots of helpful information difvided by national region. The site has a "know your region, know your role" lay out which offers excellent details for making a well-informed wild fire response plan.

http://www.fireadapted.org/

BurnsafeTN.org
BurnsafeTN.org is a good site for folks in the eastern part of the US. Their "25 Tips to Make Your Home Firewise" is a good start for wild fire planning considerations.

http://burnsafetn.org/25tips_home.html Burn safe TN.Org

FEMA
FEMA is always a great source of information. This site is for fire service personnel and has in-depth resources for fire safety, planning and safety communication. This is a good place to start when you want to find details for how to communicate with your family about fire safety.

http://www.usfa.fema.gov/citizens/home_fire_prev/wildfire/

Wildfires

B. Outlooks, Watches, Warnings, & Advisories

Remember that these alerts and bulletins are designed to inform and instruct in order to cause the public to change their behavior or take specific action for their safety. Be aware of these communications.

(US Army phtoto/ SFC Jason Kriess/Released)

Weather Alerts

The National Weather Service and its pendant offices communicate alerts in the form of *outlooks, advisories, watches, and warnings* to the public. They provide real-time notification of weather events that threaten local areas.

Emergency Management Bulletins

Emergency management agencies will broadcast *emergency management bulletins* in the case of disasters or special events when officials need to communicate public safety information or special instructions to the public. In many cases both weather alerts and emergency management bulletins will be broadcast during a disaster situation.

Outlook

Indicates the potential for significant weather events up to seven days in advance with a forecaster confidence around 30%.

Watch

Indicates that conditions are favorable for the particular weather event in and near the watch area, which may pose a risk to life and property. Watches are issued up to 48 hours in advance with forecaster confidence around 50%.

Warning/Advisory

Indicates that a particular weather event is imminent or occurring. **Advisories** are issued if the weather event will lead to nuisance conditions, while **warnings** are issued for significant weather events, which will pose a risk to life and property. Warnings and advisories are issued up to 48 hours in advance with forecaster confidence of at least 80%.

Alert Notifications

Alert notifications will come in the form the following reports. This list includes reports you are most likely to hear during a wildfire, but this is not an all-inclusive list. Be careful to listen for emergency communications and take information as you can get it. Remember that official government emergency communications may be more reliable than unofficial sources. The alerts you will want to listen for are:

Red Flag Warnings

Red Flag Warnings mean there is an expectation for explosive fire growth potential. They are issued by the National Weather Service when conditions are conducive to the formation of wildfires. Dry conditions, high winds, and low humidity are the hallmarks of weather conducive to producing large wildfires.

Fire Weather Watch

A fire weather watch is issued when fire conditions are not currently occurring, but are expected to occur.

Thunderstorm Watches and Warning

Lightning generated in dry thunderstorms can ignite vegetation. Where lightning and wind are combined with dry conditions and low humidity, fire hazards are considered critical and imminent.

Emergency Management Bulletins

These are issued by local government emergency-management agencies to inform the public of the nature and area of effect of a wildfire. These bulletins will include important information on current conditions and identified hazards, probability of additional fires or fire-speed and direction shift, road closures, location of relief centers, special instructions, and other appropriate information.

High Wind Warning

This means the expected winds will average 40 miles an hour or more for at least 1 hour or wind gusts will be greater than 58 miles an hour. Trees and power lines can be blown down. A high wind warning may be preceded by a HIGH WIND WATCH if the strong winds are not expected to occur for at least 12 hours.

Air Stagnation Advisory

Issued only at the request of the Environmental Protection Agency (EPA) whenever atmospheric conditions are stable enough to cause air pollutants to accumulate in a given area.

Dense Smoke Advisory

Issued when smoke is expected to reduce visibility to 1/4 mile or less.

Emergency Management Bulletins

These are issued by local government emergency-management agencies to inform the public of the nature and area of effect of a wildfire. These bulletins will include important information on current conditions and identified hazards, wind direction and changes in the path of the wildfire, road closures, location of relief centers, special instructions, and other appropriate information.

Wildfires

Patterns of Mortality and Injury

Wildfires tend not to kill because authorities are good at public notification of wildfire threat. When it does kill, it kills quickly and early. More people are killed by smoke than by the fire, and this is the major point emergency managers try to relate to the public. Rapid evacuation as soon as you receive notification is a significant contributing factor to your safety.

Government Response

Wildfire response is generally at the state and local level. Although there is a major national effort to fight large fires and the military is often called in to assist with firefighting on national land, the fact is that firefighting is a dangerous job that takes a developed skill set and special equipment to do well. The National Forest Service is very active in prevention, both in public education as well as land management, but do not expect to see significant federal services for public needs. Local governments are capable of responding to public needs with assistance from the state- and national-level response organizations like the Red Cross. Because wildfires are quick-onset events, the federal government is not usually involved with wildfire relief during the event. Federal relief comes in the form of a declaration of disaster, which allows access to federal resources during recovery and rebuilding.

C. Personal Plans and Readiness

The key to wildfire survival success is the ability to move quickly. This requires you to know where you keep your things of value and importance. Keep your important documents and personal valuables, like jewelry and family photos, where you can get to them fast. Remember to make plans for your pets and accommodate for their needs as best as you can.

Much of your preparedness will come in the form of property condition and readiness. Everything you want to do to protect your property will need to be done before you receive word of the wildfire. This includes, but is not limited to, keeping your property clear of overgrowth, cleaning out your gutters on a regular basis, proper building (fire-resistant) materials in and on your home, sprinkler systems on your grounds and on your roof, and having a gas-powered pump to supplement the loss of power and take advantage of the remaining water service.

By having your home prepared to be resistant to fire and being ready to move quickly to evacuate, you can ensure your safety and greatly improve your ability to mitigate the negative property effects of a wildfire.

General Description

In real-world terms, a flood is when water overwhelms a place where it is usually dry: a river or lake rises out of its banks, surface water caused by a heavy rain is left standing because the soil can't absorb the water quickly enough, or a heavy rain or flash flood causes the hills to collapse into a mud slide. But in terms of disaster declaration, a flood is not an easily definable event. In a legalistic sense, the water has to meet several criteria before being considered a flood. This is important as one aspect of a disaster is that it must be recognized as being one. Water damage that is not caused by a flood is the property owner's responsibility. Waters defined as floodwater will move the government to take action.

Floods (23)							
Effects	**Least**						**Worst**
Areas of Known Occurrence	Known	1	**2**	3	4	5	Unknown
Scales and Measurement	Before	1	2	**3**	4	5	After
Quick or Slow Onset	Days	1	2	3	4	5	Minutes
Area of Effect	Local	1	**2**	3	4	5	States
Duration of Effects	Hours	1	2	**3**	4	5	Months
Destruction of Infrastructure	Minor	1	2	3	**4**	5	Total
Disruption of Services	Minor	1	2	3	4	**5**	Total
Aftermath	Minor	1	2	**3**	4	5	Disaster

Major Threat

The major threats from flood waters are threefold. First, flood waters move with deceptive speed and force. It can easily sweep people off their feet and even cars off of roads. It can also rise faster than people anticipate, separating them from routes of escape. This combines with the second threat. Flood waters hide the ground. As the flood sweeps across the landscape, it changes it dramatically: roads are undercut and collapsed, manhole covers and storm drains are swept away, and deep channels are cut where water flows quickly. All of these changes are masked by the muddy waters of the flood. Third, the water picks up everything from building debris and bits of destruction to human waste and hazardous chemicals. You should avoid contact with flood water as much as possible, although this may be very difficult if you are trapped in a flood. Wash thoroughly after contact with flood waters.

Government Information Websites:
National Oceanic and Atmospheric Administration (NOAA) — http://www.noaa.gov/
National Weather Service (NWS) — http://www.weather.gov/
Federal Emergency Management Administration (FEMA) — http://www.ready.gov/
Centers for Disease Control and Prevention (CDC) — http://www.cdc.gov/
United States Geological Survey (USGS) — http://www.usgs.gov/

Floods

Survival Strategy

Floods do not kill with water. Floods kill with complacency. The number-one reason people die in floods is that they go near or into the water. Because water gets between where people are and where they want to be, the people go near the water and then the force of the moving water takes them away. It is a very simple and deceptively dangerous situation. The best strategy is to get away from where the water is or will be soon.

The BIG EIGHT

1. Areas of Known Occurrence, Possibility:

Floods can happen in any given year. Some areas have a general cyclic rhythm for the frequency of their floods. Annual floods are a known commodity, but names like the 50- or 100-year flood speak to the potential of an area to experience a significant flood event. Many old buildings have markers where the high water mark was during floods of the past. Be aware of these past events as indicators of future potential. The United States Geological Survey has excellent maps and surveys of the water courses in the U.S. to help you assess the risk of flood in your area. Your county assessor's office or the Corps of Engineers may have more specific local information.

This map shows areas that have flooded in the recent past and gives a generalized picture of areas of flooding in the U.S., but the real picture you need is a local map of potential flood zones. Remember that if you live in an area that can be affected by hurricanes, you are in a potential flood zone.

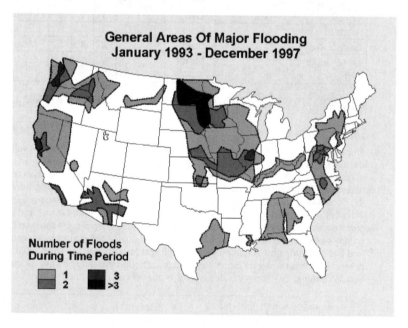

General Areas Of Major Flooding
January 1993 - December 1997

Number of Floods During Time Period

1
2
3
>3

Floods

Aspects of a Flood

(FEMA photo/ Marty Bahamonde)

To be recognized as a disaster, a flood is defined by the three major aspects of water level, duration, and frequency.

Water level

A flood is a rising and overflowing of a body of water onto normally dry land. The terms "rising" and "normally dry" are the keys to this aspect. Rising waters cause rivers and lakes to flow outside of their regular banks or shores and cover large areas with standing or flowing water. "Normally dry" areas are those areas not in a known flood plain. Even if the water floods only once every one hundred years, it is still not considered a "normally dry" place.

Duration

Flooding must be temporary. The water level must rise and then retreat to its normal level. If a river changes course without an increase in water level, it may not be considered a flood even though the damage to property is no less real.

Frequency

This aspect speaks to the idea of a flood being a surprise as expressed legally by flood plain maps. If your house is flooded every spring or even every five years to seven years, it is not really a surprise event that can be defined as a disaster, although it is undeniably a flood. It is more of a bad choice for a house location. This is a point of contention when insurance companies issue new and expanded 100-year flood plain maps and declare an area a "known flood hazard" after people have purchased the land understanding it to be a normally dry place.

2. Scales and Measurement, Predictability

Flood prediction is a well-established science. The one aspect of prediction you need to remember is that the larger the flood area, the greater the accuracy of prediction. The difficult part of flood prediction is determining how fast water will rise and how long the water will stay at flood level. This first aspect is the one you should concern yourself with. In large floods, conditions are monitored and public officials have time to issue watches and warnings, giving you time to react. In more-localized flood scenarios, the threat will develop more quickly. The warning may be of an imminent or immediate flood threat, giving you little time to react.

Floods are measured during and after a disaster event. The water level and duration are measured during the event, and property damage is measured after the event. In the case of river levels and flood stages in downstream areas, there are very good water-level and duration predictions that can give you information before the event. This ability to know what's coming is extremely useful in avoiding the hazards flood represent.

3. Quick or Slow Onset

The actual onset of flooding is not a rapid process. It takes the right conditions and time for water to gather before a flood is imminent. That said, once a flood starts, the conditions can change very quickly. Water can rise and trap people on a newly formed island in a short amount of time. Surges and rates of flow are difficult to predict and deceptively quick. The slow onset of a flood is offset by its ability to move quickly and act unpredictably.

The notable exception to this is areas prone to flash floods. The name explains the danger. Flash floods are localized, rapid-onset events and often short-duration. They are noted for the speed and power of the water.

4. Area of Effect

This is dependent on the amount of water coming into the area. Large floods can cover thousands of square miles. In 1993, several months of rain caused over six million acres of farmland and urban areas to flood across 20 states in the Midwest and Southeastern U.S. Tens of thousands of families were affected. In 2005, Hurricane Katrina dropped torrential rain for a shorter duration across five states, affecting hundreds of thousands of families.

5. Duration of Effects

Floods can last from days to months depending upon the situation specific to that flood. A short flood can last three to five days, and a long flood can last for months.

6. Destruction of Infrastructure

Floods destroy or ruin a vast majority of the infrastructure they come into contact with. Silt and mud clog, cover, or corrode everything they touch with the exceptions of steel and most types of stone. Buildings can be moved off their foundations, and interiors are ruined. Electrical systems have to be replaced, and water systems have to be unclogged, cleaned, repaired, and certified safe before they are used again. Roads are undercut and storm-water drain systems are clogged or destroyed. Bridges have to be inspected and recertified as safe for use. Power lines are brought down and must be repaired or replaced.

7. Disruption of Services

Services are denied until the water recedes to the point where there is access to the affected areas. It can also be disrupted or limited for weeks after the flood until service infrastructure can be reestablished. This includes essential services like power, fire response, police response, and emergency medical services. In addition, public services like water, sewer, and postal services are similarly limited.

8. Aftermath

Because people are forced to displace in a flood, they tend to move to places where security and rule of law are still available. Aftermath from a flood is encountered primarily in the recovery phase. After security is established and utility hazards are minimized in the flood-affected areas, people returning to their homes and businesses may encounter disease from fouled water, displaced wildlife, and the black mold that starts to grow on anything still moist and out of the sun. This last point is especially true in buildings where drywall and other building materials have soaked up water.

Electricity and water will be unavailable for several days to weeks after the flood. Infrastructure will be disrupted, if not destroyed, to the point where outside resources will be required to provide most services. Services that do arrive will be limited for several weeks and may take months to restore at the local level. Resources such as food, water, and shelter will be limited, but available from areas not directly affected by the high-water mark. Essential and public services will be stressed but available after the water recedes as state and local government do as much as possible to promote public safety and restore economic activity. Stability services such as sanitation and mail service will be suspended until the roads are reopened.

Patterns of Mortality and Injury

The initial death toll and injury count is usually small at the outset of even the largest flooding disasters. Deaths and injuries will then jump significantly as people make poor choices when encountering flood conditions and the real hazards presented by moving water and ruined infrastructure. The opposite is generally true in flash-flood situations. The quick-onset nature of a flash flood catches people by surprise, and they do not respond correctly or quickly.

In the case of either a rising flood or a flash flood, the greatest danger is from getting caught in, or going into, the water. In many cases people mistakenly believe a car will protect them from water and drive into moving water or across washed-out roads and discover too late that the water is more powerful than they believed it to be.

Government Response

Flood response is initially at the state and local level. This will include National Guard units, then there are engineering units in the state or there are significant efforts in sandbagging to protect communities and public property. The Corps of Engineers is the major federal contributor, and their efforts in levy building and flood control are all made prior to the event in an attempt to prevent or reduce flood effects. Local governments are capable of responding to public needs with assistance from the state- and national-level response organizations like the Red Cross. Federal relief comes primarily in the form of a declaration of disaster, which allows access to federal resources during recovery and rebuilding. If the governor requests federal assistance, FEMA will deploy elements and resources to help in rescue and recovery.

B. Outlooks, Watches, Warnings, & Advisories

Remember that these alerts and bulletins are designed to inform and instruct in order to cause the public to change their behavior or take specific action for their safety. Be aware of these communications.

Weather Alerts: The National Weather Service and its pendant offices communicate alerts in the form of *outlooks, advisories, watches, and warnings* to the public. They provide real-time notification of weather events that threaten local areas.

Emergency Management Bulletins: Emergency-management agencies will broadcast *emergency management bulletins* in the case of disasters or special events when officials need to communicate public-safety information or special instructions to the public. In many cases, both weather alerts and emergency management bulletins will be broadcast during a disaster situation.

Outlook: Indicates the potential for significant weather events up to seven days in advance with a forecaster confidence around 30%.

Watch: Indicates that conditions are favorable for the particular weather event in and near the watch area, which may pose a risk to life and property. Watches are issued up to 48 hours in advance with forecaster confidence around 50%.

Warning/Advisory: Indicates that a particular weather event is imminent or occurring. **Advisories** are issued if the weather event will lead to nuisance conditions, while **warnings** are issued for significant weather events that will pose a risk to life and property. Warnings and advisories are issued up to 48 hours in advance with forecaster confidence of at least 80%.

Alert Notifications

Alert notifications will come in the form of the following reports. This list includes reports you are most likely to hear during a flood, but this is not an all-inclusive list. Be careful to listen for emergency communications and take information as you can get it. Remember that official government emergency communications may be more reliable than unofficial sources. *Flood alerts* are issued when high flow, overflow, or inundation by water may cause damage.

Flash Flood Warning

Issued when flash flooding (short-term stream flooding in hilly terrain, in urban areas with rapid water runoff, or from potential dam breaks that follow within a few hours, usually fewer than six, of heavy or excessive rainfall, dam or levee failure, or the sudden release of water impounded by an ice jam) actually is occurring or is imminent in the warning area.

Flash Flood Watch

Indicates that flash flooding (short-term stream flooding in hilly terrain, in urban areas with rapid water runoff, or from potential dam breaks that follow within a few hours, usually fewer than six, of heavy or excessive rainfall, dam or levee failure, or the sudden release of water impounded by an ice jam) may become possible in or close to the watch area.

Flood Warning

Issued when flooding (inundation of normally dry areas caused by increased water levels in a river, stream, or drainage ditch or from ponding of water at or near the point where rain fell) is actually occurring or is imminent in the warning area. A flood warning will often contain river-stage (level) forecasts.

Flood Watch

Indicates that flooding (inundation of normally dry areas caused by increased water levels in a river, stream, or drainage ditch or from ponding of water at or near the point where rain fell) may become possible in or close to the watch area.

River Flood Warning

Issued for designated points (those that have formal gauging sites and established flood stages) along rivers where significant flooding is imminent or is in progress. This warning often specifies crest information, which usually occurs six hours or later after the triggering event. This type of flooding event usually is associated with widespread heavy rain or snow melt or ice jams.

River Flood Watch

Issued for designated points (those that have formal gauging sites and established flood stages) along rivers where significant flooding may become possible.

River Flood Advisory

Issued for designated points (those that have formal gauging sites and established flood stages) along rivers where minor flooding is possible.

Coastal Flood Warning

Alerts residents along the Atlantic, Pacific, and Gulf Coasts that coastal flooding is either imminent or occurring, exceeding normal high-tide levels. This flooding may impact the immediate oceanfront, gulfs, bays, back bays, sounds, and tidal portions of river mouths and inland tidal waterways.

Coastal Flood Watch

Alerts residents along the Atlantic, Pacific, and Gulf Coasts that significant coastal flooding may become possible, exceeding normal high-tide levels.

Coastal Flood Advisory

Alerts residents along the Atlantic, Pacific, and Gulf Coasts that minor flooding is possible, exceeding normal high-tide levels.

Coastal Flood Statement

Issued to provide general information pertinent to coastal flood events.

Lakeshore Flood Warning

Alerts residents along one of the Great Lakes that flooding is either imminent or occurring, exceeding normal lake levels. This flooding may impact the immediate lakefront, bays, and the other connecting waterways, such as rivers.

Lakeshore Flood Watch

Alerts residents along one of the Great Lakes that significant flooding may become possible, exceeding normal lake levels.

Lakeshore Flood Advisory

Alerts residents along one of the Great Lakes that minor flooding is possible, exceeding normal lake levels.

Lakeshore Flood Statement

Issued to provide general information pertinent to lakeshore flood events.

Hydrologic Statement

Issued after either a flood watch or a flood warning has been issued and provides the latest information on the flooding situation or event.

Emergency Management Bulletins

These are issued by local government emergency management agencies to inform the public of the nature and area of effect of flood conditions. These bulletins will include important information on current conditions and identified hazards, probability, and speed of water rise, road closures, location of relief centers, special instructions, and other appropriate information.

Floods

C. Personal Plans and Readiness

First and foremost in flood preparedness is to know about where you live. Many people are surprised and angered to learn that they live in a flood plain only after they are flood survivors. As a general rule it is wise not to live within the boundaries of a flood plain, especially in areas that are below the water level of surrounding oceans, lakes, and waterways. Distance from water is no guarantee of safety, and you should take the time to learn about the topography of where you live. Even if you are on higher ground, ensure you will not be on an island during a major flood so you can move away from the flood if required.

This brings us to our second major focus for flood readiness: the ability to move. As with other disasters, the best defense is to not be there when they arrive.

Even though sustainment and communication are still important during a flood, you should consider some extra emphasis on movement preparation. This requires you to know where you keep your things of value and importance. Keep your important documents and personal valuables, like jewelry and family photos, where you can get to them fast. Remember to make plans for your pets and accommodate for their needs as best as you can.

If you find that you live in a flood zone and are not willing or able to move, then have the following plan ready for action.

- **Get to a strong high point.** This may not be your own roof. A good option is a multi-level parking garage. They are multi-leveled to get you above the water level, strong enough to withstand flood waters, covered to provide some shelter, have a flat roof for helicopters to land on, and ramps for boats to float up to. You can secure your belongings and survival items in your car.

- **Mark your location well.** Keep a large (5X5 foot) marker panel of a bright color (red or orange) that you can use to mark your location. Even a durable canvas will not be too heavy to carry and will fold up small enough to travel well. Have a signal mirror, strobe flashlight, and a whistle ready to signal to search and rescue personnel in day or night conditions. Remember that sound, light, and motion will attract attention.

- **Be prepared to sustain yourself and your family for no less than three days.** This FEMA standard is good advice and should be taken seriously.

(Natural Disasters)
E. Volcanoes

General Description

A volcano is an opening in the earth's crust through which molten lava, ash, and gases are ejected. There are three general types of volcanoes, and the one near you will have its own characteristics. If you live near a volcano, take the time to learn about its "personality."

Composite Volcano (25)							
Effects	**Least**						**Worst**
Areas of Known Occurrence	Known	**1**	2	3	4	5	Unknown
Scales of Measurement	Before	1	2	3	**4**	5	After
Quick or Slow Onset	Days	1	2	3	4	**5**	Minutes
Area of Effect	Local	1	**2**	3	4	5	States
Duration of Effects	Hours	1	**2**	3	4	5	Months
Destruction of Infrastructure	Minor	1	2	3	4	**5**	Total
Disruption of Services	Minor	1	2	3	4	**5**	Total
Aftermath	Minor	**1**	2	3	4	5	Disaster

Major Threat

The effects are rapid, powerful, and hard to avoid if you are anywhere near the event. The power of the pressure and heat released from a volcano is so great it transforms the earth: solids act like liquids, gases act like solids, and everything in its path is destroyed.

The devastation is so great that nothing remains in the path of its destruction. There is little to no aftermath in the immediate area of the eruption because there are few living things left in the primary area of effect.

Survival Strategy

Composite cone volcanoes are a gamble. You can live in the shadow of one of these potential disasters and never be in mortal danger... unless it erupts violently in your lifetime, as in the case of Mount St. Helen, Vesuvius, or Krakatoa. But they rarely erupt without some demonstration prior to the major event, and then those eruptions are rare. When the mountain rumbles, be prepared to take everything you feel that you must take and understand what you leave behind will most likely be destroyed.

> **Government Information Websites:**
>
> National Oceanic and Atmospheric Administration (NOAA) — http://www.noaa.gov/
>
> National Weather Service (NWS) — http://www.weather.gov/
>
> Federal Emergency Management Administration (FEMA) — http://www.ready.gov/
>
> Centers for Disease Control and Prevention (CDC) — http://www.cdc.gov/

The BIG EIGHT

1. Areas of Known Occurrence, Possibility

The probability of a volcanic event at an active or dormant volcano is absolutely inevitable. Not a matter of if, but when. The probability of a volcano erupting in a significant manner during your lifetime is dependent on the grand scale of time. A volcano "lives" for thousands of years, and you live for less than one hundred. Predictability is a better indicator.

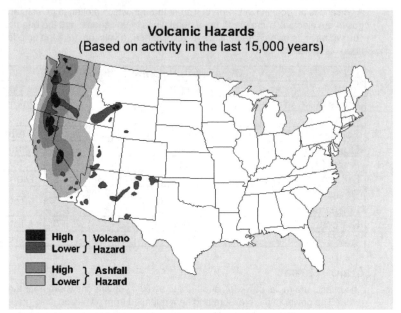

Volcanic Hazards
(Based on activity in the last 15,000 years)

High ⎫ Volcano
Lower ⎭ Hazard

High ⎫ Ashfall
Lower ⎭ Hazard

2. Scales of Measurement, Predictability

The United States Geological Survey (USGS) monitors all volcanic activity in the U.S. very closely and has proven to be adept at giving advanced warning regarding impending eruptions. The effects of a volcano are measured after the fact in earthquakes, fires, landslides, and other forms of destruction. In most cases, this would make the events less predictable. With volcanoes, this is not the case. The level of monitoring conducted in warning and study of volcanoes make their condition very well known. This is particularly true within the United States, where the USGS is very vigilant. The trick is in listening for and heeding their warnings.

There are two main volcano warning systems — color codes and alert levels. Warning systems are specific for each volcano. It is impossible to predict the date of an eruption, but few eruptions occur without some warning signs. Volcano warning systems are based on a probability of an eruption or hazard.

3. Quick or Slow Onset

In the case of a composite volcano, when it does happen, it will happen fast. The speed of pyroclastic flows, superheated gases, and mudslides will overtake everyone in the area of effect. In the case of a shield volcano, there may be a less violent primary eruption, but the threat of lava flows, superheated gases, and mudslides are just as prevalent.

Types of Volcanoes

The three types of volcanoes are shield, composite cone, and cinder cone.

Shield Cone Volcanoes

Shield cone volcanoes form over a series of eruptions. Looking like a long low shield, they can be many miles across and so large they are unrecognizable as volcanoes. They tend to have low viscosity and low gas content. Because they have a low dome, they release pressure and tend to have mild eruptions. The two examples of this type of volcano are Mona Loa in Hawaii and the Yellow Stone caldera on the border of Wyoming and Idaho.

Composite Cone Volcanoes

Composite cone volcanoes are the classic volcano shape, being proportionally taller than and not as wide as shield cones. They form over a large primary fault or fissure that feeds magma from the mantle (the molten rock under the surface) into the earth's crust, forming a chamber that builds pressure over time. The magma is viscous (flowing) and has a high gas content, which means more pressure. They tend to have fewer but more-violent eruptions.

Cinder Cone Volcanoes

Cinder cone volcanoes are much smaller versions of a composite cone that have equally proportional effects. They tend to push debris out of the cone rather than have major eruptions. This is in contrast to the volcanoes of Hawaii, which erupt and release pressure on a regular basis.

Forms of Volcano Destruction

This destruction comes in the form of lahars, tephra, pyroclastic flows, and lava flows.

Lahars

Lahars are debris flows made up of surface materials like snow, earth, wood, and stone. Hot acid water weakens the stone on the walls of the volcanic cone, and when it releases, it sends water-rich flows of stone, wood, and earth for many tens of miles. Lahars move quickly and completely destroy everything in their path.

Tephra

Tephra is the column of hot gases, ash, and coarse debris blown into the air by an eruption. It can throw large rocks for miles, and the ash can travel for hundreds of miles. The ash cloud can reach areas far away from the eruption. This causes disruptions in air travel, air quality, water quality, and other aspects of living, which can make survival difficult. Heavy ash falls and "snows" back down to the earth, making it hard to breathe and clogging machinery. At the sight of the eruption, this cloud rises thousands of feet into the air and at a certain point becomes too heavy to support itself. Then a majority of the cloud falls back down to earth as a giant cloud of incredibly hot acidic gas and ash. This is called pyroclastic flow.

Pyroclastic Flows

Pyroclastic flows are huge clouds of heavier-than-air hot gases and burning ash that can travel at more than 100 miles per hour (faster than you can drive away from it) and can extend for up to 20 miles. They incinerate and crush everything in their path.

Lava Flows

Lava flows are made up of molten rock from the earth's mantle. The pressure of the volcano pushes the magma of the mantle to the surface. Once on the surface, magma is called lava. The lava from the composite cones of the Northwest and Alaska is think and viscous. The lava from the shield volcanoes in Hawaii is thinner and flows more quickly. Either way, it consumes anything it comes into contact with.

4. Area of Effect

This will be affected by several factors. Earthquakes will be widespread. Lava flows, pyroclastic flows, superheated gases, and mudslides can be channeled by geographic features and wind direction. But there are no boundaries in events of this magnitude. Even in places where man has learned to live near volcanoes, the volcano is still in charge. On the big island of Hawaii, Mount Kilauea destroys and creates at will regardless of human habitation.

5. Duration of Effects

For the event itself, an eruption can last from days to weeks; the longer the eruption, the greater the immediate and cumulative effects. In most cases duration of effects are more in line with years to rebuild. In areas not directly affected by event devastation, the ecological effects on agriculture and wildlife can take years for recovery.

6. Destruction of Infrastructure

Anything in the path of volcanic effects is completely destroyed. Ashfall can bring down power and communication lines; collapse roofs; and seriously clog waterworks, roads, and any engine with an air intake. This last threat includes aircraft at altitude.

7. Disruption of Services

Outside of the direct effects of destruction, ashfall can disrupt electrical and water service, clog roads to the point that police and fire cannot respond effectively, limit transportation of private citizens and commerce, and limit medical services to immediate care.

8. Aftermath

Aftermath of volcanic eruption includes wildfires and aftershocks. A larger affected population will result in greater effects of aftermath. If you're in Portland, Oregon, looking at Mt. Hood, then take heed. This links directly to the ideas of limited resources and requirements for services being greater than the capacity to meet need. Resources from surrounding areas will establish security and rule of law quickly, but food and medical availability could grow into a secondary disaster scenario depending on limitations on transportation.

Power outages will last for weeks to possibly months. Most of the area will be uninhabitable for weeks or months. Infrastructure will be annihilated to the point where outside resources will be required to rescue and relocate survivors. Whole communities will cease to exist and may not return. Resources such as food, water, and shelter will be limited until it is brought in. No government services, essential or otherwise, will be available in the areas of immediate effect. Security will be lost for a limited period of time in some areas until restored with the assistance of neighboring jurisdictions, state police/state highway patrol, the National Guard, or activated federal military forces. Rule of law will be provided by neighboring jurisdictions.

Patterns of Mortality and Injury

In the initial event, the mortality rate will be high with the survivors likely to suffer some form of injury. During rescue and recovery, injuries and infection will be the primary threat. Long-term effects may include medical factors related to exposure to toxic or hot earth gases.

Government Response

As with earthquakes, help will come as rapidly as possible with thousands of responders and huge amounts of relief supplies by ground, rail, sea, and air. This

B. Outlooks, Watches, Warnings, & Advisories

Remember that these alerts and bulletins are designed to inform and instruct in order to cause the public to change their behavior or take specific action for their safety. Be aware of these communications. Because volcano eruptions can cause their own weather effects, you should be aware of weather changes during an eruption.

Weather Alerts
The National Weather Service and its pendant offices communicate alerts in the form of *outlooks, advisories, watches, and warnings* to the public. They provide real-time notification of weather events that threaten local areas.

Emergency Management Bulletins
Emergency-management agencies will broadcast *emergency management bulletins* in the case of disasters or special events when officials need to communicate public-safety information or special instructions to the public. In many cases, both weather alerts and emergency management bulletins will be broadcast during a disaster situation.

Outlook
Indicates the potential for significant weather events up to seven days in advance with a forecaster confidence around 30%.

Watch
Indicates that conditions are favorable for the particular weather event in and near the watch area, which may pose a risk to life and property. Watches are issued up to 48 hours in advance with forecaster confidence around 50%.

Warning/Advisory
Indicates that a particular weather event is imminent or occurring. **Advisories** are issued if the weather event will lead to nuisance conditions, while **warnings** are issued for significant weather events that will pose a risk to life and property. Warnings and advisories are issued up to 48 hours in advance with forecaster confidence of at least 80%.

Alert Notifications

Alert notifications will come in the form of the following reports. This list includes reports you are most likely to hear during a volcanic eruption, but this is not an all-inclusive list. Be careful to listen for emergency communications and take information as you can get it. Remember that official government emergency communications may be more reliable than unofficial sources. The alerts you will want to listen for are:

Emergency Management Bulletins
These are issued by local government emergency management agencies. They will be specific to the volcano and will include information about the type of eruption, related hazards, areas of effect, communication, road closures, and other relevant information.

will be a full-spectrum response from all government levels that are still capable of providing any services. The less-predictable nature of volcanic eruption makes them difficult to specifically prepare for in terms of gathered supplies and ready-standing response personnel unless there are significant indicators prior to the event. When there is warning, then the government will expect, or even compel, the population to follow evacuation orders. This is not draconian suspension of liberty; it's just much easier (and less expensive and risky) to make you leave before the eruption rather than to have to rescue you after the eruption. For details on evacuation plans for your area, contact your local city or county emergency management office, who will have the response plans.

Primary efforts may include the federal response of FEMA, the active-duty military, and national relief non-governmental organizations like the Red Cross. The state effort will consist of state-level and National Guard elements. This will include responding communities from outside the area of effect as well as assistance from neighboring states based upon mutual-support agreements called Emergency Mutual Aid Compacts (EMAC). These are agreements rather than contracts allowing nearby states to provide as much as they can. It is a good system. Local response will be limited and delayed due to the damage from the earthquake, but will establish jurisdictional control as soon as they are able. State and federal resources will be provided to local government to assist them. Private industry will also arrive as soon as the area is opened to public access, most notably to bring utilities back online, but also to reopen businesses. All of this will include elements to provide the immediately essential services of rescue, medical, security (police and fire), transportation, sustainment (food, water, & shelter), and communication.

After rescue is complete and security is well established, the priorities will be for electricity, water, U.S. postal services, and other services that are all vital to recovery and stability. Rule of law will be returned to local authority as soon as possible. This will be dependent on the infrastructure of police stations, legal offices, courtrooms, and jails.

Dependent on the severity of the eruption and the geographic area of effects, it may take several days for ground rescue to arrive. This may seem like a long time, but remember they have to travel to you and find you. This is different than in the case of hurricanes and earthquakes, where you will be competing with others for rescue. In the case of volcanoes, the challenge is to get into affected areas and find people buried or covered in ash. Once roads are reopened, the situation will improve rapidly.

C. Personal Plans and Readiness

While the government response is like an earthquake or hurricane, your plans should be more like those for a wildfire. The key to volcanic eruption–survival success is the ability to move quickly before the event takes place. This requires you to know where you keep your things of value and importance. Keep your important documents and personal valuables, like jewelry and family photos, where you can get to them fast. Remember to make plans for your pets and accommodate for their needs as best as you can. Once the word comes to evacuate, you will want to move quickly to avoid congested evacuation routes.

When making your movement plans, think about long-term needs and goals. You may not be able to return to living in your home soon. Plans should include more than just food and water: also important personal documents and any real property you feel you must protect. You may want to consider clearing your safety deposit box as well as volcanoes have the potential to bury large things deeply. Having a plan to transfer monitory assets to a financial institution outside of the area of effect may be a fast and easy way to protect your bank accounts. Consider making modifications and preparing your home for wildfires.

(Natural Disasters)
F. Tsunamis

General Description

A tsunami is one (or more often a series) of highly destructive ocean waves caused by undersea land movements, generally the result of undersea earthquakes, volcanic eruptions, or landslides. When these events take place, the seismic energy transfers to the surrounding water and moves across the ocean.

Effects	Least	1	2	3	4	5	Worst
Tsunami (27)							
Areas of Known Occurrence	Known	**1**	2	3	4	5	Unknown
Scales and Measurement	Before	1	2	3	4	**5**	After
Quick or Slow Onset	Days	1	2	3	4	**5**	Minutes
Area of Effect	Local	1	2	**3**	4	5	States
Duration of Effects	Hours	1	**2**	3	4	5	Months
Destruction of Infrastructure	Minor	1	2	3	**4**	5	Total
Disruption of Services	Minor	1	2	**3**	4	5	Total
Aftermath	Minor	1	2	3	**4**	5	Disaster

Major Threat

Tsunamis offer two major threats: a one-two punch of speed and power. Not only will they catch you and drown you, but they will rip apart everything in their path and make a churning, grinding blender of water mixed with everything it encounters. If you get caught in the water, chances are good you will not come out.

Survival Strategy

Tsunamis kill with water. Avoid the water completely! The force of the water is so great it will grab you and sweep you away even if you have only a part of your body in water. The water will also be filled with solids, the jagged remains of everything the wave has destroyed. This material is moving at speed and with incredible force. Get high up as fast as you can. It will need to be in a building that can withstand huge amounts of force. This means no wooden structures if you can avoid it. Concrete and steel are your best options. The height you will need is at least a three-story building, but the fourth floor or higher is better.

The water will move in, slow as it finds it's crest (or highest point of flooding), and then move back out. Do not get into the water, even in a boat, until after the water has swept back out to sea. Your best option is to wait until the water has completely receded.

Government Information Websites:

National Oceanic and Atmospheric Administration (NOAA) — http://www.noaa.gov/
National Weather Service (NWS) — http://www.weather.gov/
Federal Emergency Management Administration (FEMA) — http://www.ready.gov/
Centers for Disease Control and Prevention (CDC) — http://www.cdc.gov/

The BIG EIGHT

1. Areas of Known Occurrence, Possibility

Tsunamis can occur along any ocean coastline around the world. They are most frequent in areas of greater seismic activity. 80% of all tsunamis occur within the Pacific Rim. Tsunamis are always possible and in fact happen every day. The issue is the scale of the event.

2. Scales of Measurement, Predictability

There are undersea warning systems that identify tsunamis based on both the original seismic event and the generation of the wave at sea. The limitation on predictability is the short amount of time available to communicate that threat to the public. Even the best tsunami warning systems in the world can sometimes offer only minutes between the warning and the wave impact.

Tsunami damage is measured after the fact in loss of life and property damage. There is no accurate way to determine the size a tsunami will grow to until it reaches landfall. Advanced-warning systems can tell if they are big and fast, but that is about as specific as it can get until the wave makes landfall.

3. Quick or Slow Onset

Very quick onset. This is where awareness comes into play. A large tsunami will often first appear as a sharp swell, like a storm swell without the storm. This will be followed by a rapid outrush of water, which will expose the sea floor far below the regular low tide mark. When this happens, you will have only minutes until the first major wave strikes the beach. Do not stop to collect your things: no documents, possessions, clothing, or food. Just take hold of the hands of the people you love, do not let them go, and run for your life.

4. Area of Effect

Tsunamis can affect hundreds of miles of shoreline and penetrate miles inland, especially in low-lying areas and up rivers and streams.

5. Duration of Effects

It can take several days for the water to recede. Currents coming in and going out can be very strong. The water will also carry everything it has destroyed so the duration will include more than just the water level. Destruction and disease will be part of the duration of a tsunami.

6. Destruction of Infrastructure

As with any flooding scenario, the destruction is complete. This will include roads, bridges, buildings, power lines and poles, water distribution infrastructure, and anything else built by the hand of man. Any building left standing will be filled with mud and the bits of everything that was not left standing.

7. Disruption of Services

There will be little chance of any services in the affected areas. All assistance will have to come into the area from outside sources until recovery is well under way.

How Tsunamis Work

A tsunami is one (or more often a series) of highly destructive ocean waves caused by undersea land movements, generally the result of undersea earthquakes, volcanic eruptions, or landslides. When these events take place, the seismic energy transfers to the surrounding water and moves across the ocean.

They develop rapidly as a result of undersea earthquakes and arrive with little warning. Just as you must go underground to avoid a tornado, you must go up to avoid a tsunami. This is another case of awareness being the primary factor. The method, or building, you use to get above the water need only be sturdy enough to take the force of the water coming in and going back out. Tsunamis can affect large areas and may develop into significant aftermath until rescue and resources can arrive. The rescue effort for a tsunami is always a major undertaking as this disaster takes a heavy toll on infrastructure. If you survive a tsunami, be prepared to move as quickly as possible out of the affected area. This will be difficult and you will need all of your skills to move, sustain, and communicate to get to security and sustainment resources.

In open water this is not an issue because even large displacements have room to move or dissipate their energy. A series of tsunami waves may be several hundred miles long, be less than three feet high, and can travel at speeds up to 500 miles per hour. If you were on a ship, you would not even notice them. Even a series of waves would pass almost unnoticed as the tsunamis would pass at intervals of as little as five minutes or as long as an hour, depending on the nature of the original undersea event.

The trouble comes when the tsunamis reach the shoreline. The energy from the wave compresses, building height, and slows, stacking each wave one behind the other until it makes one very high and very deep wave with lots of power and no place to go but onto the land. This means the wave crest may be as high as 100 feet, but also the trough may be a half-mile deep. The force of the wave pushes onto the shore and releases that energy onto whatever it encounters: trees, buildings, cars, people, even the shape of the land. One aspect of the wave dynamic is that the more shallow the slope of the offshore topography, the greater the amount of energy transferred to that composite wave, what the Japanese called the "harbor wave" or tsunami. This is just like the difference of a wave hitting a rock and splashing up into the air and a wave that slides far up the gentle slope of a sandy beach. The same amount of energy is released, but the dynamic of the wave is different.

8. Aftermath

The death rate will be high, and the environmental threats will be great. Power outages will last for weeks to possibly months. Most of the area will be uninhabitable for weeks or months. Infrastructure will be annihilated to the point where outside resources will be required to rescue and relocate survivors. Whole communities will cease to exist and will not return. Resources such as food, water, and shelter will not be available until it is brought in. No government services, essential or otherwise, will be available. Security will be lost for a limited period of time in some areas until restored with the assistance of the National Guard or activated federal military forces, and rule of law will not be readily available. Those not killed by the initial tsunami or drowned in the remaining flood will face hunger, exposure to lawlessness, infection from injuries, and exposure to diseases.

Patterns of Mortality and Injury

In the initial wave landfall, the mortality rate will be high for anyone who is caught in the water. Even the survivors are likely to suffer some form of injury. During rescue and recovery, injuries and infection will be the primary threat. Long-term effects may include medical factors related to exposure to toxic chemicals or disease that mix into the water during the initial destruction. The best way to survive a tsunami, both before and after, is to stay out of the water.

Government Response

Help will come as rapidly as possible with thousands of responders and huge amounts of relief supplies by ground, rail, sea, and air. This will be a full-spectrum response from all government levels that are still capable of providing any services. The unpredictable nature of tsunamis will limit the initial government response to preposition supplies and currently available personnel for the initial response to the disaster. For details on the plans for your area, contact your local city or county emergency-management office, who will have the response plans.

Primary efforts will include the federal response of FEMA, national relief non-governmental organizations like the Red Cross, and if requested, the active-duty military. The state effort will consist of state-level and National Guard elements. This will include responding communities from outside the area of effect as well as assistance from neighboring states based upon mutual-support agreements called Emergency Mutual Aid Compacts (EMAC). These are agreements rather than contracts, allowing nearby states to provide as much as they can. It is a good system. Local response capabilities will be eliminated due to the damage of the tsunami, but will reestablish jurisdictional control as soon as they are able. State and federal resources will be provided to local government to assist them. Private industry will also arrive as soon as the area is opened to public access, most notably to bring utilities back online, but also to reopen businesses. All of this will include elements to provide the immediately essential services of rescue, medical, security (police and fire), transportation, sustainment (food, water, & shelter), and communication.

After rescue is complete and security is well established, the priorities will be for debris removal, electricity, water, U.S. postal services and other services that are all vital to recovery and stability. Rule of law provided by state agencies and nearby communities will be returned to local authority as soon as possible. This will be dependent on how quickly temporary infrastructure for police stations, legal offices, courtrooms, and jails can be established.

Dependent on the severity of the tsunami and the geographic area of effect, it may take several days for rescue to arrive. This may seem like a long time, but remember they have to travel to you and find you. The better you can mark your location, the quicker you will be rescued.

B. Outlooks, Watches, Warnings, & Advisories

Remember that these alerts and bulletins are designed to inform and instruct in order to cause the public to change their behavior or take specific action for their safety. Be aware of these communications.

Weather Alerts

The National Weather Service and its pendant offices communicate alerts in the form of *outlooks, advisories, watches, and warnings* to the public. They provide real-time notification of weather events that threaten local areas.

Emergency Management Bulletins

Emergency-management agencies will broadcast *emergency management bulletins* in the case of disasters or special events when officials need to communicate public-safety information or special instructions to the public. In many cases, both weather alerts and emergency management bulletins will be broadcast during a disaster situation.

Outlook

Indicates the potential for significant weather events up to seven days in advance with a forecaster confidence around 30%.

Watch

Indicates that conditions are favorable for the particular weather event in and near the watch area, and which may pose a risk to life and property. Watches are issued up to 48 hours in advance with forecaster confidence around 50%.

Warning/Advisory

Indicates that a particular weather event is imminent or occurring. **Advisories** are issued if the weather event will lead to nuisance conditions, while **warnings** are issued for significant weather events that will pose a risk to life and property. Warnings and advisories are issued up to 48 hours in advance with forecaster confidence of at least 80%.

Alert Notifications

Alert notifications will come in the form of the following reports. This list includes reports you are most likely to hear in the event of a tsunami, but this is not an all-inclusive list. Be careful to listen for emergency communications and take information as you can get it. Remember that official government emergency communications may be more reliable than unofficial sources. The alerts you will want to listen for are:

Tsunami Bulletin

Indicates that a tsunami (an ocean wave that may reach enormous dimensions, produced by a submarine earthquake, landslide, or volcanic eruption) is possible or imminent.

Emergency Management Bulletins

These are issued by local government emergency management agencies to inform the public of the size and area of effect of a tsunami. These bulletins will include important information on current conditions and identified hazards, probability of additional seismic events, road closures, location of relief centers, special instructions, and other appropriate information.

C. Personal Plans and Readiness

Preplanning for a tsunami is mostly about location. If you want to stay near the beach, then build strong and high. If you live in a tsunami zone, you may want to consider up to three identical survival bags: one in your home, one in your car, and one in your place of work. With only minutes to respond, you will need to have a bag immediately at hand for it to be of any use to you. Remember that your tsunami response plan is simple: find a strong building and go above the third floor as fast as you can. The bag should be equally simple and prioritized.

Priority One: Communication Items
- A whistle, a mirror, a piece of bright-colored cloth, a flashlight, and a self-powered radio.

Priority Two: Sustainment
- A couple bottles of water and some shelf-stable food (like granola bars).
- A little first-aid kit.

This is roughly the same stuff you would put into your towel bag when you go on vacation at the beach. It can be that simple. The major difference is you have a plan of action in mind should you need it. Grab the kids, grab the bag, look for the strongest building close to you, and move in a calm and purposeful manner to a place of safety.

Once you find a safe place, stay put until you're rescued. Use the resources available to you to mark your location so rescuers can find you. The last option you want to take is to go out into the destruction of the tsunami and expose yourself to the hazards and threats of aftermath.

If you are overseas on business or pleasure, once you are rescued, if you find that you need help, make contact with or make your way as quickly and safely as possible to the nearest embassy or consulate of your nation (not in the areas of destruction). They will most likely be willing to assist you in returning to your home nation. Be aware that your government may be looking for its citizens during the rescue process, and listen for announcements from your nation.

(Natural Disasters)
G. Tornadoes

General Description

The Federal Emergency Management Agency (FEMA) provides the following description of a tornado: "Tornadoes are nature's most violent storms. Spawned from powerful thunderstorms, tornadoes can cause fatalities and devastate a neighborhood in seconds. A tornado appears as a rotating, funnel shaped cloud that extends from a thunderstorm to the ground with whirling winds that can reach 300 miles per hour. Damage paths can be in excess of one mile wide and 50 miles long. Every state is at some risk from this hazard."

Tornado (21)							
Effects	**Least**						**Worst**
Areas of Known Occurrence	Known	1	2	**3**	4	5	Unknown
Scales of Measurement	Before	1	2	3	4	**5**	After
Quick or Slow Onset	Days	1	2	3	**4**	5	Minutes
Area of Effect:	Local	**1**	2	3	4	5	States
Duration of Effects	Hours	**1**	2	3	4	5	Months
Destruction of Infrastructure	Minor	1	2	**3**	4	5	Total
Disruption of Services	Minor	1	2	**3**	4	5	Total
Aftermath	Minor	**1**	2	3	4	5	Disaster

Tornadoes come from the energy released in a thunderstorm. As powerful as they are, tornadoes account for only a tiny fraction of the energy in a thunderstorm. What makes them dangerous is that their energy is concentrated in a small area, perhaps only a hundred yards across.he following are facts about tornadoes:

- They may strike quickly, with little or no warning. (Meteorologists with access to weather radar is getting very good at finding cloud rotation and debris signature.)
- They may appear nearly transparent until dust and debris are picked up or a cloud forms in the funnel.
- The average tornado moves southwest to northeast, but tornados have been known to move in any direction.
- The average forward speed of a tornado is 30 MPH, but may vary from stationary to 70 MPH.
- Waterspouts are tornadoes that form over water.
- Tornadoes are most likely to occur between 3 p.m. and 9 p.m., but can occur at any time.

Government Information Websites:

National Oceanic and Atmospheric Administration (NOAA) — http://www.noaa.gov/
National Weather Service (NWS) — http://www.weather.gov/
Federal Emergency Management Administration (FEMA) — http://www.ready.gov/
Centers for Disease Control and Prevention (CDC) — http://www.cdc.gov/

Major Threat

Wind damage and injuries resulting from flying debris constitute the greatest threat. These storms generate quickly and dissipate just as fast. If they don't kill you outright during the main event, then your chances of survival go up considerably.

Survival Strategy

Tornadoes kill with wind damage. They are quick and deadly, but they require specific conditions in order to form. Being aware of the weather and modifying your behavior accordingly during times when tornado conditions are present, you can improve your chances to escape their effects. By moving to appropriate shelter in a timely manner, even the most severe tornado is survivable. One aspect of tornadoes is that the storms are very centralized and follow a linear path. Even when they destroy whole cities, as in the case of Greensburg, Kansas, or Joplin, Missouri, the nearby towns and cities, often within just a few miles, are able to respond with no limitations. Although tornadoes have lasting effects, they very rarely create conditions that result in separate aftermath issues.

The BIG EIGHT

1. Areas of Known Occurrence, Possibility

These events are expected to happen over a thousand times a year within the lower 48 United States. Annually, they are a virtual certainty. These are common storms that are expected to develop in known areas. They most commonly occur in the spring and fall, but are not unknown during other times of the year. In the United States, they occur almost exclusively east of the Rocky Mountains. They are very common in the central plains states from Texas to Nebraska, which is known as "Tornado Alley," but are also frequent in Iowa, the interior of the Southern Gulf States, Arkansas, south central Illinois, Western Pennsylvania, and along the Eastern Seaboard in the Southern New York region.

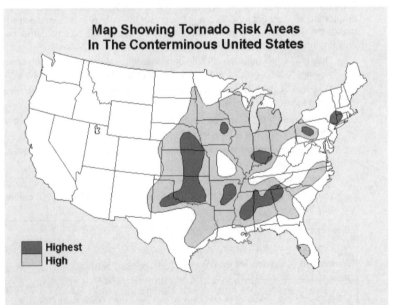

Map Showing Tornado Risk Areas In The Conterminous United States

Highest
High

The Fujita-Pearson Scale

Tornadoes are measured after the fact, which is an indicator of the difficulty in predicting specific events. That said, thunderstorms (which produce tornadoes) are measured in real time, and conditions favorable for tornadoes can be identified as they develop.

The Fujita Scale is used to rate the intensity of a tornado by examining the damage caused by the tornado after it has passed over a man-made structure.

Weak Tornadoes

F0 and F1 — 74% of all tornadoes and 4% of tornado deaths.

F0, Gale Tornado (wind speeds 40–72 mph)
Type of Damage Done: Some damage to chimneys; breaks branches off trees; pushes over shallow-rooted trees; damages signboards.

F1, Moderate Tornado (wind speeds 73–112 mph)
Type of Damage Done: The lower limit is the beginning of hurricane-wind speed; peels surface off roofs; mobile homes pushed off foundations or overturned; moving autos pushed off the roads; attached garages may be destroyed.

Strong Tornadoes

F2 and F3 — 25% of all tornadoes and 29% of tornado deaths.

F2, Significant Tornado (wind speeds 113–157 mph)
Type of Damage Done: Considerable damage. Roofs torn off frame houses; mobile homes demolished; boxcars pushed over; large trees snapped or uprooted; light-object missiles generated.

F3, Severe Tornado (wind speeds 158–206 mph)
Type of Damage Done: Roof and some walls torn off well-constructed houses; trains overturned; most trees in forces uprooted

Violent Tornadoes

F4 and F5 — only 1% of all tornadoes, but 67% of tornado deaths.

F4, Devastating Tornado (wind speeds 207–260 mph)
Type of Damage Done: Well-constructed houses leveled; structures with weak foundations blown off some distance; cars thrown and large missiles generated.

F5, Incredible Tornado (wind speeds 261–318 mph)
Type of Damage Done: Strong-frame houses lifted off foundations and carried considerable distances to disintegrate; automobile-sized missiles fly through the air in excess of 100 meters; trees debarked; steel-reenforced concrete structures badly damaged.

F6, Inconceivable Tornado(wind speeds 319–379 mph)
Type of Damage Done: These winds are very unlikely. The small area of damage they might produce would probably not be recognizable along with the mess produced by F4 and F5 wind that would surround the F6 winds. Missiles, such as cars and refrigerators, would do serious secondary damage that could not be directly identified as F6 damage. If this level is ever achieved, evidence for it might only be found in some manner of ground swirl pattern, for it may never be identifiable through engineering studios.

Tornadoes

2. Scales of Measurement, Predictability

The conditions for tornadoes are well known, and weather forecasters are capable of warning the public of the *possibility* with great accuracy.

See facing page for discussion of the Fujita-Pearson Scale.

3. Quick or Slow Onset

Tornadoes are an instantaneous event. They drop from the clouds causing immediate disaster effects. This makes it very difficult to give timely warning of an actual tornado. This short notice can be countered by the effectiveness of tornado watches and severe thunderstorm warnings. Because tornadoes require specific conditions to develop, watching for those conditions can provide adequate warning. This requires you to be aware and prepared.

4. Area of Effect

The area of effect of a tornado can vary from as small as several yards wide and a few hundred feet long to up to a mile wide and several miles long. The path of a tornado is a general line in the predominate direction of the storm that spawned it. These paths tend to meander a bit from a straight line, but usually follow a general direction. A tornado's size is NOT directly related to its intensity: small tornadoes can be very powerful, and large tornadoes can be very weak. It is the wind speed within the tornado rather than the size of the tornado that causes the destruction. Tornadoes do not always occur in singular events. Clusters of tornadoes can cause damage over large areas. In the event of large tornadoes, it is not uncommon for smaller tornadoes of varying intensity to travel in an orbit around the larger tornado. This makes it very difficult to determine where the damage is occurring until after all of the tornadoes have passed.

5. Duration of Effects

Although the average tornadoes last for about five minutes' time on the ground, tornadoes can last for just a moment or up to several hours. Because it is associated with thunderstorms, rain and flash flooding can also occur during a tornado event.

6. Destruction of Infrastructure

This aspect is highly dependent on the wind speed within the storm. An F1 tornado will not do more than superficial damage while F5 tornadoes have the potential to destroy everything in their path. Roads tend to survive tornadoes well, but bridges and buildings are very susceptible to high-wind effects.

7. Disruption of Services

Because tornadoes tend to travel in linear paths, the immediate capacity to provide services is interrupted, but the ability of nearby municipalities is not. The major issue after a tornado is the post-event debris, which hinders movement. Once the debris is moved aside, services may be limited, but should still be available. It takes very little to reestablish services after a tornado, but availability is dependent on the proximity of other communities with service to offer.

8. Aftermath

There is usually very little aftermath in terms of secondary disaster conditions developing after a tornado. Because services can come in from nearby communities, or even departments from within the affected community not affected by the storm, the potential for complications is greatly reduced.

B. Outlooks, Watches, Warnings, & Advisories

Weather Alerts. The National Weather Service and its pendant offices communicate alerts in the form of *outlooks, advisories, watches, and warnings* to the public. They provide real-time notification of weather events that threaten local areas.

Emergency Management Bulletins. Emergency management agencies will broadcast *emergency management bulletins* in the case of disasters or special events when officials need to communicate public safety information or special instructions to the public. In many cases, both weather alerts and emergency management bulletins will be broadcast during a disaster situation.

Outlook. Indicates the potential for significant weather events up to seven days in advance with a forecaster confidence around 30%.

Watch. Indicates that conditions are favorable for the particular weather event in and near the watch area, which may pose a risk to life and property. Watches are issued up to 48 hours in advance with forecaster confidence around 50%.

Warning/Advisory. Indicates that a particular weather event is imminent or occurring. **Advisories** are issued if the weather event will lead to nuisance conditions, while **warnings** are issued for significant weather events that will pose a risk to life and property. Warnings and advisories are issued up to 48 hours in advance with forecaster confidence of at least 80%.

Alert Notifications

Alert notifications will come in the form of the following reports. This list includes reports you are most likely to hear during thunderstorms and tornadoes, but this is not an all-inclusive list. Be careful to listen for emergency communications and take information as you can get it. Remember that official government emergency communications may be more reliable than unofficial sources. The alerts you will want to listen for are:

Tornado Alerts

Tornado Alerts are issued when severe thunderstorms capable of producing tornadoes are the prominent threat.

- **Tornado Warning.** Issued when a tornado actually has been sighted by spotters or indicated on radar and is occurring or imminent in the warning area.
- **Tornado Watch.** Indicates that conditions are conducive to the development of tornadoes in and close to the watch area.

Severe Thunderstorm Alerts

Severe Thunderstorm Alerts are issued when thunderstorms with hail or high winds are the prominent threat.

- **Severe Thunderstorm Warning.** Issued when a severe thunderstorm (a thunderstorm producing dime-size hail, ¾ inch in diameter or larger; damaging winds with gusts to 58 mph or greater; or a tornado) actually has been observed by spotters or indicated on radar and is occurring or imminent in the warning area.
- **Severe Thunderstorm Watch.** Indicates that conditions are conducive to the development of severe thunderstorms (a thunderstorm producing dime-size hail, ¾ inch in diameter or larger; damaging winds with gusts to 58 mph or greater; or a tornado) in and close to the watch area.
- **Storm Warning.** Issued when sustained surface winds or frequent gusts of 55–73 mph are either predicted or occurring and are not directly associated with a tropical cyclone.

Local Storm Damage Reports

Reports of actual storm occurrences and any damage they may have caused.

Patterns of Mortality and Injury

Tornadoes kill and injure during the event itself. They can sometimes cause fatalities after the event due to hazards exposed during significant destruction.

Government Response

In most cases government response is in the form of state and local rescue and assistance. The federal government does not often get involved in tornado mitigation scenarios because the state and surrounding communities can usually provide the required assistance. The state and local response will include county assets, mutually supporting neighboring communities' fire and police, state law enforcement, state chapters of the Red Cross, and the National Guard.

(Shutterstock)

C. Personal Plans and Readiness

Know where to go when a tornado strikes. The ability to find effective cover and protection from the tornado is the most important thing you can do to save yourself and your family. Personal plans and readiness should include awareness and specific knowledge of where to go if a tornado touches down. The habits of being aware of weather conditions and *modifying your behavior* during tornado watches and severe thunderstorm warnings to ensure you are not left in a position where you cannot find protective cover will be the greatest assets to your survival. This behavior modification is not high science: it is a lot like not standing in an open field during a lighting storm. If you take a few minutes to make sure you have a safe place to seek cover in the case of a tornado, you will have a greater chance of surviving one.

A minimal tornado kit should include a flashlight, self-powered radio, a small first-aid kit, and a whistle to signal to help if you're trapped. This can be kept in the safe area or in a place where it is readily and immediately available. You will have very little time to collect anything other than yourself and your loved ones should a tornado strike. If you do seek cover, stay put until the "All Clear" is announced by appropriate authority.

(Natural Disasters)
H. Drought & Famine

General Description

Drought and famine specifically relate to the non-availability of water and food. The situation we are addressing here is most often a result of aftermath, which may or may not have been caused by another disaster. This can be caused by natural forces, man-made effects, or a combination of the two.

Drought and Famine (24)								
Effects	**Least**							**Worst**
Areas of Known Occurrence	Known	1	2	3	4	**5**		Unknown
Scales of Measurement	Before	1	2	**3**	4	5		After
Quick or Slow Onset	Days	1	2	3	4	5		Minutes
Area of Effect	Local	1	2	3	4	**5**		States
Duration of Effects	Hours	1	2	3	4	**5**		Months
Destruction of Infrastructure	Minor	**1**	2	3	4	5		Total
Disruption of Services	Minor	1	2	**3**	4	5		Total
Aftermath	Minor	1	2	3	**4**	5		Disaster

Drought: A lack of water can be caused by meteorological effects (lack of rain), hydrological limitations (lack of groundwater due to overuse or non-replenishment), or agricultural issues (not enough water to grow crops). In each case, the results are similar.

Famine: A lack of availability of or access to food. A number of factors could cause famine: natural factors include agricultural drought, flood, unseasonable heat or cold, crop disease, and pest infestation. Man-made factors include war or civil unrest, economic shock, unchecked hoarding, disruptions in transportation, or population being greater than food-production capacity.

Major Threat

In this case, starvation is not the only issue. With food shortages comes desperation. Civil unrest is the universal twin of starvation.

Survival Strategy

The ability to move to where water and food are available is paramount. In the case of a slow-onset situation, ensuring that you have the resources and opportunity to move is the key to survival. If you have a vehicle but wait until the roads are jammed, you have misused your capacity to move in a timely manner. Your goal will

Government Information Websites:

National Oceanic and Atmospheric Administration (NOAA) — http://www.noaa.gov/
National Weather Service (NWS) — http://www.weather.gov/
Federal Emergency Management Administration (FEMA) — http://www.ready.gov/
Centers for Disease Control and Prevention (CDC) — http://www.cdc.gov/

be to find a place where you have access to a steady supply of food and water either using your own resources (to grow or buy) or at a location where the government is capable of providing you (and everyone else) with what they need to survive. Given a choice, the option of using your own resources is the stronger of the two as it gives you more options.

A. The BIG EIGHT:

1. Areas of Known Occurrence, Possibility

In a world where food production is dependent upon the steady availability of water, energy, processing, and transportation, a disruption in any one of these factors could trigger a food shortage. This can happen anywhere and at any time, but the greatest threat is in major metropolitan areas, where the dense population is dependent on delivery of water and food.

Given the strength of American infrastructure, a weakness in one of these four factors (water, energy, processing, and transportation) can be covered with strength in another. When two or more of these factors are weak, the possibility is greater that a failure of the supply system will take place. The more dangerous scenario includes a combination of natural and man-made factors, where overuse of natural resources intersects with a natural shortage that would otherwise be survivable. In the case of a post-disaster scenario, the situation would simply be the inability to transport enough food to a trapped population to meet their survival needs.

2. Scales of Measurement, Predictability

This is measured economically before and during the event. After the event, it is measured by number of deaths resulting from starvation or conflict. We know now that there is a "food bubble" just like there was a housing bubble. The food bubble is dependent on the ready availability of energy to create food. As long as we have cheap and available energy, we can continue to irrigate, produce, and transport huge amounts of food. These are complicated issues, and famine tends to trap affected populations before they can recognize or escape the situation.

3. Quick or Slow Onset

The situation will develop slowly, but crash quickly. The average grocery store carries three days' worth of food, and the average U.S. home has three days' (or less) in storage. This means a major metropolitan area would be out of food in less than a week.

4. Area of Effect

This is specifically dependent on two major factors: population density and limitations on transportation.

5. Duration of Effects

Once the situation collapses, it would be weeks or months until the systems of supply could be reestablished to post-event capacity.

6. Destruction of Infrastructure

It is not a matter of destruction, but the loss of the systems and functions that produced and moved water and food. Retail food outlets would suffer damage that may or may not keep them from reopening, but the lack of employees to open the store or trucks and drivers to move the food would be a major issue.

Drought and Famine

When considering drought and famine in a disaster context it is prudent to see both scenarios as a result of failures in other areas. Other factors do not cause drought and famine. The other factors allow them to become disasters.

Drought and Famine are both instances where resources run out. In each case the onset of the situation is evident and observable. As obvious as it may seem that a drought or a famine is possible or even imminent in a given area, many people still get caught in the area of effect due to other factors. Why do drought and famine become a disaster in some areas and not in others?

In the case of the American dust bowl of the 1930s the situation was a combination of agricultural practices and economic collapse. In that case the drought stressed the land to the point of ecosystem collapse and the national economic situation limited the resources of the government to respond. This predicated greater economic hardship, unchecked environmental damage, civil unrest, mass migration and humanitarian crisis.

Beginning about 2000 and moving forward the Midwest of the United States has seen a new drought of greater intensity than the one that struck the region in the 1930s. Despite incredible damage the effects of the drought have not resulted in the same levels of disruption and hardship. There are several factors that account for this. First, the lessons learned by the agricultural community and government during the first great drought have been applied in growing practices and government regulations to ensure the dust bowl did not repeat itself. Secondly, the economy is strong in the U.S. and there are resources to mitigate most of the effects of the drought. The losses are limited to reductions in cattle and agricultural production rather than a collapse of the food production system.

Compare this positive result with the repeated devastating drought and famine events and humanitarian crises across Africa over the last 30 years. In most of the cases of African drought and famine disasters there was a combination of drought, agricultural stress on the land and civil war. Of significance in each case was the inability or unwillingness of local and national governments to respond to the situation and mitigate either the causes or effects. Limitations on movement, lack of resources at the local level, armed conflict, cultural stresses and ineffective government all converged to create the disaster situation.

As the availability of clean water becomes stressed by overuse and pollution the "tipping point" that moves a water shortage from an important conservations issue to a humanitarian crisis will be dependent upon those factors that restrict actions which assist in keeping the situation from becoming a disaster. This will include cultural habits of conservation in general (not just water use), effective water conservation efforts by municipalities, effective state and national water management policies, available resources and willingness of the government to provide regulation, guidance and resources for drought mitigation, and most importantly, a civil political and cultural environment in which to apply those mitigation techniques.

B. Outlooks, Watches, Warnings, & Advisories

Remember that these alerts and bulletins are designed to inform and instruct in order to cause the public to change their behavior or take specific action for their safety. Be aware of these communications.

(Shutterstock)

Weather Alerts
The National Weather Service and its pendant offices communicate alerts in the form of *outlooks, advisories, watches, and warnings* to the public. They provide real-time notification of weather events that threaten local areas.

Emergency Management Bulletins
Emergency-management agencies will broadcast *emergency management bulletins* in the case of disasters or special events when officials need to communicate public-safety information or special instructions to the public. In many cases both weather alerts and emergency management bulletins will be broadcast during a disaster situation.

Outlook
Indicates the potential for significant weather events up to seven days in advance with a forecaster confidence around 30%.

Watch
Indicates that conditions are favorable for the particular weather event in and near the watch area, which may pose a risk to life and property. Watches are issued up to 48 hours in advance with forecaster confidence around 50%.

Warning/Advisory
Indicates that a particular weather event is imminent or occurring. **Advisories** are issued if the weather event will lead to nuisance conditions, while **warnings** are issued for significant weather events that will pose a risk to life and property. Warnings and advisories are issued up to 48 hours in advance with forecaster confidence of at least 80%.

Alert Notifications

Alert notifications will come in the form of the following reports. This list includes reports you are most likely to hear during drought and famine, but this is not an all-inclusive list. Be careful to listen for emergency communications and take information as you can get it. Remember that official government emergency communications may be more reliable than unofficial sources. The alerts you will want to listen for are:

Wind Advisory
Issued when sustained winds of 30 to 39 mph are expected for one hour or longer.

Heat Advisory
Issued when maximum daytime heat index values are expected to reach or exceed 105°F on at least two consecutive days, with intermediate low temperatures of 75°F or higher.

Excessive Heat Warning
Issued when maximum daytime heat index values are expected to reach or exceed 110°F on at least two consecutive days, with intermediate low temperatures of 75°F or higher. *An Excessive Heat Watch is issued when these conditions may be met 12 to 48 hours in the future.*

Air Stagnation Advisory
Issued only at the request of the Environmental Protection Agency (EPA) whenever atmospheric conditions are stable enough to cause air pollutants to accumulate in a given area.

Blowing Dust Advisory
Issued when blowing dust is expected to reduce visibility to between ¼ and 1 mile, generally with winds of 25 mph or greater.

Dust Storm Warning
Issued when blowing dust is expected to reduce visibility frequently to ¼ mile or less, generally with winds of 25 mph or more.

Emergency Management Bulletins
These are issued by local government emergency management agencies to inform the public of the nature and area of effect of the identified hazard. These bulletins will include important information on current conditions and identified hazards, probability of additional events, road closures, location of relief centers, special instructions, and other appropriate information.

Drought & Famine

7. Disruption of Services

Services require people, and people require sustainment. Drought and famine historically have limited or completely suspended services.

8. Aftermath

The aftermath of drought and famine is the degradation of services, limitation on essential services, social breakdown, and stress on rule of law. To get an idea of what the social and economic situation might be like during a major drought and famine disaster, John Steinbeck's book *The Grapes of Wrath* offers a sobering description. The ideas of hardship and resiliency are well represented in the book, and although there would undoubtedly be differences between the specifics of the 1930s depression-era dustbowl and a modern event, the human and economic dynamics would have similar aspects. It is interesting to point out that in the book the family finds relief in a federal assistance camp.

Patterns of Mortality and Injury

The effects of drought and famine multiply on a compound scale. In the beginning, loss of life is concentrated on the old and the very young, who would be most susceptible to illness and disease. As the situation deteriorates, the numbers rise across the board for all age groups.

Government Response

In response to a major disaster event, the federal government will join with state and local governments to provide security and move as much food and water to the distressed population as possible. This will most likely come in the form of a system of distribution centers. The intent would be to allow for controlled access, not to deny anyone resources, but to ensure that as many people receive help as possible within the limits of any particular facility. The greater the number of people at a relief center, the more difficult it becomes to service them efficiently. These relief centers may also have the capacity to coordinate transportation for relocation for that part of the population that could travel.

C. Personal Plans and Readiness

This is a long-term scenario. It would require even the best-prepared individuals and groups to make difficult decisions. The key to success is to make the decisions while there is still an opportunity to do so. This would include plans and preparations with a combination of food and water storage and transportation. The balance to the plan is having enough supplies to sustain your family, but not so much that you could not transport it in your vehicle. A little online research on the subject of food storage will tell you two things. First, that there is money to be made by companies that produce shelf-stable (long-lasting) food supplies, and second, with a little more research, you can discover how to make similar arrangements at a lower cost (but requiring more of your time to do so).

Once your sustainment issues are addressed, you should think about what it takes to move to a less-populated or better-supplied location. If you already live in a lightly populated region, like Montana, you most likely don't need to move, but if you live in a major city or sprawling suburban area, like the coast of Southern California, you may want to develop a plan to move to an area that would be less stressed by a food or water shortage. Remember that the timing of the move is important.

Chap 10

(Natural Disasters)
I. Blizzards & Ice Storms

General Description

The National Oceanic and Atmospheric Administration (NOAA) describes a blizzard as a winter storm with sustained or frequent winds of 35 mph or higher with considerable falling or blowing snow that frequently reduces visibility to ¼ of a mile or less where these conditions are expected to prevail for a minimum of three hours. The U.S. National Weather Service defines an ice storm, or glaze event, as a storm which results in the accumulation of at least 0.25 inches (0.64 cm) of ice on exposed surfaces. In both cases, transportation is limited and dangerous because rescue services are just as limited as everyone else.

Blizzards and Ice Storms (15)							
Effects	**Least**						**Worst**
Areas of Known Occurrence	Known	**1**	2	3	4	5	Unknown
Scales of Measurement	Before	1	2	**3**	4	5	After
Quick or Slow Onset	Days	1	2	3	4	5	Minutes
Area of Effect	Local	1	**2**	3	4	5	States
Duration of Effects	Hours	1	2	3	**4**	5	Months
Destruction of Infrastructure	Minor	**1**	2	3	4	5	Total
Disruption of Services	Minor	1	2	**3**	4	5	Total
Aftermath	Minor	**1**	2	3	4	5	Disaster

Major Threat

Hunger and cold (hypothermia) are the two major threats of these storms. If this event becomes a disaster, it is solely due to lack of preparation.

Survival Strategy

When these storms take place, the best strategy is to stay put. If you live in an area where these storms are possible, then take the time to prepare for them. Be aware of the weather history in your area and plan accordingly. Keep 3–5 days' worth of food in the winter months, know where your warm clothing is, and have an alternative source of heat. The issue of alternative heating is where a lot of people get into trouble. Ensure the alternate heat source is safe for use indoors or make arrangements for proper ventilation.

Blizzards & Ice Storms

> *Government Information Websites:*
> *National Oceanic and Atmospheric Administration (NOAA) — http://www.noaa.gov/*
> *National Weather Service (NWS) — http://www.weather.gov/*
> *Federal Emergency Management Administration (FEMA) — http://www.ready.gov/*
> *Centers for Disease Control and Prevention (CDC) — http://www.cdc.gov/*

A. The BIG EIGHT

1. Areas of Known Occurrence, Possibility

These storms are common and are regular annual events. Blizzards are more common the further north you live in the United States, but ice storms are possible in most parts of the U.S. with the exception of the desert southwest.

2. Scales of Measurement, Predictability

Meteorologists can predict them with accuracy several days in advance of the event. These storms are measured during and after the fact in the amount of precipitation and the duration of the storm. Some parts of the United States experience between 10 and 15 winter storms of ice or snow each year. Over the last two decades, ice storms were more common than blizzards.

3. Quick or Slow Onset

While meteorologists can predict when and where an ice storm will occur, some storms still occur with little or no warning, and the duration of a storm can evade prediction. As a general rule the presence of the storm will be announced well in advance of the event, but the severity of the storm may be a surprise.

4. Area of Effect

This is dependent upon the individual storm, but large weather systems have the potential to cover areas as small as counties and as large as whole or even multiple states.

5. Duration of Effects

The duration of effects will often be longer than the storm itself. A three-day snowstorm can take weeks to recover from, with roads and businesses remaining closed long after the storm has passed. This is especially true in the case of ice storms that cause power failure.

6. Destruction of Infrastructure

The primary threat to infrastructure during a blizzard or ice storm is damage to power lines and communication lines and towers. When power is lost, most homes lose the ability to generate heat. This should be a significant part of your planning and preparation.

7. Disruption of Services

Services will be limited or even completely unavailable during the storm itself. After the storm, services may be limited while streets and roads are cleared of snow, ice, and debris.

8. Aftermath

Near-total power loss is expected with outages that could last from several days to weeks. Infrastructure will be damaged, and services will be interrupted for several days and may be limited for several weeks. Commercial and government infrastructure will initially be limited, but not permanently damaged. Access to resources such as food and water may be delayed or limited until some stores can open again. Essential government services like police and fire will be limited. Stability services such as sanitation and mail service may be delayed for days or even weeks until roads are clear enough for unhindered mobility. Security will be maintained by local authority, but rule of law may be limited while public offices are closed.

Patterns of Mortality and Injury

Death will come from hypothermia, and injuries will be cold-related, like frostbite. Long-term exposure to cold temperatures can weaken the body, leaving it susceptible to illness and disease. Another high-percentage killer in cold weather comes from using inappropriate means of generating heat. Gas-burning heaters produce deadly gases that will kill if used in a confined space (indoors). Open fires should only be made in places specifically made for fire, like fireplaces and burn pots. Even then the issue of proper venting is important. It is better to use blankets and heavy clothing and live in a 35-degree house than to risk an unsafe heating solution. If it is not freezing (anything over 32 degrees Fahrenheit, or 0 degrees Celsius), you can survive cold with warm clothing and warm food and drink. Remember that fire response will be limited or even unavailable. If you start a fire that gets away from you, there may be no one to help you.

Government Response

The government response to these events will be initially limited to a local response. If a storm is anticipated to be exceptionally large or damaging, then state-level assets will be placed on standby for rescue and response. This will include state-level law enforcement and any National Guard assets that have capabilities helpful to disaster mitigation (i.e. heavy vehicles to clear or ford snowbound streets, armories to house those without power, personnel to assist with rescue, supply transportation, and emergency generator delivery and operation to name a few). If the governor feels the need for more help, they can request federal assistance.

C. Personal Plans and Readiness

A snow or ice disaster that catches you off-guard is the result of poor planning. This event is one of the simpler (not easier) disasters to survive because it does not involve a lot of movement on the part of the population. These events tend to last for days rather than weeks. The human body can go for three weeks without food in extreme conditions. A family trapped in a warm house could survive even a week-long storm without food. It would not be pleasant or comfortable, but it would be survivable. It is easy and relatively inexpensive to keep three to five days' worth of food in the house. You will be burning calories to keep warm while resting as opposed to burning energy through the exertion of movement. If you lose power, don't let your perishable food spoil. Take it out of the refrigerator or freezer and put it someplace safe outside in the cold. A car in the garage or close to the house makes a good refrigerator when it's cold outside.

Water would not be an issue because you have access to snow and ice, which can be made into safe drinking water by melting (to be on the safe side, boiling your water is best). If you do lose power to heat your home, then turn off the water supply and drain the water from the system if you can. This will help to keep the lines from freezing solid and bursting. Keep the water in a bathtub or in containers kept for that purpose. With a little forethought and preparation, even an apartment can be made into a comfortable and safe haven, fully stocked, ready, and warm enough for winter survival.

Heat will be a major issue, and if you're not used to working with fire, it can be a dangerous thing. Research a method for generating heat that will work for where you live. If you have a fireplace, make sure the flue is clean, the fireplace operational, and that you have an adequate supply of wood. Do not use gas-burning stoves to heat inside your home without proper ventilation. If your home is well insulated, candles may be an option. A few candles in a fire-resistant container (coffee can) will generate a good amount of heat and some welcome light. There are safety concerns with candles as well, and you need to treat them with the respect you would give any fire. Do not leave them burning while you sleep.

Blizzards &
Ice Storms

B. Outlooks, Watches, Warnings, & Advisories

Remember that these alerts and bulletins are designed to inform and instruct in order to cause the public to change their behavior or take specific action for their safety. Be aware of these communications.

Weather Alerts: The National Weather Service and Its pendant offices communicate alerts in the form of *outlooks, advisories, watches, and warnings* to the public. They provide real-time notification of weather events that threaten local areas.

Emergency Management Bulletins: Emergency-management agencies will broadcast *emergency-management bulletins* in the case of disasters or special events when officials need to communicate public-safety information or special instructions to the public. In many cases both weather alerts and emergency-management bulletins will be broadcast during a disaster situation.

Outlook: Indicates the potential for significant weather events up to seven days in advance with a forecaster confidence around 30%.

Watch: Indicates that conditions are favorable for the particular weather event in and near the watch area, which may pose a risk to life and property. Watches are issued up to 48 hours in advance with forecaster confidence around 50%.

Warning/Advisory: Indicates that a particular weather event is imminent or occurring. **Advisories** are issued if the weather event will lead to nuisance conditions, while **warnings** are issued for significant weather events that will pose a risk to life and property. Warnings and advisories are issued up to 48 hours in advance with forecaster confidence of at least 80%.

Alert Notifications

Alert notifications will come in the form the following reports. This list includes reports you are most likely to hear during severe winter weather, but this is not an all-inclusive list. Be careful to listen for emergency communications and take information as you can get it. Remember that official government emergency communications may be more reliable than unofficial sources. The alerts you will want to listen for are:

Winter Alerts are issued when frozen precipitation (snow, freezing rain, sleet, etc.) threatens.

Winter Storm Outlook

This is a statement issued when there is a chance of a major winter storm from three to five days in the future. This is meant to assist people with their long-range plans. However, since the outlook is issued so far in advance, the accuracy of the prediction may be llmited.

Blizzard Warning

Issued when sustained winds or frequent gusts of 35 mph or greater and considerable falling or blowing snow (reducing visibility frequently to less than 1/4 mile) is occurring or is expected to occur for a period of three hours or longer.

Blizzard Watch

Issued when sustained winds or frequent gusts to 35 mph or greater and considerable falling or blowing snow (reducing visibility frequently to less than 1/4 mile) may become possible for a period of three hours or longer.

Winter Storm Warning

Issued when a winter storm is producing or is forecast to produce heavy snow or significant ice accumulations. The criteria for this warning can vary from place to place.

Winter Storm Watch
Issued when there is a potential for heavy snow or significant ice accumulations, usually at least 24–36 hours in advance. The criteria for this watch can vary from place to place.

Ice Storm Warning
Issued when freezing rain produces a significant and potentially damaging accumulation of ice. The criteria for this warning varies from state to state, but typically will be issued any time more than 1/4 inch of ice is expected to accumulate in an area.

Freezing Rain Advisory
Issued when freezing rain or freezing drizzle is forecast but a significant accumulation is not expected. However, even small amounts of freezing rain or freezing drizzle may cause significant travel problems.

Winter Weather Advisory
Issued when a low-pressure system produces a combination of winter weather (snow, freezing rain, sleet, etc.) that presents hazardous conditions, but does not meet warning criteria.

Lake-Effect Snow Warning
Issued when a hazardous amount of pure lake-effect snow (not because of a low-pressure system) is falling or expected to fall.

Lake-Effect Snow Watch
Issued when a hazardous amount of pure lake-effect snow (not because of a low-pressure system) may become possible.

Lake-Effect Snow Advisory
Issued when pure lake-effect snow (not because of a low-pressure system) may pose a hazard. The criteria for this advisory vary from area to area.

Lake-Effect Snow and Blowing Snow Advisory
Issued when pure lake-effect snow (not because of a low-pressure system) may pose a hazard in combination with wind-driven snow. The criteria for this advisory vary from area to area.

Avalanche Warning
Indicates that conditions are favorable for the development of avalanches in mountain regions.

Avalanche Watch
Indicates that conditions may become favorable for the development of avalanches in mountain regions.

Emergency Management Bulletins
They are issued by local government emergency-management agencies to inform the public of the nature and area of effect of a disaster. These bulletins will include important information on current conditions and identified hazards, probable additional events, road closures, location of relief centers, special instructions, and other appropriate information.

(FEMA photo/ Norman Lenburg)

Looting and lawlessness tend to be less prevalent due to the harsh conditions. But because you will not be able to run, you may want to consider some form of self-defense. This does not need to be weapons. It could be strength in numbers by joining with another family in a communal space. Doing this allows you to share warmth, mutual support, and supplies. Scavengers and looters are opportunists and may not be as inclined to attack a group of people as they would to confront one or two.

Communication will be important. Keep a radio and a method for signaling for help ready and available. Listen to the news and be aware of changing weather conditions or opportunities for rescue and assistance.

Remember that you can survive snow and ice storms with relative ease. If the power stays on, you could change three days of worry and hunger into a nice stay-at-home holiday.

Some things to consider for your winter weather preparations:

- 3–5 days' worth of food and a container for water.
- Warm clothing including hats and gloves.
- Communication for both receiving information and signaling for help.
- Candles for light and heat (including matches or lighters).
- A method to safely warm at least one room of your home.
- Medicines you may need and a first-aid kit.

J. Outbreaks, Epidemics, & Pandemics

General Description

The descriptions for outbreak, epidemic, and pandemic can be confusing, so for the purposes of survival in a situation where disease causes illness and death within a population, we will look at effects on the population, the economy, and the ability of government to provide services (governance).

Outbreaks, Epidemics and Pandemics (30)							
Effects	**Least**						**Worst**
Areas of Known Occurrence	Known	1	2	3	4	**5**	Unknown
Scales of Measurement	Before	1	2	3	4	**5**	After
Quick or Slow Onset	Days	1	2	3	4	5	Minutes
Area of Effect	Local	1	2	3	4	**5**	States
Duration of Effects	Hours	1	2	3	4	**5**	Months
Destruction of Infrastructure	Minor	**1**	2	3	4	5	Total
Disruption of Services	Minor	**1**	2	3	4	**5**	Total
Aftermath	Minor	**1**	2	3	4	5	Disaster

The impact of disease is linked to what the disease does to humans and the scale of effects, both in the number of people affected and the area the illness affects. The disease we are concerned with would have three criteria: first, the microbe would infect and cause serious illness in humans, second, humans would not have immunity against the virus, and third, the virus would spread easily from person to person and survive within humans. The flu, or influenza, is a good example of this kind of disease.

When a disease of this type affects a greater number of people than is usual for the locality or spreads to a region where it is not usually present, it is called an outbreak. An outbreak and an epidemic are the same thing: prevalent and localized. A pandemic is a disease outbreak on a global scale: prevalent and globalized.

Outbreaks, epidemics, and pandemics do not necessarily mean disaster and social breakdown. In 1918, during the midst of World War I, Spanish influenza killed 40–50 million people worldwide. In 1957, Asian influenza killed 2 million people, and in 1968, Hong Kong influenza killed another 1 million people. All three of these events were correctly categorized as pandemics, but they did not cause the end of the world. Even today, in an average year, 5 to 20 percent of the U.S. population gets the flu, more than 200,000 people are hospitalized with flu-related complications,

Government Information Websites:
National Oceanic and Atmospheric Administration (NOAA) — http://www.noaa.gov/
National Weather Service (NWS) — http://www.weather.gov/
Federal Emergency Management Administration (FEMA) — http://www.ready.gov/
Centers for Disease Control and Prevention (CDC) — http://www.cdc.gov/

and about 36,000 people die from flu-related causes. This is the world we live in, but sometimes an illness comes along that has the potential to be devastating. In the 1917–1918 Spanish influenza events, some communities were completely wiped out; whole towns died and never returned.

The scenario we are looking at for this survival challenge is an outbreak, either regional or global, that affects enough people to have a significant impact on services. This would manifest as overcrowded hospitals, closed schools and businesses, limits on the availability of food, and restrictions on transportation, both in lack of drivers to move commercial goods and areas of quarantine.

Major Threat

The primary threat will be the initial disease. If the outbreak is significant enough to affect services, specifically sanitation services, then the secondary threats are other diseases — like typhus, typhoid fever, smallpox, dysentery, and cholera — that result from inadequate sanitation and human contact.

Survival Strategy

The methods of protection during an outbreak are social distancing to limit human contact and vigilant personal hygiene. The best thing you can do is limit your exposure by not traveling and limiting your exposure to public gatherings or places. You will still need to do some things outside the home. You may be required to go to work or buy food at the store, but these things can be done in relative safety if you take the correct measures to protect yourself from infection.

A. The BIG EIGHT

1. Areas of Known Occurrence, Possibility

These events are certain. They happen every year. The only question is the severity of the event. It is a statistical certainty that epidemics and pandemics will take place in areas of human habitation. They will most likely be associated with population centers or places where people pass while traveling.

2. Scales of Measurement, Predictability

There is no way to effectively predict the severity of an outbreak before the event. We know that outbreaks occur every year, but we will not know when an outbreak will become a disaster. These events are measured by counting infections (illness and death) after the fact.

3. Quick or Slow Onset

Although contagious diseases start within small populations, they can quickly spread; the more people that are infected, the more rapidly an illness can spread. 1 becomes 2, 2 become 8, 8 becomes 32, 32 becomes 128, 128 becomes 512; the progression is logarithmic, and although this example shows multiplications of 4, it is only an example. True virulence infects at a much higher rate.

4. Area of Effect

Diseases do not affect areas, but rather populations. This is why epidemics become pandemics. The illness does not cover the whole earth, but travels within the population.

Containment

Containment will manifest in several forms of restriction of movement: Limitations on travel to reduce the likelihood of disease migration, isolation or quarantine to contain infection within a known area or population, and entry limitations to keep infected people from entering areas where the infection has not yet migrated.

Limitations on Travel
During an outbreak, the Center for Disease Control (CDC) may recommend that people not travel into or out of areas where the disease is prevalent.

Isolation and Quarantine:
solation is the separation and restriction of movement of ill people to stop the spread of that illness to others. People in isolation may be cared for in their homes, in hospitals, or at designated health care facilities. Quarantine, in contrast, applies to people who have been exposed to a contagious illness and may be infected but are not yet ill. Separating exposed people and restricting their movements is intended to stop the spread of that illness. Quarantine can be highly effective in protecting the public from disease.

Entry Limitations
During an outbreak, a town, city, state, or any other jurisdiction believing that their population is currently free of infection could decide to deny entry or passage of people from areas or populations they believe to be infected.

Treatment
The CDC will work with local and state healthcare providers to establish methods and facilities for treatment in order to keep as few people from getting infected and to prevent, or at least reduce, the spread of illness by providing separate care facilities for the infected population. The CDC and local public health agencies will communicate instructions to the public via mass media (radio and television) and the internet. Treatment centers may not be located in hospitals. In order to contain the infection and provide for the larger numbers of patients, treatment centers may be in large public or private buildings (like sports arenas) that have lots of space, restrooms, and food-preparation areas that can handle large numbers of people, are designed for controlled entry and exit, and have adequate parking space and access to road networks for resupply. Some facilities may include temporary or mobile hospitals provided by the CDC or the military.

Epidemics & Pandemics

5. Duration of Effects

Depending on the illness, the disastrous effects of a disease can last for months or even years.

6. Destruction of Infrastructure

Infrastructure is not directly affected by an outbreak, but systems and maintenance are degraded when providers are not available to keep things in order.

7. Disruption of Services

Significant outbreak has a direct impact on the availability of services. Both essential and stability services would be limited in an outbreak. Not only would there be fewer personnel to provide services, but the requirements of additional protective procedures would slow those services that were still available.

8. Aftermath

The aftermath of disease outbreak is the degradation of social systems, limitation on essential services, social breakdown, and stress on rule of law. Exposure to unsanitary conditions may cause infections by follow-on diseases. As transportation slows, goods will not reach markets and economies will be dependent on local resources. Practices of personal protection (gloves, masks, and personal decontamination) will become commonplace. A new "normal" will develop for social contact and congregation.

Patterns of Mortality and Injury

For an event that is large enough to be categorized as a disaster, the initial deaths will be larger than can be handled by current medical and mortuary services. Illness and death would be prevalent anywhere exposure was present. This means that although larger population centers would see significant numbers of infection, smaller communities would not be less affected or safer, and in some cases rates of infection could be higher. Social distancing, hand hygiene, vigilant decontamination, and other means of disease-transmission prevention will be a greater factor in survival rates than proximity to population.

See facing page for futher discussion.

Government Response

In the case of a major outbreak, the government would concentrate on two major goals: containment and treatment (in that order). Containment is critical because stopping the spread of the disease is the primary means to control it. The number-one way a disease spreads is through population movement. In the case of a known disease, this will be people who are trying to escape infection by leaving the area of contamination. In many cases, these people will already be infected.

Patterns of Mortality and Injury

For an event that is large enough to be categorized as a disaster, the initial deaths will be larger than can be handled by current medical and mortuary services. Illness and death would be prevalent anywhere exposure was present. This means that although larger population centers would see significant numbers of infection, smaller communities would not be less affected or safer, and in some cases rates of infection could be higher. Social distancing, hand hygiene, vigilant decontamination, and other means of disease-transmission prevention will be a greater factor in survival rates than proximity to population.

Let's take a minute and examine that last statement. Can you realistically affect your chances for survival during an outbreak? The answer is YES! There are four things that determine how many people die from a disease outbreak.

First
Number of people who become infected. Obviously the number of people infected has a direct correlation to the number of people that die from the disease.

Second
The severity of disease caused by the virus (its virulence). Viruses reproduce by hijacking the cells of living organisms and turning them into little virus factories that produce more of the same virus. Sometimes this does not kill the host, but makes them an infected carrier. Other times it makes a person so sick and weak that it kills them; the more virulent the virus, the higher the rate of mortality.

Third
The vulnerability of affected populations. Here we see an opportunity to protect ourselves by making ourselves less vulnerable. We can help ourselves now by keeping ourselves healthy through diet and exercise, not smoking or drinking to excess, and by having plans made and resources collected to reduce your exposure to infected areas or populations. If you have ill, older, or very young members of your family, you may not be able to reduce their vulnerability, but you can reduce their exposure through social distancing and other methods of separation.

Fourth
The effectiveness of preventive steps. This links directly back to point number one. If you do not get infected, you will not die from infection. By learning and developing infection-prevention habits that will help you reduce your chances of infection, you can have a direct impact on your chances for survival.

What is the Flu?

Flu-like symptoms include fever, cough, sore throat, runny or stuffy nose, body aches, headache, chills, and fatigue. Some people also may have vomiting and diarrhea. According to the CDC, people may be infected with the flu and have respiratory symptoms without a fever.

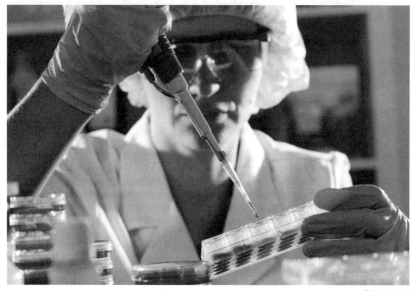

(Shutterstock)

Flu, known medically as influenza, is a respiratory infection caused by the influenza virus. The infection typically is spread by air or by direct contact from one person to another. Most cases occur during epidemics, which peak during the winter months nearly every year. Influenza virus is very contagious. Compared with other viruses, influenza can move into a large population in a relatively short time. Annually, about 25 million people seek medical care for the symptoms of flu during flu season. Some years are worse than others. The history of the flu in the U.S. includes some hard years. From 1957–1958, over 70 thousand people died, and the Hong-Kong flu of 1968–1969 killed 34 thousand people. The worst flu pandemic in the U.S. was in 1918–1919, when the Spanish Flu killed 20 to 40 thousand people worldwide and infected 25% of the U.S. population.

The danger of influenza is that the virus mutates (changes) somewhat as it moves from host to host. This change is enough to keep your body from recognizing the virus from earlier bouts, making it slow to respond. By the time your system's immune response reacts to the new threat, the virus has already infected millions of cells in your body. The weakened body is then at risk for additional infections and complications. In most cases, the combination of infections is what causes death. Respiratory failure caused by lung infections is common and dangerous.

After you have a plan, learn how to protect yourself by developing healthy habits. Modify your behavior by learning and practicing the techniques of infection protection now. A pandemic event will most likely involve a strain of influenza or an Influenza-Like Illness (ILI), so practicing protective measures for preventing this type of infection makes good habits. The methods of personal protection will work for most types of infections. Viruses are transmitted by touching and breathing.

One way to think about protecting yourself and your family is to use a layered defense against illnesses. First, keep yourself clean and healthy; second, keep your house clean; third, use medical assistance (get the flu shot); and fourth, limit your contact with people who have the flu *and* with people when you have the flu.

Keep yourself Clean and Healthy

The Centers for Disease Control and Prevention (CDC) has listed several things you can do to help prevent catching the flu bug, as influenza activity returns annually. Go to their web site at http://www.cdc.gov/flu/ for helpful tips.

- Keep hydrated by drinking at least eight glasses of water a day.
- Cover your nose and mouth with a tissue when you cough or sneeze.
- Wash your hands often with soap and water or use hand sanitizer.
- Avoid touching your eyes, nose, and mouth, as germs spread that way.

Keep your House Clean

Wash your hands as soon as you get home to get rid of the germs you bring home. Also consider reducing the number and types of things you bring home that are common-use items.

Use Medical Assistance

- Take flu antiviral drugs if your doctor prescribes them. Influenza antiviral prescription drugs can be used to treat influenza or to prevent the flu. Antiviral drugs can make the flu milder and shorten the time you're sick. They may also prevent serious flu complications. For people with high-risk factors, treatment with an antiviral drug can mean the difference between having a milder illness versus a very serious illness that could result in a hospital stay.
- Get the annual flu shot. There is a lot of discussion about the safety of these shots that is based on outdated information or misinformation. If you have questions, then do your own research to answer your questions.

Limit your Contact

Limit your contact with people in ways that will prevent the spread of illness. This does not mean you should completely avoid interaction, just forms of primary and secondary physical contact.

- Limit direct contact with people. This goes both ways; try to avoid close contact with sick people and limit contact with others to keep from infecting them if you are ill.
- If you are sick with flu-like illness, the CDC recommends you stay home for at least 24 hours after your fever is gone except to get medical care or for other necessities. If you do go out, wear a mask and keep your hands clean. You will be at greater risk of additional infections and complications if you are already weakened by infection.
- Handrails, doorknobs, public phones, coffee spoons, and other common-use items can carry a virus. Limit your use of and contact with these everyday items. Carry your own pen, use a new spoon, or if there is a significant rate of infection within the population, wear gloves when you are out and in contact with the public.
- When sharing food or drink, separate food first, and then eat.

There are many online resources that can help you identify things you will want to think about when making your plans.

B. Outlooks, Watches, Warnings, & Advisories

Remember that these alerts and bulletins are designed to inform and instruct in order to cause the public to change their behavior or take specific action for their safety. Be aware of these communications.

Weather Alerts. The National Weather Service and its pendant offices communicate alerts in the form of *outlooks, advisories, watches, and warnings* to the public. They provide real-time notification of weather events that threaten local areas.

Emergency Management Bulletins. Emergency management agencies will broadcast *emergency management bulletins* in the case of disasters or special events when officials need to communicate public-safety information or special instructions to the public. In many cases, both weather alerts and emergency management bulletins will be broadcast during a disaster situation.

Outlook. Indicates the potential for significant weather events up to seven days in advance with a forecaster confidence around 30%.

Watch. Indicates that conditions are favorable for the particular weather event in and near the watch area, which may pose a risk to life and property. Watches are issued up to 48 hours in advance with forecaster confidence around 50%.

Warning/Advisory. Indicates that a particular weather event is imminent or occurring. **Advisories** are issued if the weather event will lead to nuisance conditions, while **warnings** are issued for significant weather events that will pose a risk to life and property. Warnings and advisories are issued up to 48 hours in advance with forecaster confidence of at least 80%.

Alert Notifications

Alert notifications will come in the form the following reports. This list includes reports you are most likely to hear during an earthquake, but this is not an all-inclusive list. Be careful to listen for emergency communications and take information as you can get it. Remember that official government emergency communications may be more reliable than unofficial sources. The alerts you will want to listen for are:

Health Alert messages convey information specific to public-health considerations. They will provide both general and specific instructions for both the public and medical and healthcare providers.

- **Health Alert** conveys the highest level of importance, warrants immediate action or attention.

- **Health Advisory** provides important information for a specific incident or situation, may not require immediate action.

- **Health Update** provides updated information regarding an incident or situation, unlikely to require immediate action.

Emergency Management Bulletins

These are issued by local government emergency-management agencies to inform the public of the strength and area of effect of an earthquake. These bulletins will include important information on current conditions and identified hazards, probability and severity of aftershocks, road closures, location of relief centers, special instructions, and other appropriate information.

C. Personal Plans and Readiness

Outbreaks are a different kind of disaster, and your response to an outbreak requires a completely different set of goals. There is no running or relocation from a pandemic outbreak. This is what is called "bugging in." You will want to stay close to whatever resources you have already established, because after the event starts, the cost and difficulties of establishing a new home will be very prohibitive (if it is even possible). It has some of the same characteristics of preparation for blizzards and ice storms, but on a larger and longer scale.

(Shutterstock)

Some planning assumptions will help frame the difficulties you may encounter during an outbreak. Although it is impossible to predict the specifics, planners and medical experts on contagious disease have come to some well-informed assumptions. It is important to understand that these assumptions are not universal to all outbreaks and you will want to confirm the specifics of any outbreak event you may encounter.

When making your plans, assume that susceptibility to the outbreak will be universal with no segment of the population being immune. Assume that once infected, people may be ill for approximately two weeks (this is most likely with any version of influenza). Assume that once people start getting sick, people will stop going to work if they can't or don't have to. This would mean that up to 40% of the workforce may be absent at one time. This will affect essential services and economic activities (like trucks delivering food to the stores). No one knows how long a pandemic could last, but communities may be affected in waves of illness that last for several weeks. These waves could last for a year or more. Healthcare resources will likely be stretched beyond capacity, and separate health issues may be addressed at separate medical facilities (i.e. people with broken legs go to one hospital and people with infection go to another).

These next assumptions are very important. The balance between personal liberty and security will, by necessity, be tipped to favor security. Social distancing would be implemented during a health emergency when extraordinary measures are required to control the spread of disease or infection. State and federal laws may be modified, suspended, or enacted in response to a pandemic. Limitations on public assembly may include not only entertainment events with cancelled concerts and closed theaters, but also cancellation of school and church services, classes, and other social-support activities. All forms of social-support gatherings may need to be cancelled. This will likely lead to social and economic disruption, including shutting down or limiting mass transit and instructions asking everyone to stay at home and suspending all non-essential travel, business, and services. Curfews may be put in place to restrict nighttime travel.

Things to include in your plan:

- Stocking food and methods of getting more food. Remember that going to get food may expose you to infection. Keep your hands clean and disinfected, disinfect any food containers before you bring them into your home, and wash all fresh food with clean water. Limit your exposure by making a list and shopping only one day a week.

- Ensure you have access to clean water through purification or boiling. Water conservation measures may be enacted. If you live somewhere where you can collect rainwater, it may be an option for you.

- Make arrangements for light and heat (similar to winter-weather preparations). Power may go out for a few days at a time.

- Determine what it takes to meet your financial obligations to include bill paying and mailing.

- Have medical equipment and prescriptions on hand to meet your needs, or determine a way to meet those needs.

- Gather your personal documentation and have emergency contact information ready. Keep information of personal medical history ready, either as medical records or just lists of issues and medications. These will be important to doctors if they have to provide treatment for illness or injury. Hospital records may not be available. Keep insurance records, wills, powers of attorney, and other legal documents that can provide information about your wishes when you are unable to speak for yourself.

- Keep a basic stockpile of medical supplies (as simple as a basic first-aid kit) and protective-wear items like masks, clear safety glasses, and gloves, anything that will help you protect yourself from contact with airborne, splashed, coughed, or physical-contact infection. Also keep supplies for cleaning: disinfectant sprays and wipes, hand sanitizers, soap, and paper towels.

Man-made Disasters

This chapter provides a description of three different types of man-made disasters. The conversation starts out very general and gets more specific as each description progresses. This is done on purpose because your preparations will be based on the generalities of the type of event. Your actual survive activities during a disaster will be based on the specific situation with that particular event. This combination of general preparation and specific action is not a contradiction but rather an important method of thinking. When you understand the generalities of a man-made disaster it helps you anticipate so you can take specific actions to increase your chances of survival. You will not be able to do everything to protect yourself, your loved ones and your property, so you will need to prioritize and be able to choose the right things to survive.

(Shutterstock)

Man-made Disasters

Each Disaster type includes discussion on the following subjects:

General Description

General description provides a short introduction of the nature and general scope of the disaster type. This gives a general overview of what you may encounter.

Disaster Charts

As part of the disaster description a "Disaster Chart" is included. The Disaster Chart is a visual representation of the "Big 8" questions described in Chapter 2 and explained in greater detail later in the disaster type discussion. It is designed to give a generalized view of the effects of a disaster type. This is helpful because every disaster has aspects that are destructive, dangerous and unpredictable. That said, natural events that have the potential to cause disasters also tend to have predictable patterns of behavior.

Each type of event has some element that will allow you to avoid or reduce the impact of its effects if you take the time to be aware and prepared. To assist in expressing this idea visually, each disaster description has been provided with a "Disaster Chart". This is not high science. The Charts are subjectively based on observation and experience. They are designed to serve as a way to express an idea.

Disaster Chart (Total Points)							
Effects	Least						Worst
Areas of Known Occurrence	Known	1	2	3	4	5	Unknown
Scales and Measurement	Before	1	2	3	4	5	After
Quick or Slow Onset	Days	1	2	3	4	5	Minutes
Area of Effect	Local	1	2	3	4	5	States
Duration of Effects	Hours	1	2	3	4	5	Months
Destruction of Infrastructure	Minor	1	2	3	4	5	Total
Disruption of Services	Minor	1	2	3	4	5	Total
Aftermath	Minor	1	2	3	4	5	Disaster

The number system provided in the Disaster Chart accompanying each disaster type is not a grade to say which disaster is the worst; they are all bad. The purpose is to express the aspect of each disaster type that can be used to anticipate, prepare for, and avoid its effects. The worst disaster would have a score of 40: unpredictable, rapid onset, long lasting, with wide spread destruction, disruption and aftermath. The point to take away here is that there is no disaster

(Man-made Disasters)
A. Nuclear Events

Nuclear Events

General Description

Nuclear events fall into three general categories. In order of probability, they are accidental release from a nuclear power-generation station (nuclear plant), intentional release of radioactive material by conventional explosive device or other means (dirty bomb), and intentional detonation of a nuclear explosive device (a nuclear bomb). Exposure to radiation has two specific negative effects: cellular mutation and cellular damage.

Nuclear Events (26)							
Effects	**Least**						**Worst**
Areas of Known Occurrence	Known	**1**	2	3	4	5	Unknown
Scales of Measurement	Before	1	2	3	4	**5**	After
Quick or Slow Onset	Days	1	2	3	4	**5**	Minutes
Area of Effect	Local	1	2	3	4	5	States
Duration of Effects	Hours	1	2	3	4	**5**	Months
Destruction of Infrastructure	Minor	**1**	2	3	4	5	Total
Disruption of Services	Minor	1	**2**	3	4	5	Total
Aftermath	Minor	1	2	3	**4**	5	Disaster

Cellular mutation is caused when radiation affects the replication and reproduction of cells in the body. The much higher rate of replication and reproduction that results from radioactive exposure is almost always accompanied by mutation. Because the mutation is not caused by normal environmental stresses, the mutation is manifestly non-beneficial, usually resulting in cancer. This is especially true of glands within the body.

Cellular damage from radiation exposure is caused when genetic material in the human cell, DNA and RNA strands, are broken down, which results in premature or even immediate cell death.

It should be noted that a vast majority of radiation injuries happen because of accidental exposure. During any disaster, radioactive-containment vessels may fail, resulting in exposure to radioactivity or radioactive materials.

In the case of a nuclear detonation, as opposed to a release or a dirty bomb, an electromagnetic pulse (EMP) will cause most electronic devices to completely fail. Cell phones, cars, lights, elevators, pretty much anything electric is shorted out and will not function.

Government Information Websites:

Federal Emergency Management Administration (FEMA) — http://www.ready.gov/

Centers for Disease Control and Prevention (CDC) — http://www.cdc.gov/

Nuclear Blast — http://www.ready.gov/nuclear-blast

Major Threat

The real threat is radiation exposure. These incidences have a general pattern of a short duration (days) of very high radiation levels followed by long (years) periods of lower levels of radiation. Of course any exposure is bad, but a high level of exposure in a short amount of time is particularly harmful. A dangerous level of radiation within a specific area is known as a "Hot Zone." Exposure can cause radiation sickness, cancer, and illnesses resulting from weakness. An additional threat will be the general pandemonium of the masses of people trying to escape the Hot Zone.

A. The BIG EIGHT

1. Areas of Known Occurrence, Probability

The bombs, radioactive material, and power plants exist. It is therefore possible that that material could get out of control by accident or malice.

Areas most susceptible to nuclear events are locations near existing nuclear power-generating facilities (in the case of accidents) and large cities and population centers (in the case of targeted malice). There have been relatively few major nuclear events in recorded history resulting in directly attributed death or illness within the affected population.

- Two bombs over Japan in 1945 (Thousands of deaths and injuries with thousands more exposures resulting in deaths and illness for years after the event)
- The Mayak nuclear waste storage tank explosion in Russia in 1957 (200+ deaths and a possible 270,000 exposures)
- The plutonium burn at the Windscale facility in United Kingdom in 1957 (No immediate deaths, but 33+ from cancer)
- The nuclear generation-station meltdown at Chernobyl, Russia, in 1986 (56 direct & 4,000 after exposure)
- The tsunami damage to the Fukushima Daiichi nuclear plant in Japan in 2011 (Exposure numbers unknown, effects to be determined in time)

There are another 30 or so incidences where people died due to accidents or mishandling of nuclear material, mostly in nuclear plants and medical facilities.

2. Scales and Measurement, Predictability

These events are not predictable because we don't plan for nuclear meltdowns, dirty bombs, or surprise missile attacks. If the government knows these things are going to happen, they move to stop the event.

Radiation exposure can only be measured during the event and by following the fallout as it travels downwind. Measuring effects after the event is conducted both by dosimeter and observation of illness and effects on living things from exposure. There are several methods of measuring radiation exposure and absorption into the body. Danger and exposure communication can be expressed in rem (Roentgen Equivalent in Man), which addresses effects on humans; rad (Radiation Absorbed Dose), which looks at levels of absorption; and Roentgen, which looks at the amount of radiation in the air. For the purposes of a disaster, the communication of exposure threat can be seen as equivalent: 1000 rad is 1000 rem is 1000 Roentgens.

A sudden short dose of fewer than 50 is survivable: there will be some short-term effects on your blood and you will not feel well. 50 to 200 will most likely not kill you, but it will cause illness in how you feel both at the time of the exposure and over time. 200 to 1000 will cause immediate and serious illness. The closer the exposure to 1000, the more likely death will occur. The old, sick, and very young will suffer greater effects with less exposure. Exposures over 1000 will typically cause death.

Nuclear Incident Survival Strategy

Surviving a radiological event is directly tied to minimizing exposure to radiation. There are things you can keep in mind to reduce your exposure: remember *distance, shielding, and time.* It is important to understand that you cannot see, feel, smell, hear, or taste fallout. Having a device called a dosimeter will allow you to react to fallout levels in an effective manner. If you do not have a dosimeter, then listen to the radio for reports about fallout levels. In the case of a nuclear bomb, your radio will most likely not work due to the effects of an electromagnetic pulse (EMP). If this is the case, seek effective shelter.

Distance

This does not necessarily mean run. The distance you want is between you and the radioactive dust that is a result of a blast or release. The time to move is when the radiation levels are low, and the time to stay put is when the radiation levels are high. As an example, immediately after an event the fallout exposure levels outside of a building could be fatally high per hour, but the exposure levels in the basement may be low and survivable. This is tied directly to exposure to fallout dust.

Once you are in a safe place, stay there and do not leave until you determine it is safe to move or you have no choice but to move. Every time you open up your shelter, you potentially allow irradiated dust and air in. When it is time to move, minimize the amount of time you spend exposed to the radiation and put as much distance as possible between your family and the event. Depart the areas of effect as quickly and calmly as possible, moving upwind. Most of the danger is in the Hot Zone (the blast area), but fallout extends downwind, pushed by the prevailing winds for a considerable distance, getting less intense but still dangerous as it progresses. DO NOT drink or eat anything that is uncovered or has been exposed to open air or dust in the Hot Zone. As soon as you are out of the Hot Zone, abandon clothing and any material possessions that have been exposed to dust or fallout. This includes cars, clothing, boxes and suitcases, weapons, favorite stuffed animals, books… you get the idea.

Shielding

Anything you can do to separate yourself from the dust, debris, and fallout of a destructive blast is helpful. Remember that anything radioactive that you breathe in, eat, drink, or get on your skin will increase your exposure time and cumulative dose, even if you escape the Hot Zone. Think thick and deep when deciding on shelter.

FEMA says: "The more distance between you and the fallout particles, the better. An underground area such as a home or office building basement offers more protection than the first floor of a building. A floor near the middle of a high-rise may be better, depending on what is nearby at that level on which significant fallout particles would collect. Flat roofs collect fallout particles so the top floor is not a good choice, nor is a floor adjacent to a neighboring flat roof."

Time

When exposed to radiation, the main concern is the amount of time you are exposed to high levels of radiation. The requirements of distance and shielding can offer different protections at different times. Radiation is cumulative. That means if the radiation level outside is 30 rad per hour, within three hours you are at a dose level of 90 rad. Sometimes the best way to get distance from the radiation is not to move, but rather to seek effective shelter.

3. Area of Effect

In most cases, the area of effect would be relatively small at the initial site of the accident or blast, being only a few miles in diameter. This point is known as "Ground Zero," referring to the point of origin of the release and distance the radiation has traveled downwind. Radiation in these areas would be at high levels. The residual downwind effects could extend for hundreds of miles, resulting in large areas of land and sea that would be affected with radiation of lesser but still dangerous intensity.

4. Duration of Effect

In the case of a major nuclear event, the area of effect would be uninhabitable for years.

5. Quick or Slow Onset

These events are quick-onset. Even if there is some indication of a threat, the event itself would be immediate.

6. Destruction of Infrastructure

The initial blast of an explosive may destroy some infrastructure, but the resulting radiation will make everything that is irradiated unusable. For all intents and purposes, anything irradiated is destroyed, or at least unusable. This effect will extend into the downwind areas, but can be mitigated through decontamination (washing) procedures. Radiation is very difficult to mitigate, and access to infrastructure will be limited for weeks to months after a disaster.

7. Disruptions of Services

All services will stop in the Hot Zone. The only services that may be available in the Hot Zone could be rescue on a limited scale as people help each other escape, but this will not last for long. Services will be available to a limited extent on the edges of the Hot Zone, but will be segregated between people who are Hot (irradiated) and people who are not.

8. Aftermath

The uncertainty of a radiological event may cause people to act in a desperate or even violent manner. This will make the immediate aftermath of an event particularly dangerous if you are on the move. People will be frantically trying to escape the Hot Zone by any means while those outside the Hot Zone will be fearful of contamination and may not be as helpful as they normally would to strangers in need. There will be no government authority, although there may be representatives of government services within the affected population such as police, firemen, and civic leaders. They too will be looking to get out of the Hot Zone, but it is highly likely that they will continue to act upon their service obligations, where they can, by offering assistance and leadership where they have an opportunity and within their limited resources.

Government Response

The government will be concerned with two major aspects: containment and decontamination. The intent will be, must be, to keep radiation from spreading within the population. You may not be allowed to leave the edge of the Hot Zone until you have gone through decontamination. To do this they will set up decontamination sites and will do the best they can to clean people of dust and get them different clothing, new sustainment supplies, and new forms of identification. This will not be a simple or easy process and will most likely involve a tedious, frustrating and disjointed process. It will attempt to meet your needs, and you need to work with the process as best as you can to get what you need to preserve your life and documentation of

Patterns of Mortality and Injury

Nuclear radiation is an insidious illness. Massive exposure can sicken and kill within hours, but the greater probability is that those who are exposed will survive the initial dose only to suffer the ravages of degenerative cell mutation at a later date. For the purposes of this explanation, we can look at the U.S. military's expectation for illness and death of troops exposed to large amounts of radiation over a short duration from a bomb blast or in a Hot Zone. This will identify total exposure with onset and duration of initial symptoms and disposition. As you can see from the descriptions, effects are almost immediate and last for an extended duration.

30 to 70 R, from 6–12 hours
None to slight incidence of transient headache and nausea; vomiting in up to 5 percent of personnel in upper part of dose range. Mild lymphocyte depression within 24 hours. Full recovery expected.

70 to 150 R, from 2–20 hours
Transient mild nausea and vomiting in 5 to 30 percent of personnel. Potential for delayed traumatic and surgical wound healing, minimal clinical effect. Moderate drop in lymphocyte, platelet, and granulocyte counts. Increased susceptibility to opportunistic pathogens. Full recovery expected.

150 to 300 R, from two hours to three days
Transient to moderate nausea and vomiting in 20 to 70 percent; mild to moderate fatigability and weakness in 25 to 60 percent of personnel. At three to five weeks: medical care required for 10 to 50%. At high end of range, death may occur to maximum 10%. Anticipated medical problems include infection, bleeding, and fever. Wounding or burns will geometrically increase morbidity and mortality.

300 to 530 R, from two hours to three days
Transient to moderate nausea and vomiting in 50 to 90 percent; mild to moderate fatigability in 50 to 90 percent of personnel. At two to five weeks: medical care required for 10 to 80%. At low end of range, less than 10% deaths; at high end, death may occur for more than 50%. Anticipated medical problems include frequent diarrheal stools, anorexia, increased fluid loss, ulceration. Increased infection susceptibility during immune-compromised timeframe. Moderate to severe loss of lymphocytes. Hair loss after 14 days.

530 to 830 R, from two hours to two days
Moderate to severe nausea and vomiting in 80 to 100 percent of personnel. From two hours to six weeks: moderate to severe fatigability and weakness in 90 to 100 percent of personnel. At 10 days to 5 weeks: medical care required for 50 to 100%. At low end of range, death may occur for more than 50% at six weeks. At high end, death may occur for 99% of personnel. Anticipated medical problems include developing pathogenic and opportunistic infections, bleeding, fever, loss of appetite, GI ulcerations, bloody diarrhea, severe fluid and electrolyte shifts, capillary leak, hypotension. Combined with any significant physical trauma, survival rates will approach zero.

830 R Plus, from 30 minutes to 2 days
Severe nausea, vomiting, fatigability, weakness, dizziness, and disorientation; moderate to severe fluid imbalance and headache. Bone marrow total depletion within days. CNS symptoms are predominant at higher radiation levels. Few, if any, survivors even with aggressive and immediate medical attention.

your identity and citizenship. Receiving long-term relief will be based on this seemingly silly bureaucratic point, but the ability to prove your identity and citizenship will assist you greatly in being eligible to receive government resources.

Because information is a powerful tool in disasters such as these, the government has a very well-developed and capable chemical and radiological response network in place within the United States. Stationed at the state level within the National Guards of the respective states are special teams of highly trained responders. These Civil Support Teams (CSTs) have the benefit of being at the state level and can be on scene within hours of an event providing specific and vital information to emergency responders. They can closely coordinate with state and county emergency managers, but also have access to national-level assets like air transportation, laboratory assistance, and intelligence analysis.

C. Personal Plans and Readiness

In the case of a nuclear event, knowledge is your best resource. Consider your location, both in proximity and downwind location, to existing nuclear facilities and primary targets like major metropolitan areas of political or commercial importance. If you are in an area that may suffer a nuclear event, then invest in a radiological dosimeter. They are small, easy to use, and don't take up a lot of space. You can even learn to make a simplistic but effective dosimeter out of common household materials. Learn the basics of dose calculation and then identify places that can offer shielding. Learning to protect your supplies from radiation and electromagnetic pulse (EMP) will be helpful.

To give you a frame of reference, the following scenario is provided as an example of how the situation would unfold and how awareness, preparation, and information help you survive. This is not a story or a prediction. It is an allegory of how a little planning and preparation can make a big difference in your survival. Because a nuclear event would be so different from other kinds of disasters, the communication of the ideas for survival is also different, but the intent is the same. You need to think about what you would do *before the event* and make your *plans and preparations* accordingly. Remember that simple plans are easier to remember and follow.

On a Saturday afternoon there is a small (one square mile) nuclear blast that destroys the greater metro area of the city where you live. You are outside the blast area, but inside the Hot Zone; the Hot Zone is ten miles across. The EMP makes all telephone and radio communication stop within the effective area of the EMP, which is even larger than the Hot Zone. Now what do you do?

Assuming you can get to your supplies and equipment, you would go to your Faraday Cage in the basement (a grounded metal mesh box that protects electronics from EPM — look this up, they're easy to make and very handy) and get out your batteries, radio, and dosimeter, collect your tote box with the regular emergency supplies (just like the ones FEMA recommends) and you move your family to the interior rooms of a basement. Your dosimeter tells you that you are receiving the equivalent of 2 rad a day when you stay in the basement and away from the windows. Outside it is 20 rad per hour (not instant death, but still too Hot to move around outside). Your food was in sealed bags so you know it is safe to eat, and you drain the water heater for the fresh water that was in it before the blast. Once you drain it, you do not get more water out of it. You cannot find a broadcasting radio station with your radio.

On the second day, you scan the channels on your radio and find a repeating government message from the Emergency Broadcast System that provides information on the direction of the downwind reports and recommending that people not leave their shelter (shielding) for at least another 48 hours until radiation levels are down to survivable rem doses per hour. You know that rem and rad are close enough to be considered equivalent, so the information is useful to you. Locations of decontamina-

B. Outlooks, Watches, Warnings, & Advisories

Remember that these alerts and bulletins are designed to inform and instruct in order to cause the public to change their behavior or take specific action for their safety. Be aware of these communications. Weather will play a large role in how far and how fast radiation moves and the duration (rise and fall) of fallout intensity.

Weather Alerts

The National Weather Service and its pendant offices communicate alerts in the form of *outlooks, advisories, watches, and warnings* to the public. They provide real-time notification of weather events that threaten local areas.

Emergency Management Bulletins

Emergency-management agencies will broadcast *emergency management bulletins* in the case of disasters or special events when officials need to communicate public safety information or special instructions to the public. In many cases, both weather alerts and emergency management bulletins will be broadcast during a disaster situation.

Outlook

Indicates the potential for significant weather events up to seven days in advance with a forecaster confidence around 30%.

Watch

Indicates that conditions are favorable for the particular weather event in and near the watch area, which may pose a risk to life and property. Watches are issued up to 48 hours in advance with forecaster confidence around 50%.

Warning/Advisory

Indicates that a particular weather event is imminent or occurring. **Advisories** are issued if the weather event will lead to nuisance conditions, while **warnings** are issued for significant weather events that will pose a risk to life and property. Warnings and advisories are issued up to 48 hours in advance with forecaster confidence of at least 80%.

Alert Notifications

Alert notifications will come in the form the following reports. This list includes reports you are most likely to hear during a radiological event, but this is not an all-inclusive list. Be careful to listen for emergency communications and take information as you can get it. Remember that official government emergency communications may be more reliable than unofficial sources. The alerts you will want to listen for are:

Emergency Management Bulletins

They are issued by local government emergency-management agencies to inform the public of the nature and area of effect of a radiological event. These bulletins will include important information on current conditions and identified hazards, probability of additional events, road closures, travel restrictions, location of relief centers, special instructions, and other appropriate information.

Downwind Advisories and Warning

The public will be informed of the levels of radiation and direction of radiation travel through downwind reports. These reports will be important not only to where radiation is going, but how long high levels of radiation may remain in a particular area.

tion sites are given and strict warnings are given about people attempting to leave the Hot Zone without stopping at the decontamination sites.

On Day Three you hear that the dose level outside is only 2 doses per hour and the government radio message recommends moving to transportation collection points that have been established on the edge of the Hot Zone. These transportation points will move people to decontamination centers and then on to relocation assistance centers in other cities. You put your important documents and identification in a sealable plastic bag to keep dust off your papers, eat a meal while still in your shelter, and then check your dosimeter just outside your door to confirm the rate of exposure.

Your readings are close to the report's, so you decide it is time to move to the transportation site. Before you leave, you check your city map: you find the most direct route to the closest location given on the radio. As you start walking to the site, you see an army truck driven by soldiers in full-body protective gear and masks. They order you to get into the truck, but to leave your belongings behind. You keep your dosimeter and your sealed bag of important papers. You are no longer a planner; now you are a passenger. This is not necessarily a bad thing, and as you move to the decontamination site, you have a much greater chance of surviving the disaster At the decontamination site, they wash you and the outside your sealed bag of papers. They take the dosimeter and everything else away and give you different clothing and shoes.

Everything about the situation is either scary or frustrating. Knowing that this will be the case before you go into the situation gives you the advantage of appropriate expectations.

(Man-made Disasters)
B. Civil Disturbance

General Description

Civil disturbance includes lawlessness and violence to an extent that is beyond the ability of local law enforcement to control. It will often involve looting, fires, wanton destruction of private and public property, and violence that is random or directed at people on some broad social issue.

Civil Disturbance (29)							
Effects	**Least**						**Worst**
Areas of Known Occurrence	Known	1	2	3	4	**5**	Unknown
Scales of Measurement	Before	1	2	3	4	**5**	After
Quick or Slow Onset	Days	1	2	**3**	4	5	Minutes
Area of Effect	Local	1	**2**	3	4	5	States
Duration of Effects	Hours	1	2	**3**	4	5	Months
Destruction of Infrastructure	Minor	1	**2**	3	4	5	Total
Disruption of Services	Minor	1	2	3	4	**5**	Total
Aftermath	Minor	1	2	3	**4**	5	Disaster

Major Threat

The danger is the mob: a crowd of people who have abandoned the social contract and succumbed to the passion of destruction in order to express their emotions. This is not a melodramatic explanation. The irrational mob mentality and the willingness of the participants to conduct themselves in a manner that violates the rule of law or common conceptions of "right or wrong" is a very real danger. In this case the threat is that of violence, looting, and destruction based on random opportunity or unthinking rage directed at some scapegoat target. In either case you will want to avoid any confrontation with the mob or the inevitable appearance of people who want to take advantage of the lawlessness to commit any number of crimes.

Survival Strategy

When the mob is up and people stop thinking, then the best option is to be out of sight, or better yet, out of the area. In almost any situation of capture or confrontation, the best time to escape is before the aggressor, in this case the mob, gets organized or settled in any way. If you know a crowd is coming, the best thing you can do is to make a calm and decisive departure from the area. Some people have stayed in riot areas to protect their homes and businesses. This is a choice with many risks, and you should take the value of your life weighed against the property or possessions you want to stay and protect. Given the chance, take advantage of any opportunities to escape the troubled areas.

Government Information Websites:
Federal Emergency Management Administration (FEMA) — http://www.ready.gov/

If you can't escape the area, then the best option is to not draw any attention to yourself. This would mean staying indoors and away from windows. This is important for two reasons: first is that the rioters may see you as a target of opportunity; second is that the local law enforcement or government forces that move in to reestablish security will be in a heightened state of alert and may see you as a security competitor rather than a citizen in need of assistance.

A. The BIG EIGHT

1. Area of known Occurrence, Possibility

Civil and social unrest can happen anywhere. It is more likely in places where there is a larger population, more dependence on government assistance, large numbers of people living under the poverty line, or areas where there is a stress on resources. This is not a matter of race or class, but rather a matter of resources. Remember the example provided about Che Guevara earlier in the book. The sense of injustice, loss of voice, and little hope of change is enough to start civil unrest. Additionally, if these sentiments are present in any degree, an event offering (or denying) empowerment and emotional satisfaction may also spark civil unrest. The best example of just how ridiculous and irrational a riot can be is to look at the riots and destruction inflicted by sports fanatics brought to a frenzy in the face of a win or a loss.

2. Scales of Measurement, Predictability

In the case of civil unrest, there is usually a catalyst that serves to fuel the mob's perception of injustice. As tensions gather, it may be possible to get a general idea that the masses are dissatisfied; you may even be one of the dissatisfied masses, but when the situation disintegrates into looting, violence, and other forms of destructive chaos, it does not matter what side of the issue you were on. The event itself will generate victims by reason or chance. If you are a rioter, your chances of being hurt by your own mob are just as high as those of any other target of opportunity. The event is a yes-or-no question of the presence of rule of law. If there is no rule of law, then the aftermath is measured in deaths, destruction of property, and lost economic opportunity.

In the case of the Watts riots of 1965, the issues were perceived longstanding social and economic issues. The issues of high unemployment rates, substandard housing, and inadequate schools within the predominantly African American community were real issues that had not been addressed. The arrest of a motorist for suspected driving under the influence of alcohol was enough to spark outrage and cause civil unrest that covered over 45 square miles for 6 days. In the end there were 34 people killed, thousands injured, and just fewer than 4,000 arrested.

This is an important point. The unrest does not have to be a result of the issues of discontent. It could come in the form of a traffic stop or a soccer game — either a win or loss.

3. Quick or Slow Onset

When it does happen, it will happen fast and overwhelm local law enforcement. Although a perceptive person will be aware of the underlying issues and growing discontent of the population, the actual trigger event may not be as obvious or even related to the issues.

4. Area of Effect

This depends on the catalyst. If it is an event-based protest like Occupy Wall Street or an anti-G8 summit, then the event may be contained with police already standing by, which would limit the spread of the unrest to only a few blocks. If it is a sports event–based riot, it may be only a few blocks long, but could move a long distance, covering many blocks and leaving a path of destruction in its wake. But if it is civil unrest, based on economic or social issues, it can engulf whole communities covering square miles.

5. Duration of Effects

In the case of the Watts riots and the civil unrest after the Rodney King verdict in 1992, the rioting lasted for about six days, with some days being more active than others. Sporting-event riots tend to only last through the night, but if the sporting event is the catalyst for social and economic dissatisfaction, it could last longer.

6. Destruction of Infrastructure

In most cases the infrastructure that is destroyed is economic. Because civil unrest tends to take place in areas of economic depression, the businesses destroyed in the riots tend not to reopen. The loss of 40% to 50% of an area's economy is not survivable, and the underlying conditions that create the dissatisfaction expressed by the riot are perpetuated.

7. Disruption of Services

In the event of civil unrest, almost all services stop. Not only government services like mail and garbage collection, but also food and fuel delivery as well. Police will not be able to respond. Firefighters and medical responders will be held in their stations because it will be too dangerous for them to venture into areas where the rule of law has been lost. This will not change until security is restored to the satisfaction of local authority.

8. Aftermath

The aftermath of civil unrest is a loss of stability. This will manifest as lost economic opportunity. Stores will close and jobs will be lost.

Patterns of Mortality and Injury

Civil unrest tends not to generate massive numbers of dead and wounded. Although thousands can be affected, deaths will be limited to those who are unlucky enough to face violence at the hands of the mob or the security forces that reestablish the enforcement of rule of law. Violence is a personal thing, and individuals may well face offenders during home invasions or when attempting to do those things that are required to survive, like gathering food or seeking medical assistance, many times without assistance or protection from law enforcement. But the greatest threat to safety is when police or security forces are dealing with large crowds. By removing yourself from protests, areas of looting, and any other forms of civil agitation, you can greatly increase your chances to not be a victim of violence, either intended or accidental. During civil unrest, it is very easy to be in the wrong place at the wrong time.

Government Response

The U.S. government and local community leaders have little patience for lawlessness. Local and federal responses tend to follow three general themes.

- **First is preemptive:** to place a visible presence of officers in an area in an attempt to discourage uncivil behavior. This method is effective and works most of the time. You see it often as additional police presence at public events. In some cases they will seek out individuals they feel to be disruptive and remove them from the area. This is less about punishing the disruptive person than it is about keeping the disruptive behavior from spreading.

- **Second is to consolidate and saturate.** This method calls for police to depart the area of disruption until they can gather enough personnel to return in enough strength to provide a real deterrent to unrest. This makes a lot of people frustrated because when the unrest begins, it seems that the police just leave the area and let the situation deteriorate. The police know that small numbers of officers cannot stop widespread disruption. The method of consolidation allows police to regroup and coordinate for enough personnel to "saturate" an area. Saturation involves several different functions including, but not limited to, road blocks and checkpoints, response teams for emergency calls, escorts for fire and emergency medical personnel, and patrolling to show a strong presence. Coordinating this level of response often takes longer than it takes for unrest to escalate.

- **The third method is Show of Force and crowd control.** In this case the police "surge" a large presence into the area of unrest and exert their authority in order to contain or disperse the crowd. Containment keeps a mob from moving and doing more damage; dispersion keeps a crowd from growing bigger. This is the classic riot gear, shields, and police lines scenario that changes the role of the police officer from community liaison to paramilitary security force.

During times of civil unrest, the government may restrict freedom of movement. This will come in the form of curfews and traffic-control points. People attempting to escape the areas of unrest will be subject to questioning and search in manners they are not used to in regular situations. The government will use "special authority" in the form of restrictions on personal liberty. This is done specifically to shift the balance from personal liberty to public security. This authority will be non-negotiable as citizens encounter empowered law enforcement or federalized U.S. forces acting in a security role.

On the outside of the affected areas, organizations like the Red Cross will set up centers for displaced persons. The government may also provide transportation to relief centers away from the unrest.

B. Warnings and Advisories

Warnings and advisories will come in the form of the following reports. This list includes reports you are most likely to hear during civil unrest, but this is not an all-inclusive list. Be careful to listen for emergency communications and take information as you can get it. Remember that official government emergency communications may be more reliable than unofficial sources. The alerts you will want to listen for are:

Emergency Management Bulletins. These are issued by local government emergency management agencies to inform the public of the nature and area of effect of the civil unrest. These bulletins will include important information on current conditions and areas of danger, road closures, travel restrictions, and the location of relief centers. They will also provide special instructions, which may include directives and warnings to the public on the Rules for the Use of Force and activities that will invoke an immediate law-enforcement response (i.e. people found in closed commercial establishments will be detained as looters).

C. Personal Plans and Readiness

The best method of survival in civil unrest is departure from the area of disturbance. Earlier in the book, the issue of readiness and having available resources came up. This is the exact scenario we are speaking about. It will be unsafe to stop for gas or food in an area that is, or soon will be, in the throes of chaos. Civil unrest gives you very little time to react. Once you have your family, your supplies, and your important documents, you will want to depart the areas if you have the opportunity to do so. Avoid crowds and busy traffic, anything that may cause you to have to stop your car. As soon as you see a crowd is starting to gather, it is time to move away from the area. Do not try to drive through barricades or crowds of people in the street.

C. Explosions & Chemical Spills

General Description

This is what is meant by a hazard: a dangerous chemical or gas that is contained so as not to be harmful to the general public. When a hazard-containment system fails, regardless of if the event is catastrophic as in the case of an explosion or a failure of containment as in the case of a leak, the result is similar in regard to the threat to your health. The threats will be in the form of explosives, flammable and combustible substances, poisons, and radioactive materials.

Explosions and Chemical Spills (22)								
Effects	Least							Worst
Areas of Known Occurrence	Known	1	2	3	4	5	Unknown
Scales of Measurement	Before	1	2	3	4	**5**	After
Quick or Slow Onset	Days	1	2	3	4	**5**	Minutes
Area of Effect	Local	1	2	3	4	5	States
Duration of Effects	Hours	1	2	**3**	4	5	Months
Destruction of Infrastructure	Minor	**1**	2	3	4	5	Total
Disruption of Services	Minor	**1**	2	3	4	5	Total
Aftermath	Minor	1	2	**3**	4	5	Disaster

Major Threat

Immediate threat to life and health: burning, choking, and rapid-onset illness.

Survival Strategy

Listen to the warnings, follow the instructions, and leave the area. Information is the most powerful tool you can have in the case of an explosion or chemical release.

A. The BIG EIGHT

1. Areas of Known Occurrence, Possibility

Even with the usually effective precautions provided in hazard control, industrial and transportation accidents can happen at any time. Knowing your proximity to industrial and transportation hazards, to include downwind factors, will help you identify potential risks. There are currently over 100 million Americans who live within a potential accident area of effect. The Environmental Protection Agency (EPA) keeps an accurate list of both incidence and public information on potential hazards. This site is a valuable tool for both communities and individual families.

> *Government Information Websites:*
>
> *National Oceanic and Atmospheric Administration (NOAA) — http://www.noaa.gov/*
>
> *National Weather Service (NWS) — http://www.weather.gov/*
>
> *Federal Emergency Management Administration (FEMA) — http://www.ready.gov/*
>
> *Environmental Protection Agency (EPA) — http://www.epa.gov/TRI/*

2. Scales and Measurement, Predictability

Although great care goes into safety procedures and equipment, these systems can and do fail from time to time. The historical evidence indicates that most incidences occur in industry and during transportation. This said, because we are around these materials every day, we are used to the hazard-containment systems working. U.S. standards for containment and detection of leaks are high, and in combination with the current state of emergency management, it is highly likely that warning will be provided in a timely, but short-notice, manner.

3. Quick or Slow Onset

Some exposure issues can be slow-onset, but a disaster scenario would involve an immediate impact.

4. Area of Effect

Initially it will be the blast radius or leak radius of the event. This will injure or kill people in the immediate area of the accident. The chemical release or toxic smoke from the accident will have an additional threat aspect. It will move downwind from the site of the accident. Smoke has a tendency to rise, but many chemicals are heavier than air, which means they will stay close to the ground.

5. Duration of Effects

Although the release may last only a few hours, the chemicals could potentially remain in the air for several more days. The real effects of duration are the medical conditions caused by exposure to the chemicals. Separate from aftermath, the effects of the release lasted much longer than the event itself. Although a chemical fire may be put out in a few hours, the residual effects of exposure to chemicals could last for decades. Not only in the people initially exposed, but also to anyone who came into the area after "containment" was achieved but before clean up was completed.

6. Destruction of Infrastructure

In most cases, the actual damage to infrastructure is very minimal.

7. Disruption of Services

All services would stop in the affected areas with medical care being moved to outside of the area of toxic effects. No services could be resumed until cleanup was complete. This could take weeks or months.

8. Aftermath

The aftermath of an explosion or chemical spill is in the pandemonium of chaos that follows an event of this nature. Especially when survivors want to know how the event happened. Although the outer edges of the event will have rule of law and services, the speed and verbosity of the event will have an effect on the situation as a whole. Questions about safety and lasting effects could keep the situation destabilized for several weeks after the event itself is under control.

Patterns of Mortality and Injury

Patterns of mortality would come in three general categories: blast and fire radius, acute effects, and chronic effects of exposure. Blast and fire radius refers to the area destroyed by the initial physical blast or fire associated with the event. Death and injury are highly likely for personnel within these areas.

B. Outlooks, Watches, Warnings, & Advisories

Remember that these alerts and bulletins are designed to inform and instruct in order to cause the public to change their behavior or take specific action for their safety. Be aware of these communications. Weather will play a large role in how far and how fast airborne chemicals move and the duration of hazardous effects.

Weather Alerts

The National Weather Service and its pendant offices communicate alerts in the form of *outlooks, advisories, watches, and warnings* to the public. They provide real-time notification of weather events that threaten local areas.

Emergency Management Bulletins

Emergency-management agencies will broadcast *emergency management bulletins* in the case of disasters or special events when officials need to communicate public-safety information or special instructions to the public. In many cases, both weather alerts and emergency management bulletins will be broadcast during a disaster situation.

Outlook

Indicates the potential for significant weather events up to seven days in advance with a forecaster confidence around 30%.

Watch

Indicates that conditions are favorable for the particular weather event in and near the watch area, which may pose a risk to life and property. Watches are issued up to 48 hours in advance with forecaster confidence around 50%.

Warning/Advisory

Indicates that a particular weather event is imminent or occurring. **Advisories** are issued if the weather event will lead to nuisance conditions, while **warnings** are issued for significant weather events that will pose a risk to life and property. Warnings and advisories are issued up to 48 hours in advance with forecaster confidence of at least 80%.

Alert Notifications

Alert notifications will come in the form of the following reports. This list includes reports you are most likely to hear after an explosion or chemical release, but this is not an all-inclusive list. Be careful to listen for emergency communications and take information as you can get it. Remember that official government emergency communications may be more reliable than unofficial sources. The alerts you will want to listen for are:

Emergency Management Bulletins

They are issued by local government emergency management agencies to inform the public of the nature and area of effect of an explosion or chemical release. These bulletins will include important information on current conditions and identified hazards, probability of additional events, road closures and danger areas, location of relief centers, special instructions, and other appropriate information.

Downwind Advisories and Warning

The public will be informed of the levels of airborne chemical concentration and direction of travel through downwind reports. These reports will be important not only for where chemical effects are going, but for how long high levels of chemical concentrations may remain in a particular area.

- **Acute effects** refer to the immediate effects of direct contact with dangerous chemicals or gases. In many cases chemicals cause choking, burning skin, blurred eyesight, and other immediate physiological effects. These tend to culminate in cardiac failure (heart attack) or repository failure (drowning in fluid that fills the lungs). Acute exposure can also have lasting non-fatal effects such as blindness and severe chemical burns on the skin and lungs.

- **Chronic effects** include the long-term effects of less-than-fatal exposure resulting in burns to the skin and lungs, blindness and vision degradation, cancer or other related undesirable cell mutations, organ failures, and other general health issues resulting from physical injuries or contact with hazardous materials. These types of injuries and their related follow-on conditions can significantly degrade quality of life and shorten the life span of the afflicted population.

Government Response

Because information is a powerful tool in disasters such as these, the government has a very well-developed and capable chemical and radiological response network in place within the United States. Stationed at the state level within the National Guards of the respective states are special teams of highly trained responders. These Civil Support Teams (CSTs) have the benefit of being at the state level and can be on scene within hours of an event providing specific and vital information to emergency responders. They can closely coordinate with state and county emergency managers, but also have access to national-level assets like air transportation, laboratory assistance, and intelligence analysis.

The government also maintains mobile hospitals within the army and air force that are capable of rapid deployment and are trained and equipped to deal with these types of injuries. The capabilities of local hospitals have also improved over the last decade, and through coordination and training in emergency response, these facilities are better able to provide the specific care required for decontamination and treatment of chemical injuries.

C. Personal Plans and Readiness

If you live in an area that has the potential for an industrial explosion or chemical release, you may want to purchase personal protective equipment specific to the hazard in your area. Appropriate filtration masks, eye protection, and gloves that are resistant to the identified hazards will enhance your ability to move quickly out of the area of effect even after the effects of the release may have begun. In some cases, the best response to heavier-than-air chemical releases is to move to the higher floors of buildings. Learn what you should do. As an example, ammonia will rise and dissipate in warm weather, but depending on meteorological factors like very cold air and high humidity, it will act heavier than air. Take the time to learn about the chemicals you and your family may encounter.

Glossary of Terms and Acronyms

Adjutant General (The): The highest-ranking military officer within a state's National Guard. This officer works directly for the governor of their respective state and often serves as or with the state's Director of Emergency Management.

Advisory: An advisory is issued when a hazardous weather or hydrologic event is occurring, imminent, or likely. Advisories are for less-serious conditions than warnings that cause significant inconvenience and, if caution is not exercised, could lead to situations that may threaten life or property.

Assistance: Monies or services made available to individuals and communities that have experienced losses due to disasters such as floods, hurricanes, earthquakes, drought, tornadoes, and riots. The federal government may provide grants to fund a number of forms of assistance: the full cost for the reconstruction of certain private, nonprofit facilities and owner-occupied private residential structures; loans to local governments to cover operating expenses; free temporary housing for up to 12 months; the installation of essential utilities; mortgage or rental payments to individuals for up to one year; and food stamps, legal services, and counseling services for low-income citizens. This may include specific funding for long-range community economic recovery programs in areas devastated by disasters.

Capability: The extent of someone's or something's ability; what someone or something can do.

Capacity: The maximum amount that something can contain, perform, or create.

CBRNE; Chemical, Biological, Radiological, Nuclear, and High-Yield Explosive: See WMD

Centers for Disease Control and Prevention (CDC): The CDC is one of the major operating components of the Department of Health and Human Services. They are responsible for coordinating the expertise, information, and tools that people and communities need to protect their health through health promotion; prevention of disease, injury, and disability; and preparedness for new health threats.

Choleric, Independent Planner: Serious and intuitive. Independent Planners are motivated to develop their own plans and willing to work within networks for information and materials.

COG; Continuity of Government: COG plans are *coordinated organizational efforts within branches of government* to ensure the eight National Essential Functions (which will be described in detail soon) are continuously protected, supported, and provided.

COOP; Continuity of Operation Plan: COOPs are *individual organizational efforts* within organizations, agencies, or departments *within a branch of government* and provide guidance, both specific and general, as to how the individual organizations, agencies, or departments are to ensure they can continue to perform their respective duties.

Department of Defense (DOD): The Department of Defense (DOD) is the executive department in the federal government that is responsible for providing the military forces needed to deter war and to protect the security of the United States. The major elements of the military forces under its control are the Army, Navy, Air Force, and Marine Corps. The DOD includes the Office of the Secretary of Defense, the military departments and the military services within those departments, the chair of the Joint Chiefs of Staff and the Joint Staff, the unified combatant commands, the DOD agencies, the DOD field activities, and such other offices, agencies, activities, and commands as may be established or designated by law, by the president, or by the secretary of defense.

Director of Emergency Management: The lead administrative coordinator for emergency management in the offices of emergency management at the local, county, state, or federal level.

Disaster: Disasters are non-routine, low-probability, and high-consequence events that are *perceived* as being exceptional and requiring external assistance for recovery by *both those affected* and *those outside of the area.*

DSCA; Defense Support to Civilian Authority: It includes all Department of Defense activities, to include the Army Reserve and National Guard, conducted within the states, territories, and tribal lands in support of elected civilian authority.

ECG; Enduring Constitutional Government: ECG plans are *cooperative efforts between the three branches of government,* legislative, executive, and judicial, coordinated by the president, where each branch does its part in a mutually supporting and friendly manner to ensure the eight National Essential Functions are continuously protected, supported, and provided for the express purpose of preserving the constitutional framework under which the nation is governed.

Emergency Manager: An emergency mitigation specialist with expertise in one or more areas of emergency management: administration and personnel accountability, operations, logistics, or finance. Within these categories, there are subsets for technical specialties like firefighting, police actions, aviation support, emergency medical services, etc.

EMT; Emergency Medical Technician: A certified healthcare provider who is trained to treat and transport victims of emergencies. Emergency medical technicians (EMT) provide basic life support to victims. Emergency medical technicians may work in the emergency department, fire department, public gatherings, and factories, but most importantly the certification is aimed at providing care in an ambulance.

ESF, Emergency Support Functions: Emergency support functions are resources, program implementation, and services that are provided to save lives, protect property and the environment, restore essential services and critical infrastructure, and help victims and communities to return to normal life. It is usually provided following domestic incidents. It serves as an operational-level mechanism to provide assistance to state, local, and tribal governments or to federal departments and agencies conducting missions of primary federal responsibility. Emergency Support Function descriptions are the same at all levels of government to assist in the integration of higher level support into local mitigation efforts.

FBI; Federal Bureau of Investigation: An agency of the Justice Department responsible for investigating violations of federal laws except those assigned to some other federal agency.

FEMA; Federal Emergency Management Administration: The federal government's lead agency for national disaster preparedness. FEMA's mission is to support our citizens and first responders to ensure that as a nation we work together to build, sustain, and improve our capability to prepare for, protect against, respond to, recover from and mitigate all hazards.

Governance: The exercise of economic, political, and administrative authority to manage a country's affairs at all levels: city, county, state, and national. It comprises mechanisms, processes, and institutions through which citizens and groups articulate their interests, exercise their legal rights, meet their obligations, and mediate their differences. It includes security, essential and public services, as well as transparent and accessible government (rule of law).

Hazard: A potential or contained danger or risk of something that has the potential to physically affect a person negatively.

ICS; Incident Command System: The Incident Command System (ICS) is a standardized, on-scene, all-hazards incident-management approach that allows for the integration of facilities, equipment, personnel, procedures, and communications operating within a common organizational structure. It enables a coordinated response among various jurisdictions and functional agencies, both public and private, and establishes common processes for planning and managing resources. ICS is flexible and can be used for incidents of any type, scope, and complexity. ICS allows its users to adopt an integrated organizational structure to match the complexities and demands of single or multiple incidents.

Mandatory: Required or commanded by authority; obligatory. Used by governments to communicate situations that may cause threat to life or the expected loss or interruption of a capability to provide services.

Martial Law: Martial law is the replacement of civilian law with military legal jurisdiction in order to maintain public order in times of a crisis. It is used when the civilian institutions of justice cannot function effectively to meet the social requirements of rule of law. In the United States, only the president has the authority to impose martial law. Because martial law reduces or suspends many rights ordinarily granted to citizens under the constitution and prescribes more severe penalties than ordinary law, it is used only as a last resort and for limited periods of time. Although effective, it is expensive for the federal government and usually unpopular with the local citizenry.

MEF; Mission Essential Functions: MEFs are those tasks each governmental organization must ensure they can continue to provide or resume rapidly after a disruption. Plans for MEFs are made independently by each organization and simultaneously with other plans.

Melancholic, Loner: Introverted and feeling. Loners may distance themselves from the services and resources they need due to a general lack of trust in others over their own abilities.

Militia: A body of citizens enrolled for military service and called out periodically for drills but serving full-time only in emergencies. It is important to differentiate the definition of militia as "in support of government" as opposed to a paramilitary force of citizens who engage in activities that propose to support the Constitution rather than the elected government.

National Guard: United States Army and Air Force personnel, equipment, and infrastructure that is under the direction of the governors of the states in which these units are located

NEF; National Essential Functions: Those government functions necessary to lead and sustain the nation during a catastrophic emergency: preserving the three branches of government and the Constitution and providing visible leadership; providing for the protection of the Constitution and the United States and its interests; providing rapid response during an emergency to ensure national health, safety, and welfare needs of the United States and a stabilization of economic and financial functions of commerce.

NIMS; National Incident Command System: The National Incident Management System (NIMS) provides a consistent nationwide template to enable all government, private-sector, and nongovernmental organizations to work together during domestic incidents. The public-information systems described in NIMS are designed to effectively manage public information at an incident, regardless of the size and complexity of the situation or the number of entities involved in the response.

NOAA; National Oceanic and Atmospheric Administration: NOAA is the federal agency responsible for understanding climate variability and change to enhance society's ability to plan and respond to weather conditions. Its mission is to serve society's needs for weather and water information; to promote public safety and preservation of natural resources; and support safe, efficient, and environmentally sound commercial transportation.

NRF; National Response Framework (2008): The National Response Framework is a guide to how the nation conducts all-hazards response. It is built upon scalable, flexible, and adaptable coordinating structures to align key roles and responsibilities across the nation, linking all levels of government, nongovernmental organizations, and the private sector. It is intended to capture specific authorities and best practices for managing incidents that range from the serious but purely local to large-scale terrorist attacks or catastrophic natural disasters.

NWS; National Weather Service: The offices of NOAA that issue watches and warnings nationally to ensure public safety.

NWS, SPC; National Weather Service, Storm Prediction Center: A department of the National Weather Service that is responsible for issuing tornado and severe thunderstorm watches and warnings.

OSHA; Occupational Safety and Health Administration: OSHA directs national compliance initiatives in occupational safety and health. OSHA helps businesses protect their workers and reduce the number of workplace deaths, injuries, and illnesses through enforcement, making sure OSHA regulations are followed; assistance, outreach and training to employers and employees; and cooperation, employer partnerships and alliances through voluntary programs.

Outlook: An outlook is used to indicate that a hazardous weather or hydrologic event may develop. It is intended to provide information to those who need considerable lead time to prepare for the event.

Outrage Factors: Outrage factors are a definition of acceptable risk based upon the combination of the scientific aspects of a known hazard and the perceptual threat in the mind of the affected population.

Presidential Directive: A directive issued by the President of the United States; usually addressed to all heads of departments and agencies under the executive branch.

Primary Mission Essential Functions (PMEF): PMEF are those tasks each organization must ensure continue in a seamless and immediate manner. Plans for PMEFs are made independently by each organization and simultaneously with other plans.

Phlegmatic, System people: Logical and thinking. System people quietly work the process.

Posse Comitatus: It is a Latin term that translates to "power of the County." The doctrine comes from English common law and allows the senior law enforcement officer of the county, the sheriff, the authority to include physically and mentally fit men and women to act as a temporary police force to assist in maintaining law and order. In U.S. law, the Posse Comitatus Act restricts local authorities from calling federal forces to their aid without the consent of the state's governor and the permission of the president.

Red Cross: The American National Red Cross is registered as a 501(c)(3) non-profit organization. Working at all levels from local to national, they provide (primarily, but are not limited to) disaster relief, support to military families, health and safety training & education, blood collection, and international relief services. They are popular both for their effectiveness and neutrality, making them very accessible and acceptable to all segments of the population.

Relief: Services made available to individuals and communities that have experienced losses due to disasters. Although relief spans from the local to the federal level, it usually involves providing essential services of security, shelter, food and water, and immediate medical assistance for limited durations (days or weeks).

Relocation: The process of transporting people (as a family or population) away from a location in a long-term or permanent status based upon situations of imminent danger, inability to receive essential services or the absence of commercial viability.

Rescue: An act of saving or being saved from danger or distress.

Rules of Engagement: Military rules for how U.S. military personnel are to engage non-U.S. violent competitors and enemy combatants, specifically in respect to the use of deadly force.

Rule of Law: Rule of law is a western ideal of "Good and Just Law" based on the concepts of the supremacy of law over all men and governments, the concept of justice (law based on standards and procedures), restrictions on the exercise of discretionary powers, the doctrine of legal precedent, the methodology of common law, prospective and not retrospective law, an independent judiciary, law from the people and not from executive and the underlying moral basis for all law.

Rules for the Use of Force: Military rules for how military personnel may interact with the U.S. civilian population in times of emergency, including specific conditions on when and how force may be used.

Risk: A situation involving an *undefined possibility* of exposure to danger.

Sanguine, Relationship people: Extraverted and light-hearted. Relationship people are driven by interaction with other individuals.

Survivor: A person who survives, esp. a person remaining alive after an event in which others have died.

Threat: An indication of something impending that has the possibility to physically affect a person negatively.

United States Code (USC): The book of our national law, a consolidation and codification by subject matter of the general and permanent laws of the United States. It is prepared and published by a unit of the United States House of Representatives

U.S. Army Corps of Engineers: The U.S. Army Corps of Engineers (Army Corps) provides design and engineering services and construction support for a variety of military and civilian projects worldwide. One of the Army Corps's primary civil roles is to manage the nation's waterways and wetlands. The Army Corps's activities include, but are not limited to, constructing projects approved by Congress for flood control; commercial navigation, or shipping channel maintenance; emergency response to natural disasters; operating and maintaining flood-control reservoirs and public reclamation facilities; and regulating activities in wetlands including issuing dredge and fill permits and authorizing the establishment of wetland areas.

United States Army Reserve: Title 10 of the U.S. Code states that the Army Reserve's mission is to provide trained and equipped troops that can meet the requirements of all global operations taking place. This includes maintaining a support capability that can be called upon to assist the active component during extended operation overseas and domestically. They answer to the President of the United States, unlike the National Guard, which answers to the governors of the states.

Unified Command: In a disaster situation or event-planning process where there are multijurisdictional or multiagency situations where there are separate, or even competing, goals and responsibilities, a Unified Command offers a method where each agency gets to have input into a common set of goals and objectives that are then passed to the incident commander, who is in control of the operations to save lives, mitigate the disaster, or oversee the event and protect property and the environment. This allows for common input while still maintaining a single chain of command for operations (Unity of Command). This is commonly used in larger events and disaster situations.

Warning: A warning is issued when a hazardous weather or hydrologic event is occurring, is imminent, or has a very high probability of occurring. A warning is used for conditions posing a threat to life or property.

Watch: A watch is used when the risk of a hazardous weather or hydrologic event has increased significantly, but its occurrence, location, or timing is still uncertain. It is intended to provide enough lead time so that those who need to set their plans in motion can do so.

WMD; Weapon of Mass Destruction: Any weapon that is designed or intended to a relatively large-scale impact on people, property, or infrastructure through the release, dissemination, or impact of chemical, biological, radiological, nuclear, or explosive methods. WMD is often referred to by the collection of modalities that make up the set of weapons: chemical, biological, radiological, nuclear, and explosive (CBRNE).

Endnotes

Endnotes

1. http://www.merriam-webster.com/

2. (Quarantelli, 2002)

3. Laurie Pearce: (Canada) Dr. Pearce, MSW, MA, PhD. Dr. Pearce has participated in, and managed numerous research projects in the field in disaster management.

4. Terry Cannon: (United Kingdom) An expert in Economic and Political development, he has applied his knowledge to human geography and is a leading voice in "climate resilience". He has conducted significant work on rural disaster vulnerability and climate change adaptation, especially at community level.

5. National Commission on Terrorist Attacks Upon the United States, *The 9/11 Commission Report* (New York, NY: W.W. Norton, 2004), 281; The Oklahoma Department of Civil emergency management, *The Oklahoma Department of Civil emergency management After Action Report*, Oklahoma City, OK: 19 April 1995, 5.

6. United States Congress, Defense Against Weapons of Mass Destruction Act of 1996 (Nunn–Lugar–Domenici Amendment), Amendment No. 4349, Section 1311.

7. Kansas Highway Patrol, "Mission and Goals," http://www.kansashighwaypatrol.org, 2004.

8. Kansas Bureau of Investigation, "Our Mission," http://www.accesskansas.org/kbi, 2004.

9. United States Department of Defense, Tiger Team, *Department of Defense Plan for Integrating National Guard and Reserve Component Support for Response to Attacks Using Weapons of Mass Destruction* (January 1998), http://www.defenselink.mil.

10. Ibid.

11. National Response Team, *National Response Team ICS/UC Technical Assistance Document* (2003), http://www.nrt.org.

12. Ibid.

Index

Index

Index

Index

Unified Command, 2-10

V

Volcanoes, 10-33

W

Warning, 1-11

Watch, 1-12

Wildfires, 10-19

Worksheets, 7-
  Worksheet 1, 7-4
  Worksheet 2, 7-6
  Worksheet 3, 7-8

Related SMARTbooks
(Civil-Military / Disaster)

Disaster management (or emergency management) is the term used to designate the efforts of communities or businesses to plan for and coordinate all the personnel and materials required to either mitigate the effects of, or recover from, natural or man-made disasters, or acts of terrorism. Defense support of civil authorities (DSCA) is support provided by federal military forces, Dept of Defense assets, and National Guard (NG) forces in response to requests for assistance from civil authorities for domestic emergencies, law enforcement support, and other domestic activities, or from qualifying entities for special events.

The Lightning Press offers four specific Civil-Military/Disaster Preparedness SMARTbooks and a Homeland Defense & Defense Support to Civil Authorities (HD/DSCA) SMARTbook, plus more than a dozen related and supporting titles:

The Homeland Defense & DSCA SMARTbook
Homeland Defense & Defense Support to Civil Authority
Multi-service reference for Federal, Interagency, States & the Dept. of Defense. The military will continue to play a vital role in securing the homeland through the execution of homeland defense (HD) and defense support to civil authorities (DSCA).

Civil-Military Smartbook 1:
National Incident Management System (NIMS)

NIMS is a systematic, proactive approach to guide departments and agencies at all levels to work together seamlessly and manage incidents involving all threats and hazards.

Civil-Military Smartbook 2:
Incident Command System (ICS)

ICS is a standardized on-scene incident management system to allow responders to adopt an integrated organizational structure equal to the complexity and demands of any crisis.

Civil-Military Smartbook 3:
Disaster Preparedness

Disasters can happen at any time but with some careful thought and little preparation you can make choices before a disaster strikes that can directly improve your situation.

View, download samples and purchase online at: **www.TheLightningPress.com.** Join our SMARTnews mailing list to receive email notification of SMARTupdates, member-only discounts, new titles & revisions to your SMARTbooks!

SMARTbook
Order Form

www.TheLightningPress.com